Praise for *Britain's Revolutionary Summer*

'A refreshing, vivid account of nine of the most important days in the history of the British labour movement. Mustill puts the reader right in the centre of the action: with the working-class communities who lived and breathed the strike.'

Nadia Whittome MP

'Wealthy, efficient and enjoying broad support, Britain's ruling class in the 1920s was unrivalled for its efficiency and foresight. At the same time, the British working class was the largest, best organised and most conscious of its class solidarity. The General Strike of 1926 was an almost pure test of power and will between these two mighty forces. With narrative flair, cool passion, and a telling eye for detail, Edd Mustill tells the story of this legendary duel, those extraordinary nine days in May when all eyes worldwide turned to the class struggle on Britain's shores.'

Marc Mulholland, author of *The Murderer of Warren Street*

'Drawing on an expansive range of existing accounts, as well as previously undisclosed archival material, this book magnificently explores the multi-dimensional dynamics of what was a remarkable historical class confrontation between capital and labour. Reassessing both the sheer scale of government and state counter-mobilisation against the miners and their supporters, and the ultimate capitulation of the TUC General Council in calling off the General Strike, it also counters the narrative of British "moderation" by providing compelling evidence of the inspiring spirit of grassroots militancy, initiative and revolt – albeit unable to prevent the miners being left isolated and defeated.'

Ralph Darlington, author of *Labour Revolt in Britain 1910–14*

'A reliable, honest and comprehensive history. The bibliography alone runs to eight pages, including local histories and memoirs as well as archives, newspapers and general histories. A fascinating and outstanding work. Highly recommended.'

Mike Jackson, cofounder of Lesbians and Gays Support the Miners

ABOUT THE AUTHOR

Edd Mustill is a trade unionist and labour historian. He is the author of *The Sheffield Workers' Committee: Rank and file trade unionism during the First World War* and the editor of *The Global Labour Movement: An Introduction*. He lives in Sheffield.

Britain's Revolutionary Summer

The General Strike of 1926

Edd Mustill

A Oneworld Book

First published by Oneworld Publications Ltd in 2026

Copyright © Edd Mustill 2026

The moral right of Edd Mustill to be identified as the Author of this work has been asserted by him in accordance with the Copyright, Designs and Patents Act 1988

All rights reserved
Copyright under Berne Convention
A CIP record for this title is available from the British Library

ISBN 978-1-83643-068-1
eISBN 978-1-83643-069-8

Typeset by Geethik Technologies
Printed and bound in Great Britain by Clays Ltd, Elcograf S.p.A.

No part of this publication may be reproduced, stored in a retrieval system, or transmitted, in any form or by any means, electronic, mechanical, photocopying, recording or otherwise, or used in any manner for the purpose of training artificial intelligence, without the prior permission of the publishers.

The authorised representative in the EEA is eucomply OÜ,
Pärnu mnt 139b–14, 11317 Tallinn, Estonia
(email: hello@eucompliancepartner.com / phone: +33757690241)

Oneworld Publications Ltd
10 Bloomsbury Street
London WC1B 3SR
England

Stay up to date with the latest books,
special offers, and exclusive content from
Oneworld with our newsletter

Sign up on our website
oneworld.co.uk

For Great-Grandad (CEU), Grandad (AUEW), Mum (IPCS, APEX, Unison), Dad (NATSOPA, GMWU, Unison), Alex (SACO-SULF), Annette (NALGO, Unison), Anne (Unite), and Rebecca (GMB).

And the millions of others.

Contents

Introduction ix

Part 1: Before the Strike

1. The First Requisite of Empire 3
2. A Power Stronger Than the State Itself? 31
3. The Corridors of Power 51
4. Breakdown 75

Part 2: The Strike

5. The First Day 95
6. Volunteers 107
7. The State Responds 125
8. Who Runs the Strike? 147
9. All Out? 165
10. The State's Offensive 187
11. Surrender 209

Part 3: After the Strike

12. The Second General Strike 227
13. The Experience of Defeat 245
14. The Legacy of 1926 271

Acknowledgements 283
Bibliography 284
Notes 293
Index 316

Introduction

There has only been one general strike in British history. It began on the evening of 3 May 1926. Some workers walked off the job there and then. Others refused to show up the next morning. They were dockers, railwaymen, steelworkers, printworkers, engineers. Some train and bus drivers quietly took their vehicles back to the depots, shut them down, and headed home. They did not know how long they would be out for. They just knew they had to win.

What made them walk out? On 30 April, coalowners across the country locked out Britain's one million miners, who had refused to accept brutal wage cuts. The miners appealed to the wider trade union movement. If we are defeated, they argued, you will be next. The Trades Union Congress (TUC), an umbrella body of most of Britain's unions, answered the call. The men of the TUC were fearful of unleashing such a drastic weapon. But they felt they had no choice.

Stanley Baldwin's Conservative government had been laying careful preparations for months to deal with the strike. Thousands of volunteers were mobilised to do the work of strikers. The Army and Navy were brought in. The British Empire's establishment feared that supporters of the young Soviet Russia would use the crisis as a springboard to launch a revolution. The union leaders, they alleged, were playing a dangerous game in entertaining such risks, and posing an unacceptable threat to constitutional government. 'Sooner or later this question has to be fought out by the people of the land,' the home secretary Sir William Joynson-Hicks had said the previous August. 'Is England to be governed by Parliament and the Cabinet or by a handful of trade union leaders?'[1]

The general strike did not come from nowhere. Since 1910 Britain had seen an increasingly assertive trade union movement fighting against the abysmal conditions faced by workers. Unions grew ever larger and merged into mighty organisations representing millions. Employers responded to this perceived threat by forming their own federations. It seemed to many that a great clash between the forces of capital and labour was bound to come.

Many workers wanted a different kind of world. They believed in alternatives to the grinding poverty, overcrowded slum housing, and constant danger that were the norm for most industrial workers at the start of the twentieth century. Most who did wanted this to come through Parliament. This gradualist socialism was represented by the cautious Labour Party, founded at the turn of the century as a coalition of trade unions and political groups. But a minority, inspired by the Russian revolution of 1917, dared to dream that it could be achieved by other means. The state kept a careful watch on this nascent communist movement.

Strikes predate the rise of modern industry, but the idea of a general strike, encompassing the great mass of the working class acting together in unison, was a relatively new one. In the 1830s the Chartists, Britain's first nationwide democratic political movement, pushed for a 'grand national holiday' or 'sacred month' to achieve universal suffrage and lay the groundwork for a revolutionary congress of working-class representatives.[2] In 1842 half a million workers struck against wage cuts, but the unions were not yet strong enough to carry such an action off.[3]

By the turn of the century the industrial working class in Europe had become significantly more organised. The workers' movement debated – and implemented – the use of the general strike as a tool to win economic and political demands. In 1893, 250,000 workers in Belgium went on strike for universal suffrage, after their Parliament rejected a bill for electoral reform. Following six days involving bloody clashes with the police, the government agreed to suffrage reform. There were further Belgian general strikes in 1902 and 1913, although they failed to deliver results. In 1909 300,000 Swedish workers went on strike against wage cuts. These strikes were called – and managed – by the leaders of the trade unions and socialist political parties. Radical socialists like Rosa Luxemburg saw revolutionary potential in the more 'organic' mass strike waves, often originating in local disputes and spreading like wildfire, that occurred across the Russian Empire in 1905, forcing constitutional reform in the world's oldest autocracy. Then, most dramatically, in 1917, women textile workers in Petrograd walked out of their mills and sparked a strike wave that overthrew the tsar. Similar cataclysms, spreading from the factories to the Armed Forces, brought down the German and Austro-Hungarian Empires at the end of the First World War. By 1926, the spectre of the general strike was one and the same as the spectre of revolution.

But we do not remember the general strike in Britain as a revolutionary moment – a time when everything was up for grabs. It has now passed from living memory. Our national story is one of the triumph of the industrial revolution, gradual social reforms, and British victories in the World Wars. We are taught to feel pity for those who lived in the shadow of industrialisation's dark, satanic mills, and the unemployed workers living through the bleak decade of the Great Depression. But that millions of workers risked their livelihoods to defend the wages of Britain's miners has been curiously forgotten. If we remember it at all, we think of posh students, full of vim, making fools of themselves playing at driving buses. Nine days of madness that prove Britain's moderate temperament and common sense.

Nothing could be further from the truth. For many who lived through it, the strike appeared as the culmination of a great class struggle, a clash between two irreconcilable visions for running society. Workers saw in it the genesis of the New Jerusalem. For those loyal to the existing order, it was a threat to all they held dear.

This book seeks to reclaim the strike and those involved in it from what the historian E. P. Thompson termed 'the enormous condescension of posterity'. Of course, we can't recount the general strike without talking about those at the top: those leading the negotiations and carefully trying to keep an unpredictable situation under control. However, the real story of the general strike belongs to the working-class communities across Britain. They determined whether cargo could leave the docks, whether a train could leave a station, and whether the lights could stay on. They lived through nine tumultuous days in which the fabric of society tore apart, possibilities opened up, and no one knew when or how it was all going to end. They were, as the Welsh pitman poet Idris Davies wrote: 'Days for speeches… Days of dream and days of struggle… Days of bitter denunciation… Days for banners and for music, and beauty born of sacrifice.'[4] This is their story.

PART 1

Before the Strike

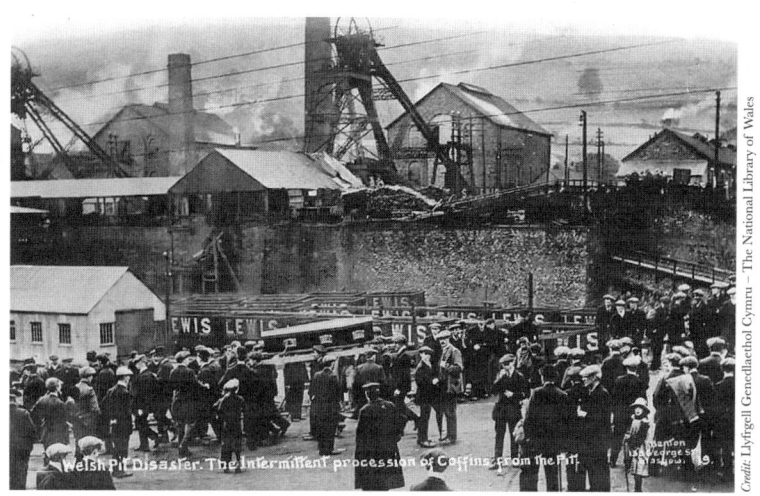

Bodies are brought up from the Universal Colliery, Senghenydd, after an explosion killed 439 miners in 1913.

1

THE FIRST REQUISITE OF EMPIRE

And the coalowners are the next on command
To arrive in hell, as I understand
For I heard the old Devil say as I came out
The coalowners all had received their rout

- 'The coalowner and the pitman's wife'

It is our real international coinage. When we buy goods, food and raw material abroad, we pay not in gold, but in coal. We pay in diamonds, except that they are black, and not in gold... We cannot do without coal. In war time it is life for us and death for our foes. Coal is the most terrible of enemies, and the most potent of friends.

- David Lloyd George to a gathering of miners and mineowners,

1915

In early-twentieth-century Britain, coal was king. Right across the land, where mine shafts were sunk, new villages and towns sprang up, creating a workforce of around one million coalminers at the turn of the century. On the eve of the First World War, 292 million tonnes of coal were mined across the country, almost thirty times the amount mined in 1800. Coal's ascent as the fuel of choice propelled Britain to new heights as an economic and imperial powerhouse.

Coal's coronation arrived by the grace of steam power and the industrial revolution it prompted. The early steam engines of Thomas Newcomen and James Watt pumped water out of mines, lessening the risk of floods, and allowing deeper pit shafts to be dug. John Blenkinsop used these innovations to pioneer the first ever steam-powered locomotive: a cast-iron railway transporting coal from Middleton colliery to nearby Leeds. It would be another thirteen years before a passenger train appeared.

The railways in turn required coal to run, thus increasing demand. Britain's metal industry was also hungry for coal, as coke – a hotter-burning fuel derived from coal – is essential to make iron and steel. By the end of the nineteenth century, a steady supply of coal was the linchpin of Britain's economy. Any disruption could throw entire industries into jeopardy through closures, short-time working, and layoffs.

Coal didn't only power Britain. It was, in the words of one contemporary commentator, 'the first requisite of Empire'.[1] By the turn of the twentieth century, about a third of all British coal was being exported.[2] The most profitable coalfields, in Durham and South Wales, were hence subject to the vicissitudes of international trade. The steamships of the Royal Navy, the pride of Britain, also ran on coal, particularly the high-quality anthracite from South Wales. An invisible workforce of below-decks stokers kept the engines of the great warships alight. The Navy required a global network of coaling stations so that ships could be refuelled and Britain's power projected across the world.

Britain's pre-eminent imperial position and the demands of competing superpowers spurred the coal industry to massive expansion from 1880. Annual output had almost doubled nationally by the outbreak of the First World War in 1914. During these years, the international arms race ensured British coal exports to Italy and France doubled, and exports to Russia tripled. But the British coal industry itself, the fuel behind the world's largest and most cutting-edge factories, remained antiquated, dominated by small employers, many of whom owned only one or two pits and lacked both the will and the capital to invest in machinery. On the eve of the war, less than ten percent of British coal was machine-cut, with the remainder being hewed by hand, more or less as it had been a century earlier. With increasing demand and little innovation, narrower, less productive, and more dangerous seams were mined by a growing force of human labour.

The three thousand collieries operating in Britain by the twentieth century formed the centre of communities, where miners and their families lived. These were more diverse than we often imagine. In the Forest of Dean, mining communities dated centuries back, governed by medieval laws beyond the advent of the industrial revolution. There were of course self-contained pit villages of the kind popularised in *Billy Elliot* and *Brassed Off*. But you could also find miners who commuted to work on the early train from the cities, where they lived alongside steelworkers, shopkeepers, and white-collar workers.

The diversity was a product of a historical quirk. Mineral rights in Britain, rather than being the property of the state or Crown as elsewhere in Europe, belonged to the landowner. Families whose claims to land dated back to the Norman Conquest found themselves sitting on stockpiles of the most coveted commodity in Britain. Naturally they snapped up the opportunities, becoming coalowners themselves or leasing the rights to mine their estates to aspiring employers. This archaism in land use rights went hand in hand with medieval working practices. In the Durham coalfield, miners were tied to their employers through an annual 'bond' until as late as 1872 in a manner resembling that of indentured labourers.[3] Mining was a lucrative income stream for Britain's largest landowners: the Duke of Hamilton, the Duke of Northumberland, Lord Tredegar, and Lord Dunraven all raked in tens of thousands of pounds a year in mineral royalties. The largest beneficiary of these payments was the Church of England, which received £400,000 a year by the 1920s.[4]

Existing mines didn't suffice to sate the Empire's appetite for coal at the turn of the century. South Wales became the site of the largest coalfield in the world, with 620 mines in operation. Here, there was more innovation and consolidation, with larger business ventures like the Cambrian Combine employing ten thousand miners. The newer pits capitalised on the latest innovations: underground canals, iron railways, and steam engines for underground haulage. Between 1880 and 1911, the population of the Rhondda grew sixfold from 24,000 to 150,000.[5] The near-guaranteed availability of work attracted youth from across the nation. At the height of this 'Rhondda boom', one miner remembered:

> Anybody could get a job in the mines. Llwynypia Colliery was all Bristol people. Boys would come here and then go home Easter-time, Whitsuntime, and Christmas-time, and then they would bring half a dozen or more back with them. Going to the top of the pit, seeing the boss: 'How many have you got?' 'I've brought six back with me.' 'All right, start in the morning.'[6]

Among these youths was the seventeen-year-old Arthur James Cook, a Baptist wunderkind from Somerset, touring congregations and chapels to preach the Gospel. He arrived in Porth with nothing but £5 in savings and a box of sermons and joined the South Wales Miners' Federation. By 1926, he would be the secretary of the Miners' Federation of Great Britain (MFGB).

As varied as mining communities were, from Kent right up to Fifeshire, miners had one thing in common: poor living conditions. They lived in houses that were usually far too small for their families, with more than four children on average crammed into tight quarters. The clay subsoil atop the coalfield made nearby housing susceptible to damp, and mine-owners' agents, tasked with overseeing the properties, had little incentive to repair or maintain the houses. Toilets were shared between multiple households as a rule, and even by the late nineteenth century sanitation left a lot to be desired. Many pit villages still disposed of excrement in open 'ash pits'. Cleaning these was the employer's responsibility. The withholding of this service during a strike or lockout was, in the words of one social historian, 'a powerful, if indelicate and rarely discussed, weapon in the employers' industrial armoury'.[7]

While the provision of free or cheap colliery housing by some employers allowed miners a relatively high disposable income, it meant that owners exerted an unusual degree of control over workers' lives. The 'truck system', whereby workers were paid part of their wage in tokens they could spend only at a company-owned store, was common despite attempts to ban it since the 1830s.

Many coalowners were small businessmen, but they were still enmeshed in the Empire's wider economic structure.[8] About a third of coal was mined by companies that also owned iron or steel mills, shipyards, and other factories.[9] The West Midlands ironmaster Alfred Baldwin acquired a colliery at Maesteg in South Wales in 1902 and made his son, Stanley, managing director of the amalgamated company. Other owners were aristocratic families who had sunk their own pits and become gentlemen industrialists, or leased the mining rights out to a third party. Such were the Earls Fitzwilliam of Wentworth in South Yorkshire. The same year that Stanley Baldwin was elevated to direct his father's company, the 6th Earl Fitzwilliam died leaving a fortune worth £3 billion in today's money and thousands of men, women, and children dependent on the mining of 'his' coal.[10]

Many lived lives of astonishing opulence and leisure on the backs of the miners' labour. The Earl of Lonsdale, who owned much of Cumberland's coal country, spent most of his life hunting, boxing, and travelling the world. The third Marquess of Bute spent a fortune decking Cardiff Castle out in gold leaf, but only stayed there a few weeks a year. In 1919 his son, a man of a rather different disposition, expressed fears that loathing of his kind was so widespread that a general strike or a revolution was surely on the horizon.[11]

More proactive owners, flush with self-importance, populated the upper ranks of Britain's two dominant political parties, the Liberals and the Conservatives. When Stanley Baldwin, who had successfully transitioned from business to politics, formed his second Tory Cabinet in 1924, it included Eustace Percy, son of the Duke of Northumberland who owned vast mineral rights across the northern coalfield. Adam Nimmo, a Scottish coalowner who in 1916 became president of the national employers' body – the Mining Association of Great Britain (MAGB) – was one of many Conservative political activists in that organisation, concerned as much with arresting the advance of socialism as with looking after their economic interests.[12]

Despite the small size of most of their businesses, the owners frequently clubbed together to pursue cartel-like practices such as price-fixing. Derbyshire owner Arthur Markham admitted to 'an understanding between certain large collieries – and he did not mind saying he took part in the plunder – to charge certain prices and only sell to certain agents. The Companies squeezed the agents and the agents squeezed the general public and high prices resulted.'[13] This sort of behaviour made them generally unpopular not only with the miners, but with the general public, and even with their fellow industrialists, who relied so heavily on coal. Even F. E. Smith, the Earl of Birkenhead, who was a hardline right-winger in Baldwin's Cabinet, said in the year of the general strike that 'it would be possible to say without exaggeration of the miners' leaders that they were the stupidest men in England if we had not had frequent occasion to meet the owners'.[14]

***

Few outside the coalfields had an accurate picture of what mining was actually like, and the half-conceptions have lingered in the popular consciousness ever since. Miners were thought of as both tough and noble, but also hard-drinking, uncouth, and even violent. They were said to enjoy morally dubious pastimes like gambling and cock-fighting. Miners' processions might be accompanied by the boarding up of shops in anticipation of trouble. Even those who never set foot in the coalfield districts were prone to seeing miners as not entirely human. Rather, they were mysterious creatures of the darkness scarred and bent out of shape by the cruel nature of their work. Those who passed their evenings in the more respectable drawing rooms of Victorian England preferred not to think about the underground toilers who provided their heat and light.

In the early days of the industry, mining was often a family affair, with the collier at the coal face supported by his wife and children loading the coal, carrying it to the surface and cleaning it. There were women and young children working underground until – and, illicitly, after – the Mines and Collieries Act 1842 banned their employment there. Women and girls continued to be employed on the surface hauling and cleaning coal, but the law and the sensibilities of Victorian social reformers had transformed mining into 'men's work' by the 1880s, when only about four thousand women remained working at the pithead.[15]

Colliery workforces were broadly divided into surface workers, 'oncost' workers underground, and hewers at the coal face. The latter are whom you most likely picture as miners. However, as many as 200,000 mine-workers – one-fifth of the total – worked at the surface at the turn of the century. Typically, a boy would start on surface work, cleaning coal and moving wagons. Then he would graduate to oncost work, fitting pit props, maintaining the underground shafts, and carrying coal from the seam to the surface. Finally, he would become a hewer. These were the best-paid and most highly skilled of all miners, extracting the coal with handheld tools. Where the seam of coal in the rock was narrow, it had to be worked crouching or even lying down. Only at the Barnsley Bed in South Yorkshire could hewers routinely work while fully standing up. To the owners, the very bodies of these miners were tools for use in hard-to-reach places, cheaper, and more expendable than modern machinery.

All mineworkers faced an ever-present risk of serious injury and death. Between 1850 and 1914 more than one thousand miners were killed at work every year. Fires and floods in the mine shafts were considered occupational hazards. Coal dust, as well as the methane gas released by mining, could easily explode in the poorly ventilated, scorching mine shafts. Miners would be familiar with a litany of disasters. At 2.20 a.m. on 8 September 1880, the middle seam at Seaham colliery, near Sunderland, exploded. One hundred and sixty-four men and boys perished underground; only sixty-seven were rescued. While many died instantaneously, some remained alive for hours, praying, until they suffocated. Miner Richard Cole wrote as he waited for the end: 'The Lord has been with us, we are all ready for heaven.'

Safety did not improve by much in the years immediately before the First World War. In Cadeby Main near Doncaster in 1912, an initial underground explosion killed thirty-eight miners, and a second killed fifty-three in the rescue party, including the colliery manager. The following year, an explosion at Universal Colliery in Senghenydd, South Wales, ended the lives of 439 miners. It remains the sixth-worst mining disaster in the world. For this, the company – which had failed to install ventilation measures as required by the Coal Mines Act 1911 – was fined the paltry sum of £10.

Most mineworkers' deaths didn't make the headlines; they were a matter of course. Prop failures, rock falls, failing machinery, and runaway rail wagons were perpetual dangers. On Arthur Cook's very first day underground, the man next to him was crushed by a fall. The seventeen-year-old Cook helped carry the man's body out and back home to his family. Herbert Smith, the Yorkshire miner who was to lead the Miners' Federation alongside Cook in 1926, saw a friend die underground at the age of fifteen.[16]

On average a miner was killed every six hours. For each death there were about one hundred non-fatal injuries. Loss of limbs and loss of eyesight were common. Breathing coal dust led to conditions like 'miner's asthma' (pneumoconiosis), 'black spit' (silicosis), and nystagmus, which caused involuntary eye-rolling and inability to concentrate one's gaze. In the absence of any health service or proper injury benefit, many owners ran compulsory insurance schemes that their employees had to pay into. Even these were used as a means to squeeze more profit. One such scheme in Clay Cross in Derbyshire took £5,000 every year in subscriptions, from which the doctor was only paid £400. These pit doctors were often unqualified or incompetent, and basic care was lacking.[17] Future Labour minister Thomas Williams later recalled being given stitches without any pain relief, after being kicked in the face by a pony.[18]

The payoff for risking life and limb was that, at least theoretically, miners received a higher wage than many other workers. At the turn of the century their income was comparable to the most highly paid trades in building and engineering: forty shillings for a fifty-four-hour week. Hewers in many coalfields could surpass this in a shorter week by increasing their output.[19] As a Lancashire rhyme ran:

Collier lads get gold and silver
Factory lads get nobbut brass
Who'd get married to a two-loom weaver
When there's plenty of collier lads?[20]

But good wages were never a given. Pay was calculated by a complex formula. Each pit had its own 'price list' for different jobs which constituted a base rate, on top of which a 'district percentage' was negotiated in each coalfield.[21] Hewers were 'pieceworkers' – paid by the weight of the coal they dug during a shift – whereas oncost and surface workers received day rates. A highly skilled hewer could increase his earnings at a forgiving seam, but they could always drop again the next week, making it difficult to plan or budget for family expenses. This variability was compounded by 'sliding scales', pegging wages to the price of coal. Miners' pay remained sensitive to the whims of the market up until the First World War.

On top of this, in many coalfields a 'butty' system sowed division among miners. This varied from place to place but essentially involved contractors employing small groups of men and boys to mine specific areas of coal within the same pit. By this system the 'buttymen' became small bosses while still being themselves exploited by colliery managers. This lasted well into the twentieth century in areas like the Forest of Dean, Kent, and Nottinghamshire.[22] The other elements that contributed to a miner's standard of living also varied massively across the country. Fines and deductions for lateness, absence, and other infractions varied from pit to pit. Injury benefits, customary holidays, and rents also made conditions in each coalfield area different.

Miners and their families did not simply endure these conditions; they sought to change them through collective action. They set up building clubs, pooling their resources to buy land and construct owner-occupied houses. The co-op became a ubiquitous feature of the pit villages, with miners and their wives forming their own associations to ensure a supply of essential goods and unshackle themselves from the employers' monopoly. Through the co-operative movement, bit by bit, mining families wrested control over their daily lives from their bosses. Whether at the meetings of the local co-operative society, the committee of the village social club, or in the parish life of the churches, mining communities burgeoned with possibilities for democratic engagement and teaching oneself, in the words of one young miner, 'the great art of self-government'.[23]

***

In the early nineteenth century, modern trade unionism emerged in the coalfields. Methodist lay preacher and miner Thomas Hepburn formed a union in the Durham and Northumberland districts in the 1820s, where miners were subject to the 'bond' – forcing them to work for a particular colliery for a year. This union achieved some quick successes, for example limiting children's shifts to twelve hours and making inroads against the truck system.

Hepburn's union was the first to attempt to build a national organisation, giving rise to the Miners' Association of Great Britain and Ireland (MAGBI) in 1841. The MAGBI called a strike in the North-East in 1844 for higher wages and the abolition of the bond. It attempted to use its national reach to prevent strikebreakers from being imported into the Durham and Northumberland coalfield, but was defeated after a five-month struggle. By 1848 the MAGBI had more or less fallen apart, but its efforts led in part to the passage of various legislation in the 1850s aimed at increasing safety in the mines. Hepburn himself was blacklisted and had to renounce his union organising in order to find work. In his last reported speech he declared:

> If we have not been successful, at least we, as a body of miners, have been able to bring our grievances before the public; and the time will come when the golden chain which binds tyrants together will be snapped, when men will be properly organised, when coal owners will be like ordinary men, and will have to sigh for the days gone by. It only needs time to bring this about.[24]

And time it certainly took. The road from these precarious early unions to a national federation of a million members was a long and hard one. It was not until around 1900 that even a majority of miners belonged to a trade union. By hook or by crook, owners tried to keep the unions out of their pits. Organisers were blacklisted or 'promoted' to jobs in which they would have little contact with their fellow workers. Bribes and free beer were used to get men to renounce union membership. During strikes and lock-outs, owners used every tool at their disposal. Threats of the sack, eviction from colliery houses, the withholding of credit at the company shop: nothing was off-limits when it came to starving miners back to work. During the 'bag muck' strike in the winter of 1902–3 at Denaby Main in South Yorkshire – a dispute over rates paid to remove waste material from the mine – seven hundred eviction notices were served on families in company-owned housing over Christmas. Workers from outside the area were brought in under police protection to replace them. One of the company's directors was overheard remarking that 'he had a square yard of gold and he'd sink it before the miners would win'.[25]

The structure of the miners' unions mirrored the structure of the industry. The local branch, known as the lodge, brought together those who worked in a single pit to elect their representatives and deal with local issues. The Yorkshire miners were the first to form a county association in

1858, quickly followed by others. The bread-and-butter issues that the miners' unions took up were common to other industries: wages, hours, and health and safety. There were, however, matters that were specific to the industry. One of the key early campaigns was for the election of 'checkweighmen'. These were miners who would weigh the coal dug by their colleagues each shift, thereby stopping the employer from cheating them out of any wages due, and stopping the miners from cheating each other, for example by the practice of switching tubs. As this was a position of incredible trust, respected men tended to be elected, and as time went on these positions were won by trade unionists, to the owners' chagrin.[26] This was the beginning of the miners' long march to wrest control of their industry from the bosses.

Miners and their unions took a keen interest in politics from an early date. Many were involved in political campaigns for the right to vote, and sympathetic middle-class allies frequently acted as lawyers and lobbyists for the unions. Laws that mandated inspections to improve conditions in the mines were a direct result of political pressure, although they were often unenforced. The miners' economic importance, coupled with the political clout of their unions, turned them into, in the words of Scottish miners' leader Alexander MacDonald, 'a power no government could afford to despise or ignore'.[27] Moreover, the first-past-the-post electoral system meant that, as the workforce increased and was often centralised in relatively small areas, the election of miners' MPs was eminently possible, particularly after the Third Reform Act of 1884 extended the franchise to many more working-class men.

In the 1880s, miners aimed to abolish the sliding scale and win the eight-hour day. This campaign paved the way for the founding of the Miners' Federation of Great Britain (MFGB) in 1888. Initially representing just 36,000 workers, the MFGB grew to over 200,000 by 1893. In June that year it was thrown into its first national struggle when owners responded to falling coal prices by invoking the principle of the sliding scale; wages were cut by twenty-five percent. The MFGB resisted and called upon its members to down their tools. A five-month strike followed, marked by occasionally violent conflict between strikers and strikebreakers.[28] Troops were deployed to protect the strikebreakers or, in their eyes, keep the peace. In Featherstone in West Yorkshire, soldiers shot and killed two young miners, James Gibb and James Duggan. When the miners returned to work in November 1893, they had won a few, valuable concessions. Although the sliding scale stayed in place, wages would be cut by only ten percent. Most importantly, this trial by fire proved national strikes could work and that the union, despite concerted attempts to crush it, could survive the pressure of a serious dispute.

This knowledge would equip the MFGB well for the industrial and political unrest of the new century. By 1900, many miners' union leaders rubbed shoulders with their employers in the local Liberal Clubs, and some had been elected to Parliament under the Liberal banner. These were largely moderate men committed to peaceful social progress. They were epitomised by Welsh miner William Abraham, known by his bardic name of Mabon, who served as MP for Rhondda between 1885 and 1920. Mabon believed in conciliation and negotiation in industrial matters, and bringing legislation through Parliament to improve the miners' working lives. For a while this strategy appeared to pay off, particularly when the Liberal Party was returned to power in 1906 with some reforming zeal. This Liberal government finally legislated for the eight-hour day in the mines in 1908, and the Coal Mines Act 1911 provided for greater oversight of safety measures. This attachment to what was known as 'Lib-Lab' politics ensured the MFGB was one of the last major unions to join the new Labour Party, only affiliating in 1908. As its MPs' politics did not change overnight, they initially had a moderating influence on Labour policy.[29]

Away from Westminster, however, a new generation of miners was growing frustrated with the slow pace of change, particularly in South Wales. The young Arthur Cook was among many union activists tiring of their leaders' caution and arguing for a more aggressive, militant policy as real wages stagnated in the 1900s. In the summer of 1910 two disputes broke out in South Wales at the Cambrian Combine and Powell Duffryn companies, both of which employed thousands of men. The issues that sparked the strikes were local, relating to the rates of pay for working in difficult 'abnormal' places and exhausted seams, but sympathy action spread across the South Wales coalfield. Mass picketing took place to prevent strikebreakers being brought in. Suspected scabs faced violence and property damage. Miners' leader Charles Stanton told a Powell Duffryn manager: 'If there is going to be any blacklegging over this there is going to be murder. My God, I mean it.'[30] He insisted he meant it not as a threat but as a mere statement of fact.

This augur proved prescient, but not in the way Stanton perhaps intended. The miners were pitched into a head-on confrontation with not only the coalowners but the forces of the state. Police were drafted in, and during rioting at Tonypandy the miner Samuel Rhys died from injuries sustained by a blunt instrument, almost certainly a policeman's baton. Local chief constable Lionel Lindsay asked for military intervention. The man who had to make this decision was Winston Churchill, then home secretary in the Liberal Government. Although reluctant to inflame the situation, Churchill did authorise the deployment of cavalry along with units of the Metropolitan Police. Ironically, it was the latter who behaved more like an occupying army in the Rhondda, provoking more violence. In 1926, Churchill would not be so reticent about the use of the military.

The Cambrian dispute ended, after nearly a year of hardship, in defeat for the South Wales miners. But it served to draw together the new radical tendency at the grassroots. While the strike was still on, a group of militants calling themselves the Unofficial Reform Committee began to meet to discuss new forms of organisation and strategy. This group included Arthur Cook, who had been involved in organising the feeding of striking miners' families during the dispute.[31] The URC produced a manifesto, *The Miners' Next Step*, arguing for a much more militant industrial policy and a more centralised union.

The authors argued that 'the system of long agreements, with their elaborate precautions against direct action, cramp the free expression of the might of the workmen and prevent the securing of improved conditions, often when the mere exhibition of their strength would allow it.'[32] They proposed an organisation set up for conflict rather than negotiation, with regular delegate conferences to decide policy and instruct miners' MPs how to vote in Parliament. The aim of this would not be to throw miners into a perpetual state of strike action, but to make it clear to employers and the government that the whole of the union would be prepared to take action over a local or sectional dispute. Alongside the traditional strike, they advocated methods like widespread sympathy strikes, and the 'irritation strike', or go-slow, whereby miners would remain at work but deliberately decrease production.

Influenced by this new radicalism, and determined to move away from the sliding scale wage system, the MFGB redoubled its efforts to achieve a national minimum wage. This would, the union reasoned, finally prevent miners from falling into penury during years of lean demand and low prices. Over the Christmas and New Year period of 1911–12, the MFGB ran a ballot for a national stoppage 'to establish the principle of a minimum wage for every man and boy working underground in the mines of Great Britain'. Members voted to strike by a margin of almost four to one.[33] After the owners again rejected the idea of a minimum wage, the country's first fully national miners' strike came into effect on 1 March 1912. Faced with a coal shortage causing a general stoppage of industry, the Liberal government wasted no time in intervening and rushed the Coal Mines (Minimum Wage) Act through Parliament. Although the law still stipulated that the actual minimum would be decided by joint boards on a district-by-district basis, the MFGB had at long last won the principle of a minimum wage. The MFGB turned its attention to its other great goal – public ownership and control of the mines – just as the outbreak of war would bring this previously unachievable aim closer than ever before.

***

The economic and political ramifications of the First World War overhauled Britain's coal industry. The initial rush of willing volunteers to the colours in 1914 caused an acute labour shortage; twenty-six percent of miners had joined the forces by 1917 and their replacements, if any, were boys and old men.[34] On the outbreak of war, pressure was brought to bear by both the government and the trade union leaders to bring existing industrial disputes to an end. This industrial truce was formalised in the Treasury Agreement of 1915 by which most union leaders agreed to cooperate in increasing production, suspend various privileges, and sacrifice strike action in favour of compulsory arbitration for the duration of the war.

The MFGB, though not signing up to the Treasury Agreement, encouraged its members to resolve disputes without strikes. In wartime conditions, however, the cost of food and everyday goods had shot up by twenty-five percent by the end of 1914. Faced with this price squeeze, the miners put in for a cost-of-living increase. In South Wales, against the advice of the MFGB's national executive, they struck for it and within a few days Lloyd George had conceded to almost all their demands.[35] He was criticised by colleagues, who thought this would encourage a strike-first-ask-later mentality, and the miners, for their trouble, were denounced as German stooges by the wilder factions of the press.

By flexing their muscles, the miners demonstrated how crucial they were to the war effort. Along with other industrial workers they were awarded pay rises to more or less offset the increased cost of living for the remainder of the war. But they had shown that, even under wartime conditions, they were prepared to press their claim for ever greater control of the industry.

While Asquith's Liberal government would initially have preferred to keep a *laissez faire* approach to private property, the demands of total war and the militarisation of the country rendered this a pipe dream. On the Western Front, the war was one of equipment and materiel, of heavy guns and shells. In the early months, it became clear that Britain's industry was not equipped to keep pace with the output of gigantic German firms like Krupp, with fatal consequences for British troops. The resulting scandal of the 'shells crisis' led the state, spurred on by David Lloyd George and Winston Churchill, to take an increasing role in the organisation of industry to put the economy on a war footing. For the mines, this initially meant enforcing export limits and price controls from 1915.

Asquith's government collapsed at the end of 1916, largely due to its failure to fully militarise the economy. Lloyd George replaced him as prime minister at the head of a wartime national coalition including Liberal, Tory, and Labour ministers. One of the first acts of the new government was to bring in state control of the mines under the Defence of the Realm Act. This move was motivated largely by the failure of existing conciliation methods to sort out disputes in the South Wales coalfield, and was also a response to general working-class sentiment against war profiteering.

While outright opposition to the war was muted during its first two years, there was great anger at both the capitalists who continued to turn enormous profits and the government whose measures were encroaching on the hard-won liberties of the British worker. Arthur Cook expressed this in April 1916:

Daily I see signs amongst the working class with whom I move and work of a mighty awakening. The chloroforming pill of patriotism is failing in its power to drug the mind and consciousness of the worker. He is beginning to shudder at his stupidity in allowing himself to become a party to such a catastrophe as we see today. The chains of slavery are being welded tighter upon us than ever. The ruling classes are over-reaching themselves in their hurry to enslave us… Comrades I appeal to you to rouse your union to protect the liberties of its members. An industrial truce was entered into by our leaders behind our backs which had opened the way for any encroachment upon our rights and liberties. Away with the industrial truce! We must not stand by and allow the workers to be exploited and our liberties taken away.[36]

Cook went further and faster than most trade unionists in his opposition to the war. His speeches and articles became more explicit and, in the eyes of the authorities, more seditious. Chief Constable Lindsay implored the government to take action to 'punish a conceited upstart of this type'. Lists of socialists and syndicalists were provided to the Home Office by the police and colliery managers, and in March 1918, Cook and his friend and fellow miner George Dolling were arrested under the Defence of the Realm Act. Cook was jailed for three months (he served two). This only served to increase his standing among the South Wales rank and file.

***

The war resulted in a curious form of pseudo-nationalisation whereby the mines were left formally in private hands but the government regulated wages and conditions and instituted controls on prices and profits. In February 1918 a further law codified this control and provided a 'national pool' of profits so more profitable coalfields could subsidise those that were struggling – a measure that, before the war, the coalowners had always insisted was impossible. It also legislated for the existence of joint pit committees which, while limited to questions of output and absenteeism, gave the miners a formal measure of control over management of their workplaces for the first time.[37]

The war had proven that national terms and conditions, price caps, and state control were in fact eminently possible. The owners' and politicians' protestations about their impracticality now rang hollow. Nationalisation of the mines, and of the mineral wealth within, had gone from a fringe demand to a central plank of the MFGB's programme. Short of this, it wanted reform that would level up miners' terms across the coalfields and modernisation that would eradicate the need for miners to work on dangerous narrow seams. Crucially, it also sought to defend and extend the principle of national bargaining, including for a nationwide minimum wage.

Yet the state of the industry in the years between the end of the war and the general strike caused constant frustration for governments, the country, and the miners themselves. The 'coal crisis' was the subject of seemingly endless parliamentary debates, editorials, and commissions as successive administrations tried to balance the competing claims of the miners and the owners with the needs of the country as a whole.

The MFGB was now prepared to strike for nationalisation – 'the mines for the nation'. In January 1919 the miners put forward a set of radical demands: a thirty-percent pay rise, public ownership, a six-hour working day, and immediate demobilisation of miners in the Armed Forces.[38]

As the mines were still in government hands, it was Lloyd George, not the coalowners, who had to handle the situation. To head off the threat of a national coal strike he established a royal commission on the future of the industry, ostensibly to deal with the question of reorganisation and ownership once and for all. High Court judge Sir John Sankey was appointed as its chair. Three miners' representatives sat on the commission along with three sympathetic public intellectuals: the Fabian Sidney Webb, the socialist historian R. H. Tawney, and the aptly named Liberal economist Leo Chiozza Money. The mineowners were also represented by three of their number alongside a trio of other industrialists. Sitting to hear evidence in the House of Lords, the miners and their allies sat to Sir John's left, and the coalowners to his right.[39]

Predictably, such a mish-mash of opposing interests could not agree on recommendations, and the commission produced no fewer than four reports. By a majority of one – Sankey himself – they supported nationalisation. Sankey, however, opined that it must be accompanied by a system of compulsory arbitration to prevent strikes, which the MFGB could not accept. For their part, the owners protested that nationalisation would neither increase output nor reduce the price of coal, and recommended that things remain essentially unchanged albeit with some input from the miners on joint committees. They did, however, concede a reduction of the working day from eight hours to seven. The fourth report, solely authored by one member of the commission, Sir Arthur Duckham, recommended the nationalisation of mineral rights while leaving the mines themselves in private hands.[40] A chemical engineer, Duckham had faith in private enterprise as the salvation of the industry but believed it needed wholesale reorganisation on a rational, scientific basis.

Lloyd George exploited the lack of consensus on the commission, an inevitable result of his own decisions, to kick the issue of nationalisation into the long grass. He chose to proceed with 'decontrol' – the return of the industry to full private ownership. The date of decontrol was set for April 1921 in strained economic circumstances. The wartime pay awards meant that miners' average cash wages were significantly higher than they had been before government control, and the owners pleaded poverty. Evan Williams of the Mining Association protested that, if the owners were obligated to continue paying current wages without state support, 'there is not a single colliery in the country that would have been able to carry on without loss, and in the large majority of cases at such a loss as the colliery companies themselves would not be able to bear'.[41]

To square the circle, in 1920 the government insisted on a pay deal linked to increased output. This was overwhelmingly rejected by the miners who decided to strike against this proposed 'datum line' in October. This very quickly forced the government to up their cash offer but without abandoning the datum principle. Against the wishes of the majority of members, the MFGB executive settled the dispute after two weeks. In South Wales, Cook and the other militants, who had spent the strike urging workers to occupy the pits, were incensed by what they saw as a sell-out.[42] This experience increased their resolve to persuade the MFGB of a more militant policy, and they redoubled their organising efforts.

The datum line strike had not, however, resolved the key question of what was to happen upon the date of decontrol. It appeared as though a major conflict was inevitable, and it would not involve only the miners. A few months before the outbreak of war in 1914, the MFGB had formed a 'Triple Alliance' with the National Union of Railwaymen (NUR) and the

National Transport Workers' Federation (NTWF), which represented dockers, carters, and drivers. The principle was that each union would support the demands of the others, if necessary by industrial action. The Triple Alliance was an early victim of wartime patriotism and had fallen into abeyance, but it was revived in 1919. Now, there was a very real possibility that if the mines were handed back to the owners on terms the miners found objectionable, a miners' strike would see at the very least a refusal by other workers to handle coal, and at most sympathetic walkouts that could take on the dimensions of a general strike.

On the date of decontrol, the owners responded to the industry's problems the only way they knew how – by issuing savage wage cuts. They pointed out the industry was running at a loss of £60 million a year, a black hole equivalent to four shillings per shift per miner. But they discounted out of hand the MFGB's proposal to maintain the wartime profit pool.[43] The national agreements that characterised the era of government control were ripped up. It was a return to the bad old days. The MFGB could not accept it. It instructed its members not to work under the new terms and asked the NUR and NTWF to prepare sympathetic strike action. It was agreed that the full power of the Triple Alliance would be brought to bear and their members called out on Friday 15 April.

The moderate leaders of the railwaymen and transport workers were, however, none too pleased with the idea of throwing their members into a struggle at the miners' behest. Ernest Bevin was at the time spending most of his considerable energy welding their disparate unions into one mighty amalgamation, which would emerge in the form of the Transport & General Workers' Union (TGWU) the following year. He was convinced that the machinery of the Triple Alliance was not ready for such a struggle. It was not clear who would have the authority to call a strike on or off. And would the miners be the sole negotiators or would their allies have a seat at the table?[44] Such issues would trouble Bevin just as much five years later. Jimmy Thomas was the dominant figure among the railwaymen. Despite having led strikes himself, during which he had been known to appeal to other unions for help, he was a firm believer in constitutional politics and openly fearful of any industrial situation that could spiral out of his control.

On the eve of the proposed strike MFGB secretary Frank Hodges was questioned by a group of MPs in Parliament. In the course of his answers he appeared to concede that the miners would be happy to negotiate on wages independently from the issue of a national pool. It is possible he misspoke – he offered to resign at a stormy meeting of the MFGB's executive the next day – but the other Triple Alliance leaders took this as a window of opportunity to withdraw their proposed strike notices at the last minute. On the morning of the proposed strike Jimmy Thomas cheerfully informed journalists waiting outside his union's headquarters (somewhat tragically, in the circumstances, called Unity House): 'It's all off, boys.' This volte face, the apparent disintegration of the Triple Alliance, was soon christened 'Black Friday' by the miners and the movement's rank and file. The memory of this capitulation, they determined, would have to be expunged.

The MFGB fought alone for three months before returning to work on the owners' terms. There was great hardship in the coalfield communities, where conditions at times resembled life under military occupation. In South Wales, Cook's house was raided by police and his correspondence seized. His windows were smashed by unknown assailants and he temporarily sent his twelve-year-old son to live with relatives. On the strength of the confiscated documents, Cook was once again arrested, for allegedly inducing safety men – who traditionally were kept at work with union permission during strikes to prevent pits from flooding – to leave work. He spent another two months in prison. Of 1921, he wrote:

> I have had a unique though trying experience this year, my adventures taking me to the Downing Street parlour, Police and Assize Courts, and finally to the prison cell as a guest of His Majesty. Several lodge officials and myself have been separated from their loved ones, compelled to wear the broad arrow, and treated precisely the same as the lowest of low criminals. All this, doubtlessly, is intended to forcibly demonstrate the Coalition [Government]'s contention that there is no class war.[45]

This failure in 1921 helped to propel the more radical elements to the leadership of the MFGB. Throughout the 1920s this leadership would be embodied by Cook and Herbert Smith, who were products of the MFGB's two most radical constituencies: South Wales and Yorkshire respectively.

Herbert Smith was a no-nonsense Yorkshire miner who became president of the MFGB in 1922. He was born in a workhouse in 1862, the year in which 204 miners were killed in the Hartley Pit disaster. An older man than Cook, he was not of the radical left and had not opposed the war. But his dedication to expressing the views of his members was well known. Smith became known for his softly spoken but unmistakable catchphrase when asked in negotiations to make concessions: 'Nowt doin'.' Towards the end of the war, Smith's son Ernest had been wounded on the Western Front, and Smith had maintained a constant presence at his bedside, even in the midst of the threatened national strike in spring 1919, until Ernest's death in September.[46] It was an experience familiar to many families in the mining communities. Those who had volunteered to fight had escaped the dangers and rigid class hierarchies of colliery life to find those same hierarchies replicated in the Army and encounter horrors that even the pit could not have prepared them for.

The whims of international economics once again changed the miners' fortunes, as production in coalfields abroad picked up following the disruption caused by the end of the war. In Europe, the Silesian coalfields, which had been torn between Germany and the young Polish republic, began to produce coal for export after Poland made peace with Soviet Russia in 1921. In 1923–4 the Dawes Plan restructured the debilitating reparations scheme that had forced Germany to provide coal to its former enemies for free, allowing German coal to be exported for profit once again and therefore in higher quantities voluntarily. In the USA, where a series of large and violent coalminers' strikes had significantly reduced the availability of American coal, the United Mineworkers of America signed a new contract. On top of these pressures, alternative fuels, most importantly oil, began to be used for industrial and military purposes.[47] Consequently, significant numbers of British miners earned no more than the minimum rates imposed in 1921 in the ensuing years, especially in South Wales and Lancashire. Only inland districts shielded from the export market fared better.[48]

Compounding this export crisis was the position of the pound sterling, the value of which had been decoupled from gold due to the rampant inflation of the war years. In peacetime, economic orthodoxy reasserted itself, and it became totemic in the corridors of Whitehall and the City of

London that the pound should be returned to the gold standard as soon as possible so that it could 'look the dollar in the face'. Winston Churchill, who was appointed chancellor of the Exchequer by Stanley Baldwin in 1924 despite a distinct lack of economic experience, enthusiastically adopted the gold standard policy. In his eyes, the move would restore stability and prestige to the British economy. But there was a catch: pegging the sterling back to gold would overvalue it by as much as ten percent.[49]

To offset this, the cost of producing staple goods for export markets had to be driven down. In the case of coal, wages comprised between two-thirds and three-quarters of this cost. For the mineowners, especially those in the export districts, this meant that they came to see a concerted and ruthless effort to drive down wages as a fight for their own survival. The government's policy attracted fierce criticism, most famously by the young economist John Maynard Keynes, who in his polemic *The Economic Consequences of Mr Churchill*, noted:

> Those who are attacked first are faced with a depression of their standard of life, because the cost of living will not fall until all the others have been successfully attacked too; and, therefore, they are justified in defending themselves. Nor can the class which are first subjected to a reduction of money wages be guaranteed that this will be compensated later by a corresponding fall in the cost of living, and will not accrue to the benefit of some other class. Therefore they are bound to resist as long as they can; and it must be war, until those who are economically weakest are beaten to the ground.[50]

Both the miners and the mineowners certainly saw themselves as waging war. The MFGB, along with many of its members, had suffered debt and financial hardship in the aftermath of the defeat in 1921, but by 1924 it was once again ready to take on the bosses. The miners voted overwhelmingly to junk the 1921 'agreement', and that same year, Arthur Cook defeated Yorkshire miner Joseph Jones by 217,000 votes to 202,000 to become the MFGB's general secretary.[51] He embarked on a nationwide speaking tour that at times resembled a religious revivalist movement. Speaking without the aid of any notes but with his intimate knowledge of the industry, Cook articulated the demands and desires of the miners: public ownership, reorganisation, and a living wage. He told them that next time they would not be alone; Black Friday would not be repeated.

In order to pursue their wage cuts policy, the Mining Association gave notice on 30 June 1925 that it wished to terminate the national wages agreement signed the year before, effective from the end of July. The principle of a national minimum would be abolished altogether, and harsh wage cuts were the order of the day unless the miners would agree to an increase in the working day back to eight hours. These terms, they knew, would be unacceptable to the MFGB, which rejected them, by conference vote, three days later.

July saw a series of frenetic discussions involving the miners, the other union leaders, the coalowners, and the government. Baldwin's initial reaction was to propose a Court of Inquiry – a tool for arbitration that had been established by an Act of 1919 under the Lloyd George government – but the miners were in no mood to accept yet another government investigation which would side with the employers. In discussions with the union leaders Baldwin reportedly told them: 'All the workers in this country have got to take reductions in wages to help put industry on its feet.'[52] Though he denied making this exact statement, he almost certainly said something similar. This was like a red rag to a bull for the trade union rank and file, who became convinced that if the miners went down, they would be next.

The General Council of the TUC issued a relatively forceful statement that endorsed the miners' position, accused the owners of deliberately provoking a confrontation, and informed the government and general public that it would be 'without qualification and unreservedly at the disposal of the Miners' Federation to assist the Federation in any way possible'.[53] Behind the scenes, negotiations continued. The king even asked to meet the MFGB leaders in a last-ditch effort to find a compromise. Cook treated this idea with contempt. 'Why the hell should I go to see the King?' he asked Walter Citrine, a mild-mannered Liverpudlian electrician who had been appointed assistant general secretary of the TUC in 1924. 'I'll show them they've got a different man from Frank Hodges to deal with now.'[54]

The TUC organised a meeting between the rail, transport, and sailors' unions that agreed that, in the event of a strike or lockout in the coal industry, no worker would move any 'blackleg' coal. This was no idle threat. Instructions were issued: 'Wagons containing coal must not be attached to any train after midnight on Friday, July 31st.'[55]

This decision to embargo coal sufficed to get the government to back down. Baldwin met with the owners and asked them to withdraw their notices in exchange for a subsidy to assist unprofitable pits that would last until the end of April 1926. In the meantime, yet another commission would be assembled for 'a full investigation into the methods of improving the productive efficiency of the industry for the purpose of increasing its competitive power in world markets'.[56] The owners, as ever mostly concerned with their profit margins, accepted this, and the miners, although exhausted by the endless merry-go-round of inquiries, commissions, and reports, saw the withdrawal of the notices as a victory. The prospect of united action between miners and transport workers had bought the former a few months of breathing space. The date of the agreement, 31 July, was soon christened in the labour movement as 'Red Friday', vanquishing the ignominious memory of the Triple Alliance's disintegration.

Why did the Triple Alliance stand firm in 1925 and why did the government concede, however grudgingly? Suffice to say that the failure to solve the coal industry's perennial problems since 1918 had forced both the TUC and the government into a position of conflict that they could not extricate themselves from. The conservative press was outraged at what it saw as a government capitulation, with the *Daily Mail* calling the concession of the subsidy 'A Victory for Violence'. Never one for understatement, Churchill, who opposed the subsidy, informed Cook: 'You have done it over my blood-stained corpse. I have got to find the money for it now.'[57]

Because the subsidy came with a deadline attached, all parties knew this was a ceasefire, not an armistice. The government fell back on the tried-and-tested method of setting up yet another commission, but with a twist. Rather than representatives of the miners and owners, the commission would comprise only 'a few distinguished men of business'.[58] The chaos of Sankey's multiple reports would not be repeated. It was to be chaired by Sir Herbert Samuel, a veteran Liberal politician whose latest role had been high commissioner in the British Mandate of Palestine. Alongside Samuel sat the economist Sir William Beveridge, General Sir Herbert Lawrence, and Kenneth Lee, who chaired a Manchester cotton company. None of these eminent individuals was likely to support public ownership of the mines, and the MFGB approached proceedings with extreme scepticism. It saw the Samuel Commission as primarily a delaying tactic. This was confirmed in Cook's mind when reports of disputes over piecework rates started to reach him from across the northern coalfields in September. He complained to the government that the owners were 'trying to enforce the proposals they put forward pit by pit, district by district'.[59]

From October 1925, the Samuel Commission took evidence, and familiar arguments from miners and coalowners were once again rehashed. The owners stressed the need for lower wages and longer hours to make the industry competitive again. They alleged that the current dispute over working conditions was a smoke screen to push a campaign for nationalisation of the mines. They also suggested that the wages of railwaymen needed to be reduced to bring down transport costs. Such was the stubbornness of the Mining Association that one progressive coalowner complained of 'the evil spirit which appears to vitiate and befog all their utterances; and their total inability to realise that it is their business to attempt to help the Commission and not to make their task more difficult'.[60]

Samuel soon began to despair of prospects of a breakthrough, and Beveridge took it upon himself to invite Arthur Cook and Herbert Smith to a private dinner at his flat. It was made clear to the miners' leaders that the commissioners had already made up their minds not to extend the subsidy, but Cook and Smith remained intransigent, sticking by their slogan of 'Not a minute on the day, not a penny off the pay.' An exasperated Beveridge described Smith's mind as 'granite' and Cook's as 'having the motions of a drunken dragon-fly'.[61]

The Samuel Commission published its report on 10 March 1926. There was a voracious public appetite for this dry three-hundred-page government report. A staggering 100,000 copies were sold and an additional print run ordered. Such was the importance of coal to a nation keen to understand the coming conflagration. The report slammed the current organisation of the industry as inefficient but, as expected, discounted public ownership as a remedy. Rather, it proposed that the state should acquire the mineral rights, and smaller private companies should amalgamate into larger, more efficient enterprises. The commission also recommended the establishment of a National Wages Board and a handful of reforms like pithead baths and paid holidays. It rejected the owners' calls for a longer working day – why increase the supply of coal which was proving such an ordeal to sell? The crucial question, therefore, was one of wages. Samuel accepted the mineowners' case that wage reductions were necessary, even if only temporarily, and that the principle of different wage rates in different districts should be upheld.

Within days of the report's publication the miners and owners were reiterating their old positions. The owners wanted draconian wage cuts and the miners would not accept any. The fleeting hope that the Samuel report could provide the basis for a settlement vanished into the spring air, and the government looked to wash its hands of the situation by saying it would only accept the report if both parties did likewise. When, in late March, the miners and owners met face to face, the result was predictable; the miners would not talk about wages until reorganisation was discussed, the owners would not countenance reorganisation until wage cuts had been agreed. The industry, and the country, was at an impasse.

Tom Mann addresses workers during the 1911 Liverpool transport strike.

2

A POWER STRONGER THAN THE STATE ITSELF?

They were local strikes in your day, where the men could see and hear you. Now things are dealt with on a national level by officials whom many of the rank and file may never have seen... We have accepted without question the policy of national agreements and large-scale organisations. Nowadays we cannot have a small strike in some obscure locality like Penistone without its involving the threat of a national lockout.

- Walter Citrine to John Burns, 1924

The struggle for economic possession is bound to come. How shall it come? Will public opinion welcome an expansion of possession and with it the extension of responsibility among the workers in industry? Or will public opinion, especially among the employing classes, be negative at best, at worst retrogressive and obstinate? That will mean revolt and probably violence and disaster.

- Ernest Bevin speaking at Oxford, 1924

While the miners in some ways lived a world apart, many of their tribulations, fears, and hopes were shared by their comrades who made up the rest of industrial Britain. Workers of all stripes were no strangers to squalid housing, industrial accidents, and low wages. Like the miners, they had experienced decades of struggle against intolerable conditions, and like them suffered from the Empire's relative industrial decline.

In some ways the miners' nearest cousins were the hundreds of thousands who kept the country's transport network moving. Railwaymen, from engine drivers and firemen through to platelayers, porters, and station staff, comprised the bulk of this number. Most worked sixty hours a week or more when work was available. Danger was ever present. In the decade up to 1907 industrial accidents claimed the lives of over 5,000 men on the railways and caused a staggering 146,000 injuries.[1] In the great sprawling docklands of London, Liverpool, Hull, and elsewhere, which all Britain's valuable exports passed through and where the raw materials of the Empire were brought into the country, work was so casualised that men would literally fight each other for a shift during the hectic and humiliating 'call-on' scrum at the dock gates each morning. The unloading of ships was a labour-intensive and physically demanding job done largely with handheld tools.

Manufacturing work, in which around a third of the workforce was employed, was as varied as the products it created.[2] Many industries included a bewildering array of specialised jobs performed by highly skilled workers who often looked down on the labourers, whose efforts were just as crucial to production. After many years of apprenticeship and learning a trade, one could move from company to company almost at will to find the best job. During a downturn in trade, however, skilled men would find themselves laid off, 'out on the stones' alongside the lowliest labourer. Sometimes, whole industries relied on 'sweated' labour, toiling for paltry wages in filthy and unsafe surroundings that barely qualified as factories. In 1910, a strike of chainmakers in the Black Country was organised by the National Federation of Women Workers. Using innovative methods including showing video footage at meetings around the country, they exposed the conditions of women forced to work in cramped workshops or even in their own homes with young children and babies looking on from the cot.[3]

Much of the industrial working class lived together in close physical proximity. The landlord was a ubiquitous foe; at the outbreak of the war, eight out of every ten homes were privately rented and only one percent of housing was local authority.⁴ Although some wealthier skilled workers were moving into new suburbs, the urban slums were tight-knit, which meant there was a strong imperative to stick together. If you chose to break a strike, you could expect your neighbours to shun you, at the very least.

The First World War created another shared experience, of a sort, within the working class. All who survived knew somebody who had not: sons, fathers, friends, colleagues. Many who joined local battalions fought alongside men who they had also worked with. And upwards of one million more people, most of them women, gained firsthand experience of industrial or ancillary work.

After the war, women were turfed out of most of these jobs during a short-lived post-war boom. Then, as other countries began to challenge Britain's economic supremacy, mass unemployment became an endemic feature of working-class life; it stood at 16.9% in 1921 and remained above ten percent for most of the interwar period.⁵ In 1921 the coalition government instigated an austerity programme – the infamous Geddes Axe – to balance the nation's books on the backs of the poor. It had promised a 'land fit for heroes', but this never materialised. Instead, the unemployed were not only hit financially but demonised. 'The ex-Serviceman who lost his temporary employment', observed Robert Graves, 'was no longer a hero but a good-for-nothing living on public charity.'⁶

***

There was no question of the working class simply enduring such conditions without a fight. Workers have come together in combinations or unions for as long as they have had bosses, but the story of modern industrial trade unionism in Britain begins in the late nineteenth century.

In July 1888, women and girls working at the Bryant & May match factory in East London went on strike – their fourth strike of the decade. The immediate trigger was the sacking of a colleague, although the poverty wages and the fines the company imposed for minor infractions undoubtedly further incentivised them to strike. After two weeks of all-out strike action with donations pouring in from across London, the workers won their demands and the Union of Women Matchworkers was formed.⁷

Their success inspired other workers. At the Beckton Gasworks nearby, the semi-literate stoker Will Thorne launched a campaign for an eight-hour day and signed up eight hundred men to his new union in one day, 31 March 1889. Here, they didn't even need to strike. The astronomical growth of the union made the employers cave to the demand within three months.

Simultaneously, workers in the capital's huge complex of docks and harbours were organising. Many of these men were Irish immigrants in the East End with family connections to the matchwomen and sympathy for radical and socialist politicians who were supporting Irish Home Rule. Through the tireless organising of the loquacious Bristolian Ben Tillett, who had been attempting for several years to form quayside unions with limited success, eighteen thousand London dockers had enrolled in a union by August 1889. Their demands were for the 'docker's tanner' – sixpence an hour – and some regulation of the extremely casualised system of employment whereby dockers were hired at crowded gate meetings several times a day, known as the 'call on', sometimes for extremely short jobs, while regular work was hard to come by.

Many assumed that such precarious and 'unskilled' workers could never be organised into effective unions, but through the summer of 1889 the dockers proved them wrong, going from scrapping with each other at the dock gates for work to standing by one another in mass demonstrations of tens of thousands. They marched daily from the slums of the East End through the City of London, drawing attention to the dire poverty and inequality in the world's richest city, both impressing and horrifying respectable opinion. Processions past the employers' offices carried red flags and union banners, with brass bands playing the revolutionary anthem the *Marseillaise*, and effigies depicting a starving docker's child contrasting with a well-fed child of the boss.[8] The London dockers won their 'tanner' but the strike was only the beginning of a decades-long struggle to end casual labour.

New unionism was a national phenomenon. The general unions extended, with greater or lesser success, first to other ports and then to most large cities and towns around the country, enrolling gasworkers, tramworkers, quarriers, builders, and many others. In Cardiff the seamen, organised in their new National Sailors' and Firemen's Union (NSFU), encouraged flour millers and other factory workers to formulate their own demands and agitate for them.[9] As far away as Derry, shirtmakers applied to join Thorne's National Union of Gasworkers and General Labourers.[10]

In the 1890s the employers struck back, refusing to recognise the new unions and going on the offensive to smash them. This period saw the first effort to set up organised strikebreaking operations like the National Free Labour Association, which worked with shipping and railway employers to provide non-union labour during strikes. Many of the unions shrank to a membership comprising more highly paid skilled workers who were less at risk of being disposed of.[11] Despite this, a number of significant organisations survived and established themselves. These included the forerunners of the TGWU and the National Union of General and Municipal Workers (NUGMW), both of which would play a central role in the events of the 1920s. The period also saw the emergence of the first national unions for white-collar workers like teachers, shop assistants, and office clerks.

Many of the leaders of the new unions were avowed socialists. Socialism in Britain had not achieved the dimensions of a mass movement like it had in Germany and some other countries on the continent, but in the 1880s, as the Empire's relative economic decline kicked in, socialist ideas began to gain more of a hearing. The bread and butter of groups like the Social Democratic Federation (SDF) and the Socialist League was simply to propagandise – to explain to the workers at open-air meetings and in pamphlets how the future socialist society would be an improvement on the current squalid capitalist misery. They believed an extension of democracy would inevitably lead to working-class voters electing a socialist government in their own interests. To some, like the SDF's Henry Hyndman, strikes and trade union organising were at best a distraction from this goal and at worst actively harmful. 'Inevitable as they may be,' he wrote, '[strikes] are but the least valuable weapon at the disposal of the workers.'[12]

Nonetheless, the socialists' activity gained recruits among industrial workers who were also active in their trade unions. John Burns, a Battersea engineer, became known as 'The Man with the Red Flag' for leading a mass demonstration of unemployed workers through the well-heeled streets of London's West End in February 1886.[13] Fellow engineer Tom Mann, who had worked as a colliery trapper in Warwickshire as a boy, cut his political teeth in the SDF where he clashed with Hyndman over the importance of supporting trade union struggles.¹⁴ Mann and Burns would both join fellow SDFer Ben Tillett on his dockers' strike committee in 1889. Will Thorne, who founded the gasworkers' union, was also an SDF member. In this he was assisted by Eleanor Marx of the Socialist League, Karl's youngest daughter. Marx in particular was keen to bring together the political socialist movement with the new mass workers' organisations, lest they remain on the fringes of working-class politics. In this she was somewhat successful; her socialism was reflected in the preamble to the union's rules:

> The interests of all Workers are one, and a wrong done to any kind of Labour is a wrong done to the whole Working Class, and that victory or defeat of any portion of the Army of Labour is a gain or a loss to the whole of that Army, which, by its organisation and union is marching steadily and irresistibly towards its ultimate goal – the Emancipation of the Working Class. That Emancipation can only be brought about by the strenuous and united efforts of the Working Class itself. Workers Unite!¹⁵

***

In the 1890s the trade union movement suffered setbacks but also continued to grow and extend into more parts of the economy. This inevitably spurred a debate about whether the working class would most effectively wield its power by political or industrial means. The Labour Representation Committee (LRC) was founded in 1900 and became the Labour Party in 1906. It involved pre-existing socialist groups like the Independent Labour Party (ILP) and the gradualist Fabian Society, but was dominated by the trade unions. Trade unionists had been elected to Parliament in small numbers under the Liberal Party banner before, but the pressure from the grassroots for workers to have their own party became too great to ignore. The arguments in favour of political action were strengthened by legal cases like Lyons v Wilkins, which set a precedent to outlaw even peaceful picketing, and most infamously the Taff Vale judgement of 1901 which allowed unions to be sued for damages for losses incurred by companies during strikes, which spelled financial catastrophe. It seemed to many trade unionists that the only way to secure their rights was to get the movement to a position where it could pass Acts of Parliament. By 1903 unions representing 861,000 workers were affiliated to the LRC.¹⁶

After 1906, the Labour Party in Parliament acted as a slightly more radical prop to the reforming Liberal government, from which it wrung some concessions. For the unions, the most significant of these was the Trade Disputes Act 1906, which provided legal protection for those going on strike and became a popular bugbear of the Tory right. Beyond this, however, the impact of the advance of the Parliamentary Labour Party was limited, and disillusionment soon set in among the grassroots.

The pendulum of working-class action swung back from Westminster politics towards collective action. In the years immediately before the First World War, Britain witnessed an unprecedented drama of industrial strife, of which the Cambrian Combine strike provided the opening act. A recession in 1907–9 had been followed by a recovery during which workers were keen to press their advantage. The years 1910–14 would come to be known as the Labour Revolt or the Great Unrest, cut short only by the outbreak of the First World War.

In June 1911 the NSFU went on strike. It was facing a well-organised body of employers determined to shut the union out of the industry altogether. The NSFU's ultra-moderate leader Havelock Wilson hired the revolutionary Tom Mann to head up an organising campaign over the winter months.[17] Neither of them anticipated the extent to which their strike would spark action. Dockers at ports around the country then walked out, initially acting in sympathy with the sailors, but soon formulating their own demands for pay rises and recognition of their unions. The spirit of 1889 had returned to the waterfront.

It showed no sign of stopping there. As the ports acted as major transport hubs, the strike soon spread to carters, drivers, and railway workers. In Liverpool, Mann called on all workers to refuse to handle any goods 'to demonstrate our loyalty to the principles of industrial solidarity', and thousands readily agreed. After a police riot injured hundreds and sparked a massive protest, troops were called in and two workers were shot dead. Winston Churchill ordered the armoured cruiser *HMS Antrim* to sail into the Mersey and aim its guns at the docks.[18]

The unofficial strike action on the railways soon spread so widely that the leaders of the four most significant unions felt compelled to call a national rail strike – the first in their history – if the employers refused to meet them for direct negotiations. The official strike lasted only three days before a settlement was reached, but in this time troops had shot and killed a further two picketers at Llanelli in South Wales. Four people died in the ensuing riots when strikers attempted to blow up a train, unaware it was carrying munitions.

Overall, nearly one million workers took strike action during 1911, and the government feared that the country was approaching revolution. The Army was mobilised and its normal regulations on the use of force suspended.[19] The newly crowned King George V, deeply worried about the survival of the monarchy, urged the government to act to prevent sympathetic strikes.[20] Almost all the settlements reached between strikes and bosses that year involved significant concessions to the workers. The rapid spread of the strike wave had caught the establishment off guard, but, most importantly, the unprecedented unity had been the key to success. Workers insisted that no grade or section would return to work until all the others were satisfied with their settlements. When the strike spread to the London docks it was so complete that Ben Tillett claimed a sort of embryonic alternative government existed in the strike committee: 'The seats of the mighty had shifted to Tower Hill… It was on the Hill our Strike Committee issued orders of war, of treaty; we governed more than the ten million people of the Thames Valley.'[21] The press denounced the strike wave as a nihilistic assault on society and civilisation itself.

The following year, the unions attempted to corral this militant, explosive unionism with mixed results. In 1913 the most prolonged and bitter dispute of the pre-war years occurred in Dublin, when the city's most influential businessman, William Martin Murphy, locked members of the Irish Transport and General Workers' Union (ITGWU) out of working in all the parts of his business empire – including the Dublin United Tramway Company, several newspapers, and the Imperial Hotel. When most of the city's other big employers followed his example, a seven-month-long, often violent, civil conflict ensued. Two men were killed during a police baton charge, and Alice Brady, a sixteen-year-old worker at the Jacob's factory, died of a tetanus infection after being shot by a strikebreaker during a riot. The London-based TUC provided food and money for the locked-out Irish workers, but stopped short of ordering an embargo on goods to and from Dublin. In an extraordinary broadside of criticism against the British union leaders, the ITGWU's Jim Larkin called them 'about as useful as mummies in a museum' with 'neither a soul to be saved nor a body to be kicked'.[22]

Millions of industrial workers had taken strike action between 1910 and 1914, sometimes more than once. According to official estimates, in these five years, over eighty million working days were lost to strike action. The government deployed the Army and police frequently, and workers across Britain faced the violence that had been inflicted upon their fellows in the coalfields periodically since 1893.

The pre-war unrest owed something to the growing popularity of syndicalism in Britain. This was a militant approach to class struggle focused on workers' self-organisation, hostile to both cooperation with employers and appeals to the state. Syndicalists were prepared to walk off the job without giving notice, instigate 'go-slows' to decrease production, and foment widespread sympathy action. They were willing to jettison previous agreements with employers as soon as they felt strong enough to get better terms, and to criticise the leaders of the movement for timidity. Arthur Cook and his fellow South Wales radicals were probably the best-organised syndicalists, but there were similar reform movements among the engineers and metalworkers. Many historians have stressed that only a minority of workers were ever ideologically driven syndicalists in this period. This is true, but it misses the point that syndicalism was not so much an ideology as an approach to trade unionism, one which was, albeit briefly, adopted by hundreds of thousands of workers. This was acknowledged by activists at the time like Tom Mann who wrote: 'It does not follow that all the men who have so taken action are highly intellectual class conscious revolutionaries, but it does warrant the conclusion that they are exactly the right kind of material out of which revolutionaries are made.'[23] The idea of class-wide solidarity – that the whole working class should mobilise in support of one section of it – took root, and would manifest again in 1926.

The unrest also hastened calls for the merging of unions into larger and more powerful industrial organisations. A National Transport Workers' Federation was formed which paved the way for the amalgamation of many unions into the TGWU after the war. On the railways, three of the biggest unions merged into the National Union of Railwaymen (NUR) in

1913, an 'all-grades' union that aspired to represent all except the white-collar workforce. Even in engineering, where a plethora of specialist craft unions still existed, the unrest spurred the formation of an Amalgamation Committees Movement and calls for greater cooperation that would be put to the test during the war years.

This was industrial unionism, the idea that all workers in an industry should be part of the same organisation. For some revolutionaries, the amalgamations presaged the 'One Big Union' that would encompass the whole class and be powerful enough to take over the functions of the state. Even for many moderate pragmatists, though, amalgamation seemed long overdue. Ernest Bevin was a key instigator in welding countless local transport unions together into the TGWU. Some leaders, guarding their own unions' histories, traditions, and privileges, preferred federations to mergers. Others pushed for looser alliances whereby unions remained distinct but would aid each other in times of need. It was the latter attitude that birthed the mighty Triple Alliance in March 1914. The historian George Dangerfield argued that a potentially ruinous general strike in 1914 was only 'forestalled by some bullets at Sarajevo'. This view somewhat oversells the alliance's organisational strength, but he was right to see it as the result of rank-and-file pressure when he wrote: 'The Trades Union Congress, left to itself, would never have forged so potent a weapon.'[24]

***

If the bullets at Sarajevo put the Triple Alliance on ice, they also heralded a revolution in industrial relations. As in the mines, many workers volunteered to fight at the outset of the war. Unlike the miners, workers absent from the factories and transport network found their jobs filled by women and 'unskilled' men. As we have seen, this change was formalised by the Treasury Agreement of 1915 and an acceptance of industrial peace 'for the duration' by most union leaders.

In exchange for their quiescence, the unions were treated as necessary partners in the war effort, particularly after Lloyd George entered Downing Street in December 1916. He adopted policies that the unions had been calling for since 1914, like state control of the mines and of shipping, oversight of food supplies to prevent profiteering, and the establishment of a new Ministry of Labour.[25] While industry was still privately owned, the government could designate 'controlled establishments' where it regulated wages and profits. Robbed of the ability to withdraw their labour to secure a pay rise, workers were instead granted pay awards by courts of arbitration. Trade unions thus became to some degree incorporated into the machinery of the state, acquiring new respectability and political clout, but sacrificing some of their independence.

This was a sore point for the more syndicalist-inclined members, who began to reassert themselves. In munitions factories on the Clyde and in Sheffield unofficial and illegal strikes broke out against the 'dilution' of skilled labour and the calling up of men into the Army. A system of grassroots workers' committees developed across the country, culminating in a national strike of engineers in May 1917. Over the winter of 1917–18 this movement began to extend to labourers and to women, forcing the government to grant the 'war bonus' – a 12.5% pay rise – to a broad layer of workers in a successful attempt to mollify the movement before it took on a more radical and anti-war character.

In 1917, when the February Russian revolution overthrew the three-hundred-year-old Romanov autocracy, a new world of political possibilities was born. With the appeal of the Petrograd Soviet to the peoples of Europe for 'concerted, decisive action in favour of peace', opposition to the war in Britain finally came into the open. In June, in Leeds, a convention of disparate forces of the left – syndicalists, socialists, pacifists, and senior Labour and trade union figures – came out in favour of peace. The Leeds Convention also resolved to set up 'Workers' and Soldiers' Councils for initiating and co-ordinating working class activity...to work strenuously for peace...and for the complete political and economic emancipation of international labour.'[26]

On the left, the Leeds Convention was all things to all people. For moderate but anti-war socialists like Ramsay MacDonald it was primarily a means of mobilising anti-war public opinion across classes. For some of the syndicalists it appeared to be an acknowledgement, if not a wholesale adoption, of the idea of rank-and-file workers' committees by the wider movement. Some revolutionaries even saw it as a sign the British labour movement was prepared to entertain a road to power that did not involve winning a parliamentary majority.[27] This muddle ensured that the resolutions remained mostly on paper.

Nevertheless, the revolutionaries had been galvanised. When the second revolution of November 1917 appeared to place state power in Russia into the hands of the Soviets, this appeared to them to vindicate the strategy of the workers' committees in Britain. Over the course of the next few years the labour movement experienced a growing division between those committed to the parliamentary road and those who looked to Russia for inspiration. The spectre of the Russian revolution would haunt the minds of governments, state officials, and union leaders alike.

When the war ended with victory in 1918, the free-marketeers in government were keen to give back controlled industries to the private sector but terrified of the reaction this would provoke among a confident and increasingly radical working class. Lloyd George pushed the development of systems of arbitration and conciliation to give the unions a stake in industry and try to prevent widespread strikes. His short-lived National Industrial Conference brought employers and unions together in 'a Parliament for industry' and was welcomed by many moderate Labour leaders.[28]

More long-lasting were the Whitley Councils, committees of employer and union representatives that aimed to deal amicably with industrial problems. Unions that had struggled to achieve voluntary recognition from employers, like the NUGMW which represented labourers across many different industries, welcomed the Whitley proposals. Where there were long-established collective bargaining mechanisms, often involving skilled workers like engineers, unions were more distrustful of this state intervention.[29]

Nor was this turn to conciliation accepted by many workers on the ground. Miners, engineers, and other key industries refused to engage in the Whitley system. The engineers campaigned for a shorter working week to ensure work for demobilised men, and this was pushed as far as strike action by shop stewards in Glasgow and Belfast in January 1919. The press denounced mass demonstrations supported by demobilised soldiers in Glasgow as 'terrorism'. Violent clashes occurred between strikers and police and the strike leaders were arrested. 'The police have once more been used as hirelings to bludgeon the workers,' stated the Glasgow strike bulletin.[30]

But unrest even spread to the police in this period. Metropolitan Police officers had walked out in August 1918 in response to the dismissal of a constable who was a member of the National Union of Police and Prison Officers (NUPPO). General Nevil Macready, a veteran of Tonypandy and the Irish Troubles, was brought in to break the union. An attempted national police strike in the summer of 1919 was confined to London and Liverpool. All the strikers were summarily dismissed and, despite many years of campaigning afterwards, never reinstated. The Police Act 1919 was rushed through to establish the Police Federation as an alternative to genuine trade unionism, and the NUPPO was smashed.

Throughout the summer of 1919 there was no abatement as workers attempted to force down the length of the working week and force up their wages. The situation was febrile and local strikes could easily be provoked by a change in shift times or the disciplining of a colleague. Most significantly, a strike of almost half a million textile workers across the north of England successfully achieved a forty-eight-hour week – down from 55.5 – and a thirty-percent pay rise.[31]

Discontent on the railways had been rumbling on all year, as the NUR formulated a national programme to raise the pay of those in lower grades. The government, which had not yet decontrolled the railways and therefore was responsible for the workers' conditions, prevaricated until after the miners' dispute was settled and then, instead of a raise, proposed draconian wage cuts. Jimmy Thomas, who had been looking for any excuse to avoid a strike, was forced by pressure from below into calling one. At midnight on 26 September the nation's railwaymen walked out in their first national strike, with engine drivers from the Associated Society of Locomotive Engineers and Firemen (ASLEF) joining in sympathy. After a week, the strike was settled with the railwaymen maintaining their old terms and wages.

The 1919 strike wave kept both the government and the unions on tenterhooks. Mass strike waves had forced the German kaiser to abdicate in November 1918 and contributed to the collapse of the Austro-Hungarian Empire. Each side in Britain was well aware that large-scale strikes could spark revolutionary conflagrations. At key junctures, there was a risk of events spiralling out of union leaders' control, which would have been disastrous for both parties. Their attitude is best summed up by an account of a meeting between the Triple Alliance leaders and Lloyd George that year, relayed by miners' leader Bob Smillie to South Wales miner Nye Bevan. The prime minister summoned the union leaders and told them:

> Gentlemen, you have fashioned, in the Triple Alliance of the unions represented by you, a most powerful instrument. I feel bound to tell you that in our opinion we are at your mercy. The Army is disaffected and cannot be relied upon. Trouble has occurred already in a number of camps. We have just emerged from a great war and the people are eager for the reward of their sacrifices, and we are in no position to satisfy them. In these circumstances, if you carry out your threat and strike, you will defeat us. But if you do, have you weighed the consequences? The strike will be in defiance of the Government of the country and by its very success will precipitate a constitutional crisis of the first importance. For, if a force arises in the State which is stronger than the State itself, then it must be ready to take on the functions of the State, or withdraw and accept the authority of the State. Gentlemen, have you considered, and if you have, are you ready?

'From that moment on,' Smillie told Bevan, 'we were beaten and we knew we were.'[32]

***

After 1920, the short-lived boom turned into another slump. As they had in the 1890s, employers went on the offensive and attacked terms and conditions with a view to making British industry more internationally competitive. Real wages were driven down across most industries. In 1922, having victimised many of the militant shop stewards and smashed the workers' committee movement, the engineering employers felt strong enough to effect an industry-wide lockout to claw back some of the concessions they had made during the war. A quarter of a million engineers were locked out for three months and, with little support from workers outside the industry, were forced back to work on worse terms.

This slump, coupled with the decontrol of wartime industries, had a huge effect on union membership, which declined from a post-war peak of 8.4 million in 1920 to 6.6 million in 1921 and 5.6 million the following year.[33] This posed burning questions about trade union strategy and organisation. One response to this was the continued amalgamation of unions into larger organisations. The Amalgamated Society of Engineers merged with nine smaller unions in 1920 to form the Amalgamated Engineering Union (AEU) with nearly half a million members and syndicalist Tom Mann as its first general secretary. Will Thorne's union merged with two other general unions in 1924 to form the NUGMW.

A relative latecomer to amalgamation, but a formidable force, was the TGWU. The road to amalgamation among transport workers was a long one that required the tireless organisational capacities of the Bristol docker Ernest Bevin. Tough talking, physically strong, and, like Cook, a former Baptist lay preacher, Bevin was thrust into the limelight during his role at the Shaw Inquiry into dockers' working conditions in 1920. The 'dockers' KC', as he came to be known, first brought the rival waterfront unions around to the idea of amalgamation, then extended the scheme to include those working in inland transport. At 300,000, the resulting union was smaller than some of its peers but had members in strategically key and well-organised workplaces. The TGWU, however, failed to extend to all transport workers; most significantly Havelock Wilson's seamen's union stood aloof.[34] This would have disastrous consequences in 1926.

These strategic debates did not just concern individual unions. They also caused a shift in the TUC. Since its founding in 1868, it had seen its role as that of a political lobbying group: campaigning for improved labour legislation and supporting trade unionists in their bids for elected office. Tellingly, its leading body was called the Parliamentary Committee.

In the early 1890s, new unionists had turned up to the TUC's annual congresses and, through forthright and sometimes fierce arguments, pushed it to support the eight-hour day and move towards independent labour politics. But the organisation's focus remained firmly on the political rather than the industrial field. It was only in the post-war landscape of the 1920s, after the failure of the Triple Alliance, that the movement required the TUC to function as an industrial organising centre. In 1919–20, Bevin and others began to push for the formation of a 'General Council' to replace the Parliamentary Committee. Set up in 1921 after the debacle of Black Friday, it comprised thirty members from across the movement, and was tasked with preventing inter-union disputes and developing relations with unions in other countries. Crucially, its proposed role included promoting common action between unions, including industrial action if necessary.[35]

The founding of the General Council only opened up new arguments about the scope and nature of its powers. Its structure was somewhat of a compromise, with seats reserved for unions from specific industries. This meant that even the mammoth Miners' Federation had only two representatives whereas a number of tiny specialist unions, for example the National Union of Gold, Silver and Allied Trades, were more or less guaranteed one each. As the experience of the Triple Alliance had shown, few unions wanted to abrogate their decision-making to an outside body, still less give an external organisation the power to call their members out on strike. It would, after all, be the unions and not the TUC that would have to pay the strike pay, and the unions' own officials who would have to organise such a strike. For Bevin, the point of creating such a 'general staff of the army of labour' was to make industrial action less likely; he reasoned that such an organisation would naturally extend its power across industry and would, at most, have to threaten strikes to achieve its goals.

Those on the left of the movement, however, looked to the General Council to provide a more active and militant leadership. In 1920, inspired by the Bolshevik revolution, the Communist Party of Great Britain (CPGB) was founded, largely as a fusion of existing socialist groups and wartime syndicalists. While it numbered only a few thousand, it drew into its ranks many of the most militant trade unionists including those who had been central to building the workers' committee movement such as Sheffield's Jack Murphy and Willie Gallacher and Tom Bell from Clydeside. This gave the party a significant base in the engineering unions. Crucially, the CPGB also attracted miners to its ranks, particularly in South Wales and the north-east of England. Arthur Cook briefly joined and, even after formally leaving, remained close to the party and continued to describe himself as a communist.[36]

The CPGB provided a pole of attraction for those who wanted to strengthen and centralise the trade union movement's leading bodies. The General Council, wrote Communist leader Harry Pollitt, should be invested 'with power to direct the whole movement, and not only with power, but under responsibility to Congress to use that power'.[37] To ensure such power was not simply centralised into the hands of people who wanted to do nothing with it, the CPGB argued at the same time for strengthening the voice of the rank and file. To this end they would also work to strengthen the trades councils – umbrella bodies of union branches in different towns and districts. Trades councils were arguably closer to the feeling of workers on the shop floor than remote – often London-based – union leaders. In the view of Communists and other radicals, they could function as 'working-class parliaments' where issues of strategy, policy, and organisation could be freely debated.[38]

Churchill kept a watchful eye on such developments. At a speech to a gathering of City of London worthies in 1920 he expressed the fears of Britain's establishment that this radicalism might spread and the hope that 'responsible' trade union leaders might contain it:

> There is a growing feeling that a considerable section of organized Labour is trying to tyrannize over the whole public and to bully them into submission, not by argument, not by recognized political measures, but by brute force.
>
> I think that the trade unions will have to review their position very carefully in the next few years if they are to preserve the great and, on the whole, beneficent influence which they have exercised for so long in British public and industrial life. There is an active and very voluble minority which is always trying to grab the control of the organization, and this minority has a perfectly definite and avowed intention of trying to wreck the whole system of society, and to wreck it by any means, however violent and however wicked, that may be within their reach.
>
> The responsible leaders of trade unions have very great difficulty in standing up to these hotheads. We must make all allowance for the difficult position in which leaders of the Labour movement are placed in these circumstances.[39]

The Communists did not confine their agitation in the unions to calling for a more centralised and powerful general council. They also set up an organisation – the National Minority Movement (NMM) – to bring together radical elements at the grassroots, argue for the unions to pursue a militant policy, and support left-wing candidates in union elections. As its name suggests, the revolutionaries knew they were in a minority and saw it as their job to convince the broad layer of trade unionists of the wisdom of their position. After its founding in 1924, Minority Movements were set up in different industries. They found most success in mining where they supported Cook's successful campaign to become general secretary of the MFGB. Through the NMM, the Communists reached a significant number of trade unionists with their argument that the mining crisis was part of a general ruling class offensive for which the workers had to prepare. They avidly disseminated bulletins to this effect at an increasing number of factory gates and pitheads.

At the TUC's annual congress in Scarborough in September 1925, it seemed as though those on the side of a stronger General Council were winning the argument. The left-wingers had, throughout the early 1920s, found unlikely allies in moderates like Bevin who recognised that the trade union movement's nineteenth-century machinery was no longer adequate to deal with disputes in an era of interconnected industries, government intervention, and powerful national employers' associations. When it came to a discussion of exactly what powers to give the General Council in light of the coal situation, though, congress prevaricated. The National Union of Vehicle Builders proposed a motion that would empower the council 'to call for a stoppage of work, by an affiliated organisation, or part thereof, in order to assist a union defending a vital trade union principle', and to impose a levy on affiliates for a strike fund. Arthur Cook was the only union leader to speak in support of this. At this crucial moment Bevin hesitated and stated he would have to consult the TGWU's executive, and the proposal was kicked into the long grass.[40]

Despite this setback, delegates were buoyed with confidence provided by the temporary victory of Red Friday and mindful that a battle was likely looming upon the expiration of the coal subsidy the next May. They backed a number of left-wing, even revolutionary-sounding, positions. Motions were passed opposing imperialism and calling for the overthrow of capitalism. Outgoing president Alonzo Swales of the engineers proclaimed:

> We are entering upon a new stage of development in the upward struggle of our class… The new phase of development which is worldwide has entered upon the next and probably the last stage of revolt. It is the duty of

all members of the working class so to solidify their movements that, come when the time may for the last final struggle, we shall be wanting neither machinery nor men to move forward to the destruction of wage slavery and the construction of a new order of society based upon co-ordinated effort and work with mutual good will and understanding.[41]

With such rhetoric members could perhaps be forgiven for believing their leaders were making all possible preparations for the struggle ahead. More important than the radical phrase-mongering at Scarborough, however, was the change in the personnel of the members elected to the General Council itself. Swales was replaced as chairman by the moderate steelworker Arthur Pugh. Jimmy Thomas, allergic even to the thought of coordinated industrial action, returned to the General Council having briefly stepped down to serve in the 1924 minority Labour government. This strengthened the movement's right wing, who were perfectly happy to adopt a wait-and-see approach to the Samuel Commission and its findings. Ernest Bevin was, for the first time, elected to represent the TGWU, and Walter Citrine became the General Council's acting general secretary upon the sudden death of the incumbent, Fred Bramley. While acutely aware of the deficiencies in the movement's organisation, they did not forcefully argue for a different policy. Although Citrine produced a circular early in 1926 urging the General Council to begin making preparations, this was largely ignored.

There were now few avowed left-wingers on the General Council, and those still there, such as Alf Purcell of the furnishing trades, were just as content to play the waiting game as their moderate colleagues. Most believed it would reflect badly on them if they seemed to be pre-empting the report of the Samuel Commission. They were also concerned that openly making any preparations for a strike would simply give the government the opportunity to counter them. Despite persistent urging from the grassroots, the 'general staff' of the trade union movement more or less lapsed into inactivity. As 1926 dawned, it seemed power had been invested in a leadership who were determined not to wield it.

A cartoon in the newsletter of the Rufford
Pit Communist Group, 1925.

3

THE CORRIDORS OF POWER

The need for complete secrecy in regard to the organisation has, to some extent, disappeared but there are many details which it is undesirable to disclose.

- GOVERNMENT INSTRUCTIONS TO THE VOLUNTEER SERVICES COMMITTEES, 22 DECEMBER 1925

Just show the Parasites what you think of it all when they pass here in a few minutes. We have been living in Hell for the past four years but the Great Red Dawn is not far away when there will be a reckoning.

- THOMAS JAMES, TWENTY-SEVEN-YEAR-OLD COMMUNIST, AT AN OPEN-AIR MEETING DURING THE VISIT OF PRINCESS MARY TO ROTHERHAM, SEPTEMBER 1925

The overthrow of the tsar in March 1917 and his replacement with a broadly liberal government headed by Alexander Kerensky was almost universally welcomed in Britain, whose wartime leaders had long been embarrassed by their alliance of convenience with the world's most notorious autocrat. However, eight months later, when the Bolsheviks stormed the Winter Palace, the capitals of Europe started to tremble. As Vladimir Lenin negotiated peace with Germany, in November and December 1917, British newspapers spent their time denouncing the illegitimacy of the new Russian government. European rulers were aghast to find that Lenin was there to stay, and, moreover, workers across Europe seemed to want to follow the example of the soldiers and sailors in Petrograd. By the time of the Armistice, strikes, uprisings, and mass revolt had swept away 'all regimes from Vladivostok to the Rhine'.[1] The British state worried revolution might still spread further west. Arthur Cook, then still working as a miner in South Wales, reportedly said at one meeting following the October Revolution: 'To hell with everybody bar my class… Russia has taken the step, and it is due to Britain to second the same and secure peace and leave the war and its cost to the capitalist who made it for the profiteer.'[2]

As Russia erupted into civil war between the new government and the counter-revolutionary 'Whites', lurid tales of Red atrocities began to appear in the British press. These ranged from reports and exaggerations of things that actually happened, such as the murder of the tsarist Archbishop of Perm, to more fantastical tales. From late 1918 the newspapers' favourite Red scare story was the supposed abolition of the royal family and the 'nationalisation' of women to turn them into common property. That this was an obvious lie that had found its way to the *Daily Telegraph* from various 'White' tsarist forces did not stop it from being raised in the House of Commons on multiple occasions.[3]

The killing of the deposed tsar and his family in July 1918 appeared to confirm these tales of Bolshevik barbarism, and was personal for the British royal family, who were cousins of the Romanovs. The spectre of communism became an ever-present feature of the popular press and literature, and a pervasive anti-socialist feeling, fanned deliberately by the Conservative Party, took hold among middle-class, white-collar, and some industrial workers. The charge of Red sedition was levelled at those far beyond the ranks of the Communist Party of Great Britain. Mainstream labour figures were caught in the net. One Conservative Party leaflet described the post-war strike wave of 1919: 'A plot by a minority to destroy the House of Commons, to make the vote valueless, and to establish a dictatorship in this country.'[4] The Tories were setting themselves and their voters up as the stout defenders of the constitution against the red menace.

Those who did not indulge in such hyperbole were more at pains to emphasise the distinction between the solid, sensible, moderate British working man and the sinister figure of the communist agitator. The former was concerned primarily with feeding his family, keeping his house, and 'getting on'. The latter was a shiftless professional agitator in the pay of a foreign power. This worldview created a tension. If the innate respectability of the British worker meant that he had no truck with radical or revolutionary political views, then why was communism such a danger? One newspaper squared this circle succinctly:

> This country is the least Socialistic in the world, because the best governed. Left to itself it would never adopt the wild theories of Marx or Lenin. Such theories could never hope to win their way here by open challenge. They can only be propagated by subtle and underground methods. Naturally the most obvious of these is the 'capture' of the trade union organisation. Here there is a splendid set of machinery ready to the extremists' hands. All they need to do is gain absolute control over it, then on some fine day to issue a sudden secret order, and we shall wake up to find the country in the throes of revolution in the Russian style, with misery, ruin, famine, starvation and death facing this great and once prosperous country.[5]

Many in the British establishment were seized by this conspiracist worldview in the 1920s. They could not understand how working-class radicalism had grown out of harsh material conditions, the experience of war, the tyranny of the bosses in the workplace, and self-education. It could only have been imported by nefarious outside agitators.

The idea that the Communist International in Moscow was using its small British section, the CPGB, to gain influence in the mainstream labour movement was not entirely far-fetched. The International was in these early years certainly concerned with exporting the revolution, and the British Empire, still just about the world's predominant power, was a key target. From 1920 a number of high-profile labour leaders visited Soviet Russia and returned with more or less favourable impressions. From 1924, under the influence of Grigory Zinoviev, the International embarked on a campaign for international trade union unity. To this end, an Anglo-Russian Trade Union Committee, with representatives from the union organisations of both countries, was formed. The CPGB accepted this but reserved the right to make criticisms of the leaders. Unfortunately, to outside observers, unbothered by the nitty-gritty of revolutionary strategy, this seemed to confirm their worst fears: the Bolshevisation of the mainstream trade union movement. In reality, the enthusiasm of Zinoviev for the Anglo-Russian Committee as a short-cut to fomenting revolution in Britain prompted the CPGB to tone down its denunciations of mainstream trade union leaders in the months leading up to the general strike. For instance, furnishing trades union leader and prominent General Council member Alf Purcell, because of his willingness to sit down with Soviet trade unionists, was hailed in the Communist press. The party's newspaper described Alonzo Swales as showing 'the simple and rugged strength of a far-seeing and courageous leader'.[6]

To counter the Red menace, real or imagined, the British state fell back on authoritarianism. The wartime Defence of the Realm Act had made it an offence to 'by word of mouth or in writing spread reports likely to cause disaffection or alarm among any of His Majesty's forces or among the civilian population'. Cook himself was briefly imprisoned under the act; however, fearful of sparking further unrest, authorities avoided widespread sedition trials. These new powers became a permanent weapon in the government's arsenal through the Emergency Powers Act (EPA), passed by the Lloyd George government in 1920. The EPA gave the king – in practice, the government – the power to declare a state of emergency and draw up wide-ranging regulations that would have the force of law. While these 'emergency regulations' would have to be reviewed by Parliament, in practice a government with a large majority would have little problem passing and maintaining whatever measures for as long as it deemed necessary.

The regulations ensured that, during any emergency, essential goods could be moved, with military assistance if necessary, but stopped short of banning strikes or peaceful picketing altogether. Breaking these regulations could result in a three-month prison sentence with hard labour.

The EPA was first invoked by Lloyd George during the 1921 miners' dispute. He mobilised the Army Reserves and created a volunteer 'Defence Force' of seventy thousand men with Churchill's enthusiastic backing.[7] When the short-lived Labour minority government of 1924 was faced with the possibility of a dock strike by the TGWU, it prepared a proclamation for a State of Emergency, but the dispute was settled before it was brought into force. Only in 1926 did Britain witness emergency regulations deployed on a mass scale outside the coalfields, with thousands of workers falling foul of a law specifically designed to cripple strikes.

***

With the fear of revolution came the rise of the security state. From the start of the twentieth century, the police, the military, and the nation's young security services increasingly concerned themselves with what they called the 'labour problem'.

There were those in the military establishment like Sir Henry Wilson, chief of the Imperial General Staff, just as committed to stamping out Bolshevism as were their political masters. Wilson wrote in his diary just before the Armistice that 'our real danger now is not boches [i.e. Germans] but Bolshevism' and pushed Lloyd George towards active intervention.[8] By this time, British forces had already been on revolutionary Russia's territory for several months. Churchill, who became secretary of state for war after the 1918 election, was the most hawkish interventionist, consistently excusing White atrocities in the name of the greater good. The British government knew of extra-judicial killings, mass rapes, and consistent anti-Jewish pogroms being carried out by White forces, yet continued to arm and fund them.[9] For Churchill, Bolshevism was 'this world-wide conspiracy for the overthrow of civilisation and for the reconstitution of society on the basis of arrested development, of envious malevolence, and impossible equality', spearheaded by Jewish revolutionaries lacking national feeling.[10] Consequently, it was an existential threat to the British Empire and had to be stopped.

Churchill's Russian adventure ended in abject failure. This was not simply the fault of White generals' military ineptitude and utter disunity, which even significant foreign aid was not able to overcome. At home, the weight of public opinion was opposed to the intervention. When, early in 1919, more fighting broke out between Soviet Russia and the newly created Polish republic, the labour movement rapidly mobilised a 'Hands Off Russia' campaign, which encompassed all shades of opinion from pro-Bolsheviks to moderate Labour Party leaders. None of them wanted Britain to be drawn fully into another war, nor a repeat of the movement's failure to prevent it as in 1914. Veteran suffragette and socialist Sylvia Pankhurst launched a persistent propaganda campaign in the East End that resulted in London dockers refusing to load a consignment of weapons onto a ship, the *Jolly George*, bound for Poland. Their stance was given official union backing by Ernest Bevin.

When, in August 1920, Lloyd George appeared to be moving towards a pro-war position as Red Army troops pushed towards Warsaw, the Labour Party and the TUC formed a National Council of Action threatening to use extra-parliamentary means to prevent Britain joining the war. They warned the Government that 'the whole industrial power of the organised workers will be used to defeat this war'. Some 350 local Councils of Action were set up. They were urged to keep a look out for the movement of war materials and form subcommittees for strike arrangements while 'not in any way to usurp the powers of Trade Union Executives, especially so far as the withdrawal of labour is concerned'.[11]

This raised, briefly but alarmingly, the prospect of widespread industrial action up to and including a general strike in support of revolutionary Russia. As well as a threat, it was also an opportunity for the right to skewer the labour leaders as agents of Bolshevism. Ramsay MacDonald, who had paid for his anti-war stance by being booted out of Parliament during the 'khaki election' of 1918, argued that 'when people talk of this Council being unconstitutional, they talk nonsense. Everything necessary to protect the Constitution is constitutional, if constitutional means anything at all except passive obedience to any outrageous acts done by men who happen to be Ministers.'[12]

The arch-moderate union leader Jimmy Thomas disagreed. At the special conference called to institute the Council of Action, he told the assembled trade unionists they were abrogating their executive authority to determine the best course of action. 'When you vote for this resolution,' he continued, 'do not do so on the assumption that you are merely voting for a simple down-tools policy. It is nothing of the kind. If this resolution is to be given effect, it means a challenge to the whole Constitution of this country.'[13] He did not want it, he declared, but as Parliament would not act against the war, the workers would have to.

In the event, the Polish victory over the Red Army – 'the miracle on the Vistula' – rendered the situation moot. The question of whether the moderate trade union and labour leaders were prepared to call a general strike for a political goal remained, for now, unanswered.

Just as concerning for the authorities was the discontent manifesting in the military itself. The year 1919 saw an unprecedented series of mutinies in the Army and Navy. The immediate cause was the slow and uneven pace of demobilisation. The bulk of troops were not professional soldiers and they wanted to get back to their civilian lives as quickly as possible. Having been through the horrors of the war and defeated the enemy, they reasoned, there was no need for them still to be in uniform. Many were trade unionists. They resented the extension of class boundaries to the Army, where most of the officers were their social superiors.

In January ten thousand troops at Folkestone refused to obey orders to embark for France. Within days, as many as 52,000 soldiers were effectively on strike. Some of these actions took on the characteristics of a trade union dispute, with committees being elected and pickets placed at harbour gates.[14] An army circular issued at the end of January asked officers to report back on the following questions:

> Will troops in various areas respond to orders for assistance to preserve the public peace?
> Will they assist in strike-breaking?
> Will they parade for draft to overseas, especially to Russia?
> Whether there is any growth of trade unionism among the units under your command?
> The effect outside trade unions have on them.
> Whether any agitation from internal or external sources is affecting them.
> Whether any Soldiers' Councils have been formed.[15]

Sailors on the *HMS Kilbride* mutinied and hoisted the red flag when commanded to join the Russian campaign, and in the Baltic a series of similar rebellions affected several ships later in the year. Several death sentences were passed against mutineers, but not carried out for fear of sparking a general conflagration. Major-General Sir Wyndham Childs later summed up this acute nervousness: 'I feel sure that we sent back into the ranks of labour, dissatisfied men by the thousand – men who afterwards took an active part in the strikes and industrial upheavals which were the natural and ultimate sequel of war.'[16]

As well as the military, another arm of the state increasingly concerned itself with the organised labour movement. The security services were relatively young and still behaved as a kind of roguish gentleman's club. The Secret Service Bureau was founded in 1909, primarily concerning itself with counter-espionage against the kaiser's spy network. After 1917, and particularly following the defeat of Germany the following year, the security services' emphasis shifted to the red menace emanating from Soviet Russia. By 1923, agents of MI5, as the Secret Service Bureau was by then known, had successfully infiltrated the CPGB and were working closely with a shadowy organisation of private businessmen, the Industrial Intelligence Bureau, to monitor suspected communists in workplaces.[17] Many of the reports produced by these would-be gentlemen spies were far removed from the plane of reality. Childs, who headed up the Metropolitan Police Special Branch after the war, recalled having to discard at least eighty percent of the information he received as too fanciful to be taken seriously. One informant, 'a well-known public man', claimed to have information from directly inside the CPGB that four battalions of communists were forming up in South London intending to march on Buckingham Palace and chloroform the guards.[18]

It was the Special Branch and its colleagues in the police who took on the lion's share of the work of monitoring internal dissidents. These officers were by and large men for whom communism was beyond the pale of acceptable opinion, and in whose worldview any sort of trade union militancy was merely a Trojan horse for the Bolshevik threat. Sir Basil Thomson, head of CID at the Metropolitan Police, who, in 1919, was given the task of coordinating the various intelligence agencies, described Bolshevism as 'an infectious disease rather than a political creed – a disease which spreads like a cancer, eating away the tissue of society until the whole mass disintegrates and falls into corruption'.[19] These attitudes were almost always accompanied by an antisemitic worldview in which the threatened global revolution was being propagated by 'Jewish Bolshevik' agitators.

State agencies therefore disproportionately busied themselves with the activities of foreigners and immigrants, or 'aliens' in the language of the time. In December 1925 the chief constable of Glasgow wrote to the Home Office with a list of 'alien Communists' he recommended for deportation. These were largely Russians and Lithuanians, including miners. Where they were 'Russian Jews' this was inevitably pointed out. All but four of them had been resident in the country for more than twenty years, many with children born in Scotland. The Home Office official in receipt of the report complained: 'It is not much use the C[hief] C[onstable] continuing to send up batches like this and the fact that the grounds for suggesting deportation seem ludicrously inadequate in some cases tends to throw doubt on the wisdom of his recommendations. He has already been asked to come up and discuss a previous batch and said he would – but has not done so.'[20] Clearly the red scare had taken hold among some to the extent that it was becoming counterproductive.

***

The spectre of revolution and the fear of industrial unrest, in the years following the First World War, convinced those more sober individuals in the corridors of power of the need to devise a comprehensive plan to keep the country moving during a general stoppage of work. Faced with a potential stoppage in the mines and a strike on the London Underground in the spring of 1919, Lloyd George's coalition, at Lord Curzon's urging, set up a permanent interdepartmental cabinet committee, initially known as the Industrial Action Committee. This would be an alternative to Winston Churchill's favoured method of simply using the military to suppress strikes.[21] By avoiding deployment of troops, Curzon reasoned, the prospect of a major strike developing into serious social conflict would be reduced.

The first test was the national railway strike in September 1919. During this week-long strike, the mass enrolment of volunteer workers that would be repeated in 1926 was piloted, with local Rotary Clubs, Scout groups, and the Automobile Association (AA) offering assistance.[22] Following the railway strike, the organisation was made permanent under the more innocuous name of the Supply and Transport Committee (STC). Its aim was primarily to ensure that food and other essentials could still reach shelves during a national strike, and that the lights could be kept on by the maintenance of power supplies. Moreover, it would undertake the work of attempting to break any general strike through the recruitment of volunteer labour and the inducement of strikers to remain at work.

Between October 1919 and November 1921, the STC met forty-six times. It agreed a three-stage approach to government action during any general strike. First would come the gathering of state forces and the calling up of volunteers, followed by an intensification of activity and an increase in police forces through the calling up of reserves or recruitment of special constables. Finally, the military would be used to quell civil disturbances if necessary.[23] There was broad agreement with this strategy although debates occurred on various points. Churchill, for example, wanted a heavier reliance on special constables or some other form of volunteer police force to keep the peace, so that the Army could be concentrated to deal with any attempted insurrection in the capital. And there were disagreements over the extent to which volunteer labour should be advertised for in advance, in case this looked too obviously like government strikebreaking.

Eventually a scheme was arrived at whereby the country would be divided into ten districts, plus Scotland which would have its own similar arrangements. In each district a junior member of the government would be appointed as civil commissioner, reporting to a chief civil commissioner in Whitehall. Each commissioner would have a number of underlings with different responsibilities. There would be food officers responsible for maintaining supplies and clamping down on any hoarding or profiteering. Road officers would bring together local private companies in Haulage Committees to ensure goods could be moved in the event of a rail strike. Other officials would liaise with the police, local authorities, and the eighty-eight Voluntary Service Committees across the country whose job would be to sign up strikebreaking labour.

After Black Friday and the subsequent temporary ebbing of trade union militancy, the STC remained in place but its activities somewhat lapsed. When Stanley Baldwin succeeded Bonar Law as Conservative leader and prime minister in May 1923, he immediately set about reviving the STC under the able stewardship of his own private secretary J. C. C. Davidson, MP for Hemel Hempstead, who was made chief civil commissioner. As a former civil servant, Davidson was intimately familiar with the workings of Whitehall. He impressed upon everyone there the importance of secrecy to the success of the emergency organisation. Departments were advised that 'disclosure of details should be avoided so far as possible' and people 'should only be told what is essential to enable them to perform their duties'.[24] In this cloak-and-dagger environment, Davidson was not paid a salary for his chief civil commissioner role and so, remarkably, received £500 per year for this work directly from Conservative Party funds.[25]

When the Labour minority government assumed office in January 1924, Davidson was urged by a close friend and ally not to turn his papers regarding the Supply and Transport Organisation (STO) over to the new government but rather to give them to senior civil servants for safekeeping, on the understanding that these civil servants might also keep them from the incoming government. The reasoning behind this was that 'the Chief Civil Commissioner appointed by that government might very well be a prominent trade unionist, like Mr Smilie or Mr Frank Hodges. In this event, whoever was appointed would at once become acquainted with all the machinery for quelling the crisis which he himself, when in opposition, may have done his best to foment.'[26]

In the event, the chief civil commissioner of the Labour government was not a trade unionist but Josiah Wedgwood, scion of the pottery dynasty and a personal friend of Davidson. Shortly after coming into office Wedgwood produced a memo arguing:

> It would be well, now that a Labour Government is in power, if the whole system of dealing with these emergencies could be recast. There has been an almost melodramatic air of secrecy about the whole business, as though a revolution were being combated, rather than a straightforward effort made to keep the essential services going... It might be better to rely more upon the Local Authorities and upon the open statement of what the Government requires and what it means to secure in the case of emergency.[27]

Discussions were initiated with the transport unions to attempt to elicit their cooperation in a less secretive supply and transport scheme, to no avail. The situation was not helped by the threatened transport workers' strikes in spring 1924 during which the Labour government indicated its willingness to use both the Emergency Powers Act and the existing STC organisation. 'MacDonald and his ministry', observed Lloyd George, 'not only took it over, but were ready and even anxious to use it.'[28]

When, along with the rest of the Labour government, Wedgwood was ejected from office ten months later, he told Davidson: 'I haven't destroyed any of your plans. In fact, I haven't done a damn thing about them.'[29] Not only had the emergency plans remained intact, but the wider labour movement had not been made aware of the details of them. The reasons for this are not entirely clear. Perhaps the newly respectable Labour ministers feared breaching the Official Secrets Act, deferring to what they assumed were administrative norms. Or perhaps, bruised by facing down the transport unions themselves, they were keen for such meticulous plans to remain in place, once they made a triumphant return to power.[30]

***

The government of Stanley Baldwin took office in November 1924 in a landslide victory following an election beset by the spectre of communism. Labour had come to power at the beginning of that year without a parliamentary majority, and it was a question of when, not if, the other parties would force a vote of no confidence. An article in the CPGB's newspaper *Workers' Weekly* precipitated the crisis. The Communists had begun to produce propaganda aimed at convincing the rank and file of the Armed Forces not to fight in any imperialist war or allow themselves to be used against strikers. Their 'Open Letter to the Fighting Forces' stated:

> Soldiers, sailors, airmen, flesh of our flesh and bone of our bone, the Communist Party calls upon you to begin the task of not only organising passive resistance when war is declared, or when an industrial dispute involves you, but to definitely and categorically let it be known that, neither in the class war nor a military war, will you turn your guns on your fellow workers, but instead will line up with your fellow workers in an attack upon the exploiters and capitalists, and will use your arms on the side of your own class.[31]

For this, a case was prepared against the paper's editor, John Ross Campbell, under the Incitement to Mutiny Act 1797, and the attorney general advised prosecution. Charges were, however, withdrawn after political pressure, but Ramsay MacDonald denied having anything to do with this in the House of Commons. As a result, a vote was brought by the prominent liberal MP Sir John Simon calling for an inquiry into the matter. MacDonald made it clear he regarded this as a vote of confidence in his government and, when he inevitably lost, had to go to the country.[32]

To much respectable opinion, the Campbell case seemed to prove that even a moderate Labour leader was at the end of the day in thrall to the movement's 'extremist' wing. This was compounded during the election itself by an act of political manipulation involving the security services and Conservative Party headquarters. Four days before polling day, the *Daily Mail* published a document purported to have been written by Grigory Zinoviev, a leading figure in the Communist International, giving instructions to British communists. The content of the letter was in fact relatively innocuous, urging communists to increase their agitation among the military and to pressure the Labour government to ratify its proposed general treaty with the USSR. It was however splashed in the *Mail* as 'Civil War Plot by Socialists' Masters: Moscow Orders to our Reds'.[33] It was taken up by the rest of the right-wing press as further proof that the Labour administration was a catspaw for Moscow.

The letter was just the latest in a line of forgeries that had been passed to British intelligence officers in the Baltic by White Russians. The intelligence services then passed it on to the government giving absolute assurances as to its authenticity, and leaked the letter to Conservative Central Office who in turn passed it to the press.[34] The Labour Party, which would probably have lost the election in any case, went down to a crushing defeat, even though its share of the vote actually increased. The Zinoviev letter rallied anti-socialist opinion behind the Conservatives, who won 412 seats, and thereby accelerated the decline of the Liberals, who won just 40.

Thanks to the red scare, Baldwin was back in office with an apparently unassailable majority. He was, in Tory terms, a moderniser with a business background. His father, Alfred, a Liberal who defected to the Conservatives in the 1870s for religious reasons, ran the family's iron and steel business in the West Midlands in a relatively progressive fashion. His Wilden ironworks was among the first in the area to introduce eight-hour shifts, and was known to take industrial safety seriously. Strikes at the works were said to be unknown. Alfred remained resident in the village where most of his workmen lived, albeit in a somewhat grander house, and considered himself to know the minds and desires of his men well.

After Alfred's death in 1908, Stanley entered Parliament unopposed for his father's Bewdley seat. A competent and moderate Conservative, he rose steadily through the party's ranks. He inherited his father's paternalistic sympathy for the workers, ensuring that the Wilden workers were paid allowances for six weeks when the works were shut due to the 1912 coal strike. For Baldwin, trade unions, albeit tamed ones in which the radical elements had been neutralised, were crucial to a harmonious system of industrial relations. He also recognised trade unionists were an important constituency of voters, remembering all too well the Liberal landslide in 1906, after the Tories upheld the Taff Vale ruling, effectively making strikes financially catastrophic for unions.[35] This made him cautious, even as prime minister, about pursuing anti-union legislation before the general strike.

Despite his impeccable capitalist credentials, in many ways Baldwin was the perfect spokesman for the white-collar middle class of the new English suburbs. He spoke softly and behaved modestly. He cultivated an anti-intellectual persona despite moving in a social circle of artists and writers. On the campaign trail in 1923 he expressed his desire to retire to Worcestershire 'to read the books I want, to live a decent life, to keep pigs'.[36] His rapid rise through Tory ranks had reached its pinnacle the year before when Prime Minister Bonar Law stepped down due to illness. Against the much larger character of Lord Curzon, the king, partly at J. C. C. Davidson's urging, appointed the unassuming Baldwin as Bonar Law's successor. It was a sign of the changing times and the febrile post-war atmosphere that having a prime minister sitting in the House of Lords would be intolerable to much of the electorate.

Baldwin's politics were indicative of an attempt at the turn of the century to build a mass popular conservatism. As a young man he had joined the Primrose League, an organisation dedicated to spreading conservative principles and loyalty to the Empire among the middle and working classes. Unlike some of the more reactionary and aristocratic elements of his party, Baldwin reconciled himself to the extension of the voting franchise. He was convinced that conservatism could be made popular by extolling the virtues of free enterprise and individual liberty, and giving more people a stake in society through home ownership and savings. As prime minister he took to claiming the newly coined phrase 'property-owning democracy' for his vision.[37]

Others in the government had views that were at odds with their prime minister's professed desire for industrial peace. The puritanical Home Secretary William Joynson-Hicks was an implacable opponent of organised labour. When not concerning himself with the suppression of West End nightclubs and the works of D. H. Lawrence, Jix – as he was popularly known – obsessed over the dangers of socialism. Virulently antisemitic even by the standards of the time, Jix had spent his career railing against the evils of Jewish immigration from Eastern Europe, that is to say, refugees from pogroms. After the Russian revolution he became an avid believer in the idea that there was a global Judaeo-Bolshevik conspiracy against capitalism, and the British Empire in particular. It was this behaviour that earned the home secretary the nickname 'Mussolini Minor'.[38]

This worldview perhaps helped reconcile Jix with his old adversary Winston Churchill. The two had faced each other in a by-election for the Manchester North West seat in 1908, after Churchill had abandoned the Tories for the Liberal Party. At the time, Jix had pronounced: 'There is between him and our party a gulf fixed, which enables me to declare that, while there is seedtime and harvest we will never have him back.'[39] After 1924, however, the pro-White foreign interventionist was back in the Tory fold, having been elected for Epping Forest as an anti-socialist 'constitutionalist' candidate. Churchill was appointed chancellor by Baldwin so that, as the prime minister told his friend the artist Kathleen Hilton Young, 'he wouldn't be able to talk about Labour, nothing but finance'.[40]

This hardline faction in the government was spoiling for a fight with the trade union movement. Their concerns went far beyond the relatively small forces of British communism. They wanted to straitjacket the unions by either rolling back or substantially amending the Trade Disputes Act 1906. This law, passed by the Liberals with Labour support, ensured that unions could not be found liable for damages resulting from strikes, as long as the industrial action was done 'in furtherance of a trade dispute'. In other words, employers could not sue unions if their workers went on strike. The Tory hardliners also wanted legislative reform to weaken the trade unions' funding of the Labour Party. In March 1925 the backbencher Frederick Alexander Macquisten introduced a private member's bill attacking unions' political levy. Anxious to avoid a political conflagration with the unions at this point, Baldwin leant on Macquisten to withdraw his bill. However, even Lord Birkenhead, the enforcer Baldwin had relied on to nip the bill in the bud, wrote to a peer: 'We shall have no peace until the matter is fought out to a victory... which will involve a complete reconsideration of the exceptional legal status conceded to the Trades Unions and which they seem to me, under the influence of extremist elements, to have so grossly abused.'[41]

Just as Red Friday gave confidence to the union membership, it increased the determination of those like Birkenhead, who saw it as an unacceptable climbdown in the face of trade union thuggery. Some have disputed claims by Baldwin and others that the government's emergency organisation was not ready for a confrontation in the summer of 1925, instead suggesting the government did not risk confrontation then because public opinion was with the miners and the unions.[42]

In such a situation a general attack on trade unionism would have been politically foolish. But, the government reasoned, the Communist Party did not enjoy widespread sympathy and could take advantage of the industrial crisis to push its revolutionary agenda. J. C. C. Davidson's biographer commented in 1969 that 'the extent to which Conservative Ministers were convinced of the presence of a gigantic Communist plot now seems somewhat unreal'.[43]

At the first Cabinet meeting after Red Friday 'there was general agreement that the activities of Communist agents in this country should be carefully watched in the present industrial situation'.[44] The following week, posters directed at soldiers were found affixed outside barracks, including in the military town of Aldershot, and Cabinet agreed to prosecute the printers if they could be identified.[45] In early September, the *Mail* claimed that orders had been given to arrest 'Red Agitators' who were preparing to disrupt a military training exercise. 'Statements in the *Mail* and *Sketch* today regarding police action in connection with manoeuvres are merely a triumph of imaginative journalism,' Jix's permanent under-secretary telegraphed to him: 'But we are not issuing any contradiction.'[46]

The government was, in fact, preparing for the arrest of red agitators. By October, the director of public prosecutions advised that evidence existed to arrest leading Communists and that convictions would be likely. These arrests were pre-approved at the highest level of government.[47] The charges would be seditious libel and incitement to mutiny under a law dating back to the Napoleonic Wars. At exactly 5 p.m. on 14 October, the CPGB's King Street headquarters was raided. The police went through the building from top to bottom, seizing twelve leading Communists along with thousands of documents. Shortly afterwards, raids followed at the offices of the Young Communist League and the Minority Movement. In Scotland, leading Communists Tom Bell and William Gallacher were picked up by the Glasgow police and sent to London under escort.

At the trial some of the Communists conducted their own defence while the rest were represented by Sir Henry Slesser who had been solicitor general in the MacDonald government. Speaking for himself, using the courtroom as a soapbox, John Ross Campbell denied that the Communists were interested in carrying out a minority coup, but were trying to build a mass movement. 'I would deplore it', he exclaimed irreverently, 'if the jury have the attitude that our organisation is one of gunmen like the Fascisti or the Ulster Volunteers.'[48] It was to no avail. Five who had previous convictions, including Gallacher, were sentenced to twelve months. The other seven defendants were given the option to disavow the Communist Party and avoid going to prison. They all refused and were jailed for six months.

The Communist trial became a *cause célèbre*. The guilty verdicts delighted the right-wing press. 'Prosecution or persecution of political opinion is repugnant to the British tradition,' claimed the *Daily Express*. 'But when people take to tampering with the disciplined loyalty of the Army and Navy they exhaust the stock of legal tolerance. The trial has taught a salutary lesson. The law of England regards sedition as illegal. Those disciples of Lenin who try to apply his methods here are now warned that they cannot count on immunity.'[49]

The labour movement, including many who had little sympathy with the Communists generally, saw the arrests differently, as a flagrantly political move. Thousands joined demonstrations to Wandsworth Prison and 300,000 signed a petition calling for the release of the twelve. Protesters were careful to couch their support for the twelve as support for freedom of speech and fair play, rather than for communism. When a crowd of supporters was attacked by police outside the courtroom, their treatment riled much respectable opinion. 'I am not aware that to sing "The Red Flag" is illegal, and the police had no right to attack these men,' one bystander stated to the *Herald*. 'I am a law-abiding citizen with a dislike of disorderly scenes, but in my opinion the action of the police in this instance was despicable.'[50]

The arrests were obviously intended to decapitate and disorient the CPGB. But although the party no doubt suffered organisationally from having much of its senior leadership jailed, the trial also had the effect of increasing its membership and intensifying its public meetings on the coal crisis in the winter of 1925–6.[51] As for the police, they congratulated themselves on a job well done. The officer in charge was commended by Met Commissioner Sir William Horwood who could not resist a sideswipe at the 1924 Labour government:

> Those of us in the know realise that the case was the culminating point of four years' real hard work by Chief Inspector Parker and his subordinates – work which was often made harder by the excuses that were made openly by some who were for the time being in authority over us. But, as always, loyal work and the honourable traditions of the Force have prevailed in the long run.[52]

***

Entertaining or enraging as the Communist trial might have been, it was something of a sideshow. In the run-up to Christmas, the real political pressure on the government was coming from its right. Since Red Friday, hardliners had been attacking Baldwin for rolling over in the face of union militancy. The press barons Lord Rothermere, owner of the *Daily Mirror* and *Daily Mail*, and Lord Beaverbrook, of the *Express*, had never warmed to Baldwin as leader of the Conservative Party, considering him too avuncular and indecisive.[53] They were joined in the chorus of criticism by many Tory MPs and grassroots activists, as well as the Duke of Northumberland, who criticised Baldwin for 'drifting helplessly towards the abyss, hoping until the last moment that something will turn up to avert the inevitable catastrophe'.[54] The home secretary, receiving deputations of businessmen, complained that 'our own people are getting so savage thinking that nothing is being done'.[55]

In reality, Baldwin was far more active. The emergency organisation was stepped up immediately after the government's begrudging extension of the coal subsidy. It was perhaps the veil of secrecy over the STO that explained the impatience of those Tories who were outside immediate government circles. This was slightly lifted in the second week of

August. Although much publicity was to be avoided until after the Coal Commission's terms of reference had been decided, offices were opened in each of the districts and civil servants were seconded to these from the Ministry of Health. The eighty-eight Voluntary Service Committees, each chaired by 'a gentleman of local influence', were convened for the registration and recruitment of volunteers.

One of the few areas where volunteer recruitment was not left to this decentralised network of local committees was in the power stations. This was particularly true of those in London, where a detailed plan for the use of exactly 663 naval ratings to operate the boiler rooms already existed. Volunteer lists of technical workers and students at various engineering schools had been kept and periodically updated since 1919, and 'the more responsible of these volunteers [had] been allocated to definite posts in the Stations'.[56] Much depended on a relatively tiny number of highly skilled technical staff remaining at their posts. If these men showed more loyalty to the trade union movement than to the state, and joined a general strike, there would need to be much more direct military intervention to keep Britain's lights on.

The question of law enforcement preparations was a thorny one. There was no way that the small regular police forces could be expected to keep order if widespread rioting or violence broke out in the major population centres. There were 100,000 special constables – volunteer police officers who could be called up in emergencies – across England and Wales but they were overwhelmingly middle-class men and it was noted that 'generally very few are available in the industrial districts'.[57] It was decided that police forces should hold their men at a central location in their town or county, ready to be sent to trouble spots as and when necessary. A list of potential vulnerable spots, like petrol stations and railway signal boxes, would be provided to the Supply and Transport Committee, but Joynson-Hicks noted somewhat ruefully that, as home secretary, he had no direct power to compel one police force to come to the aid of another if necessary.

However much planning went into the emergency organisation, though, it could only be tested in the heat of conflict, as the Cabinet acknowledged: 'While the organisation was complete, it was only a skeleton and could not be put in operation until volunteers had come forward. Volunteers, however, could not be called for until an emergency was proclaimed… Until volunteers had been enrolled and sorted out, the organisation could not function, and this would require a few days.'[58]

Put bluntly, even if the emergency machinery were perfected as much as possible in advance, the government would still need to mobilise public opinion to staff it up. The question of exactly when and how to advertise for volunteers caused some debate in the Cabinet. Lord Eustace Percy, himself from a family of aristocratic coalowners in the North-East, suggested drawing up lists of all firms engaged in maintaining essential supplies and providing them with a Royal Proclamation at the outset of any emergency, informing their workers that they are working under government direction and calling on them to remain at work. He even suggested that the workers could be given special badges to incentivise their loyalty.[59] This proposal was deemed needlessly provocative and remitted to the Supply and Transport Committee, there to be quietly shelved.

The volunteers would be necessary in different roles. Some would directly replace striking workers on the railways and the docks. Crucially, others would form an armada of private vehicles as the government looked to the emerging road transport sector to circumvent the need for rail freight in the event that the heavily unionised railway network was paralysed. Car ownership was still largely restricted to the affluent, and so motorists were a natural constituency for the government to court. Discussions had already taken place with the Royal Automobile Club and the Automobile Association, of which the home secretary was a former chairman.[60]

In order to prevent the government appearing to take sides in an industrial dispute that it professed to be committed to preventing, the enrolment of these volunteers would be farmed out to external organisations. In October, Cabinet noted approvingly: 'Various unofficial organisations had been formed for this purpose, including the OMS, the Chambers of Commerce, the Fascisti and the Crusaders, and it was understood that the persons who volunteered under these unofficial organisations would, in case of emergency, be at the disposal of the government.'[61] Jix told Baldwin he had met the Fascist leaders several times and was sure they could be relied on.[62]

The most significant of these was the Organisation for the Maintenance of Supplies (OMS), an avowedly non-state and non-party group whose leadership nevertheless read like a roll-call of establishment figures. Its president, Charles Hardinge, 1st Baron Hardinge of Penshurst, had been the viceroy of India for six years. He was joined on the national council by the Earl Jellicoe, who had served as first sea lord during the war. The existence of the OMS was announced through the letters page of the *Times* on 25 September. It claimed to oppose industrial action only where it would cause significant social harms: 'If, however, in order to secure a particular end, an attempt is made to inflict severe privation on the great mass of the people who have no part in that industrial dispute, this Organisation of Citizens, serving the interests of the general community, will place its entire resources at the disposal of the constitutional authorities'.[63]

Despite the OMS fervently maintaining that it only cared about public welfare, the links between it and senior Conservatives were clear from the beginning. As early as August, a memo from the minister for transport had argued that 'an organisation outside the government could do a very great deal in enrolling in advance capable and willing volunteers and giving them instructions where to report and for what duties' and 'such men would not be deterred by the intimidation of pickets'.[64]

One week after its existence was made public, Joynson-Hicks gave overt backing to the OMS in the *Times*. Admitting that he had known about the organisation for some weeks, he stated 'it would be a very great assistance to us to receive from the OMS, or from any other body of well-disposed citizens, classified lists of men in different parts of the country who would be willing to place their services at the disposal of the Government'.[65] There was some dissension from the minister of labour who urged that the government should do nothing that would make it look as though it was directing the OMS's activities. The government would spend the next few months walking a tightrope, adamantly insisting that the responsibility of keeping the country going through a strike would be theirs alone and that the OMS was nothing to do with them, while at the same time tacitly encouraging its activities.

Much smaller than the OMS, but just as keen to help the government, was Britain's nascent fascist movement. It was inspired by Benito Mussolini's so-called March on Rome in 1922, after which a wave of violence and terror was unleashed against socialists and trade unionists across Italy. Established in May 1923, the British Fascists (BF) could boast of links to the highest echelons of the establishment. A Tory MP sat on the BF's Grand National Council and several others were supportive.[66] Several high-ranking military officers, serving and retired, were members. In March 1925 Harry Pollitt, a leader of the NMM, was hauled off a train at Edge Hill station on his way to address a meeting in Liverpool and held overnight by five BF members. It was an action that echoed the kidnapping of Italian socialist politician Giacomo Matteotti by the fascist political police in Rome nine months earlier. While Matteotti was stabbed to death trying to escape, Pollitt was released the next day by his captors who apparently meant to prevent him from addressing the meeting but not to cause him any physical harm. At their subsequent trial, despite admitting their involvement, the five claimed it had been a harmless practical joke, and were acquitted.

Another, smaller group, the National Fascisti (NF), was more militaristic, parading in uniforms and adopting the Roman salute. In 1925 they physically attacked several Communists in London and stabbed a tailor, Max Adler, at an unemployed workers' meeting in September.[67] The following month four NF members hijacked at gunpoint a delivery van carrying 8,000 copies of the left-wing *Daily Herald* newspaper. The assailants were merely given a dressing down by a magistrate and released. The contrast between their treatment and that of the twelve arrested Communists – who had committed no violent acts – caused some unease even in the mainstream press.[68]

The views of fascists and their associations with violence were by no means unconscionable for the government. Their paramilitary trappings and independent organisation might have been irritating, but ultimately they were on the side of the angels, defending 'the community' against the threat of anarchy and revolution.

For trade unionists, with an eye on the paramilitaries effectively conducting street executions of their counterparts on the continent, any concordat between the Conservatives and the fascists at home seemed to portend hard times ahead. Already convinced that Baldwin was dead set on reducing their living standards, and seeing the home secretary embrace the OMS, workers were left to wonder just how far the government was prepared to go to defeat the general strike, if it came.

Miners' leaders including Herbert Smith (left) and A.J. Cook (second from right) attend the Samuel Commission.

4

BREAKDOWN

If, next May, there is a general strike in this country, it will be a national calamity, and once you let loose the passions of men no one can prophesy where it will end.

- ARTHUR COOK TO A MEETING IN BIRMINGHAM, 22 MARCH 1926

The General Strike is the last resource of steady responsible men to prevent the degradation of working class life to an impossible level.

- INDEPENDENT LABOUR PARTY NOTES FOR SPEAKERS, 3 MAY 1926

From the publication of the Samuel report on 10 March 1926, there was a six-week window in which to avoid a confrontation before the expiration of the coal subsidy. It was clear to all that if an agreement was not reached, some sort of industrial crisis would erupt. At a minimum, this would be a national lockout of the country's one million miners. At most, it would be a general strike. With the miners and owners digging into their entrenched positions, much depended on the attitude of the government and the miners' putative allies in the TUC.

Although some in government wanted Baldwin to grasp the nettle, accept all Samuel's recommendations, and get on with reorganising the industry, Churchill warned that the nationalisation of mineral rights would be ruinous to the public purse. But the government could not be seen to offhandedly reject the findings of a commission that it had itself set up. George Lane-Fox, the minister for mines, proposed an innovative solution. Samuel's proposals for reorganisation would be accepted in theory by the government, but nothing would actually be done unless the other parties accepted the report in full.[1] This was, as he was fully aware, putting the ball back into the court of the miners and owners, neither of whom wanted to play. On 24 March Baldwin told the warring parties:

> Nevertheless, in face of the unanimous Report of the Commission, and for the sake of a general settlement, the Government for their part will be prepared to undertake such measures as may be required by the State to give the recommendations effect, *provided that those engaged in this industry – with whom the decision primarily rests – agree to accept the Report and to carry on the industry on the basis of its recommendations.*[2]

By the time this abrogation of responsibility had been communicated, two of the six weeks had been lost.

Keen though Baldwin was to leave the coal industry to its own devices, this was never really a viable option. Miners' working hours were set by law so, if they became part of any negotiations, the government would necessarily be involved. The sort of reorganisation proposed by Samuel would also likely get nowhere without some sort of government incentives and investment. When the owners first met the miners to negotiate on the report on 31 March, therefore, they kicked all the questions of reorganisation back to the government. At this meeting the Mining Association also confirmed its position, in contravention of the Samuel report, in favour of lengthening the working day.[3]

It was not just the prime minister who was taking things easy. The TUC drifted towards the storm in an even more lackadaisical manner than the government, although it did offer its services as an alternative mediator between the miners and owners. The Miners' Executive was adamant that it could not take wage cuts. 'Not a penny off the pay, not a second on the day' was the slogan reiterated by Cook as he embarked on another energetic speaking tour. But the TUC's Special Industrial Committee was slow to provide the backing the miners needed. Early in April it told Cook weakly that it was unable to take a definite position on miners' wages because to do so would 'prejudice negotiations'. Pugh and Thomas were not confident that their members would respond to a strike call on the miners' behalf, or even just to support the extension of the subsidy.

By contrast, there was a solid expectation among the rank-and-file that the other unions would come to the miners' aid. Discontent was bubbling up in other industries. In January the railwaymen narrowly rejected a pay offer from their National Wages Board. Jimmy Thomas had to win the NUR delegates round with a personal appeal, averting a potential national strike just three days before it was due to start. For this he won the praise of his biographer Gregory Blaxland:

> It was a very closely won verdict which might easily have gone the other way if Thomas had not refrained from changing for an Empire dinner at the Savoy which he was due to attend as soon as the meeting ended. 'I don't apologise for not being in evening dress,' he told them at the dinner. 'I won by a few votes. What would have happened if I had appeared respectable?'[4]

Just weeks later there was a breakdown in talks between engineering unions and bosses, and an unofficial strike at a London firm threatened to spiral into a national lockout which was only stopped by the intervention of the union leaders. Throughout the spring, the industrial situation remained delicate and an explosion of unrest in one area could easily have rapidly escalated. Cook was acutely aware of this and tried to push the TUC down the road of solidarity action by claiming publicly in late March that an agreement had been reached not to handle any coal in the event of a lockout.[5] Although this was not true, the TUC could hardly deny it without alienating the mass of workers.

On 21 March the Minority Movement convened a 'special conference of action' in the Communist stronghold of Battersea. Tom Mann made a stirring speech, supporting the formation of a Workers' Defence Force to protect pickets from fascist or police attacks. He implored friends and relatives of soldiers on leave to talk to them about the workers' demands.

Delegates claiming to represent nearly one million workers were present. They were miners, metalworkers, labourers, builders, transport workers. Some came from the ranks of the unemployed.[6] They adopted a compelling analysis that saw the developments of the previous months, including the arrest of the Communist leaders, the employers' offensives on the railways and in engineering, and the looming coal crisis, as part of an all-encompassing class struggle. They entreated the General Council to take a lead in this struggle, while also urging local trades councils to turn themselves into Councils of Action.[7] This was a significant achievement in taking radical policy far beyond the ranks of the Communist Party, urging those attending to strengthen their shop-floor organisation. 'There is no doubt', wrote one of the plainclothes officers observing proceedings, 'the conference was a success from the Minority Movement's standpoint.'[8] Nevertheless, it did not manage to push an indolent TUC leadership into any further action.

On 12 April the coal negotiations reached a deadlock. Three days later, the district associations of coalowners terminated the contracts of all miners in effect from 30 April and posted new wage rates. Essentially, any miner who did not agree to resume work under new terms in two weeks' time would be sacked. We now know this practice as 'fire and rehire'. If the miners refused the cuts, they would be 'locked out' from 1 May. The employers invited the MFGB's regional representatives to discuss new minimum rates in each coalfield, a direct challenge to the union's position of maintaining a national minimum wage. They were clear that the new terms would involve significant wage cuts and longer hours. At this point, Cook appeared to waver. He told Tom Jones, the deputy secretary to the Cabinet who was fruitlessly trying to prevail on the more moderate mine-owners to assert themselves in the negotiations, that he recognised the miners might have to take a reduction on the national minimum, but that it must remain a *national* minimum.[9]

Although the lockout notices set both sides on a very clear path to confrontation, the government still dragged its feet in intervening. Not until 23 April did Prime Minister Stanley Baldwin meet with representatives of both the miners and the employers in Downing Street. He opened the discussion inauspiciously: 'I have very, very few words to say to you this morning.'

Claiming to represent the country as a whole, Baldwin simply wanted, he said, to hear the case put forward by each side. For the owners, Sir Evan Williams bemoaned the MFGB's intransigence. Nevertheless, he acknowledged that in districts where much of the coal was exported to the international market, 'it is a matter of absolute impossibility for the industry to provide a wage other than one which...I did not shrink from describing as miserable'. More economically competitive districts would, he argued, be able to pay a good wage if the hours of work were lengthened.[10]

Herbert Smith stated the miners' case in his typically forthright manner. 'You said you spoke for the nation. I realise your position,' Smith told Baldwin. 'We speak for a million or more men who have had conditions put down for them to work under that we cannot and would not attempt to recommend them to consider for one moment.' He flatly refused to countenance any discussion of district-based minimum rates. The conditions of miners in each district already varied dramatically; Smith argued in favour of levelling them up. Quoting from the employers' own material, Smith accused them of wanting to roll back local customs and agreements that had been won over the years, such as the practice in South Wales of paying 'six shifts for five' to those who worked nights.[11]

These direct tripartite talks produced no results. Baldwin went on holiday for the weekend. On his return to Downing Street, the prime minister summoned the TUC's Special Industrial Committee for talks separately from the coalowners. This group of eight men included the TUC general secretary Walter Citrine, Jimmy Thomas, train drivers' leader John Bromley, and veteran union official Ben Tillett, but no miners' representatives. They arrived at Downing Street at lunchtime on 26 April, slightly depleted in number due to the lateness of the summons, to begin days of frantic shadow-boxing negotiations. In his frustration at the deadlock, Baldwin reluctantly took the talks out of the hands of the miners and the coalowners. The TUC would speak for the former and the government for the latter, but neither with any surety that any concessions they made would be accepted by anyone outside the room.

Industrial relations in the mines, opined Baldwin, were the worst of any sector he had seen. No government since the war had satisfactorily overseen a proper settlement, and it was crucial for the country to reach an agreement, particularly as others were 'liable at any moment to have the economic circumstances of their industry altered by disputes in this one great and fundamental industry'. He reiterated that the government stood by the recommendations of the Samuel report. Baldwin was likely hoping that the TUC committee would be amenable to suggesting to the MFGB leaders that they make some concessions before he met with the miners and owners again. Meanwhile, the TUC committee was looking to the government to find the middle ground with a proposal of its own. Jimmy Thomas stated that if such a proposal could not be put before a conference of trade union executives, due to meet in three days' time, then the movement would have no choice but to back the miners' position.

Sir Arthur Steel-Maitland, minister of labour, agreed that if the miners and employers were brought back into a room together without an agreed basis for negotiations, 'they would merely go at one another like terriers'. The trade unionists suggested that pay only be talked about once some agreement had been reached on the reorganisation of the industry. They also suggested that other industrialists who would be affected by a coal stoppage be brought in, to act as a moderating influence on the mineowners. Baldwin seemed amenable to both these suggestions.[12] He had himself confided in officials that he hoped to sidestep the wages question by securing an agreement on lengthening the working day. Increasingly anxious for a settlement, Thomas pointed out to Baldwin that night that there was only time for one full day of negotiations before the miners' delegates met. The two parted with a promise to prevail upon each side of the dispute to resume direct negotiations. 'We both of us have difficult tasks,' said Baldwin, 'and we were none of us brought up as circus riders.'[13]

The prime minister met the coalowners later that night, who were less than pleased at the prospect of having trade unionists from outside their industry intrude on the negotiations. They did, however, inform him the next morning that they were prepared to discuss anything with the MFGB, including the issue of a national minimum wage if it was tied to a longer working day. Baldwin attempted to secure more concessions from the employers, arguing for a national minimum wage that would be set by arbitration and could be altered by the employers in a given district by making an application to a wages board.[14] But this proposal was rejected and Baldwin did not push back. After he apologetically explained to the Industrial Committee that it would not be able to join the talks, the TUC men proffered advice to him on how best to approach the discussion. Thomas, who did the bulk of the talking for the TUC in these meetings, strongly urged the prime minister to convene the negotiations before the miners' delegates assembled in London, as he feared the outcome of a delegate meeting at which no progress could be reported. Turning to the

Industrial Committee's chairman, Arthur Pugh of the steelworkers' union, Baldwin asked whether it would be better to summon the miners before or after they had eaten. 'It all depends', replied Pugh, 'on how long it is since they had the previous meal.'[15]

The following day, 28 April, the miners' delegates met. Exercising tight control over their leaders, they mandated their negotiators not to accept any wage cuts without first bringing any proposals back to them for a vote.[16] Direct negotiations that afternoon went nowhere. In the evening, when Baldwin met the TUC representatives again, his frustration was palpable. He argued for a simplification of wages across the whole industry once the current trouble was settled, saying of the current pay structure: 'I do not believe anybody understands it. If you ask either side what a man is getting they always give you different answers and neither believes what the other says. The men will be going out by the hundred thousand and you have no idea what they are going out for.'[17] The government side, which included Steel-Maitland and George Lane-Fox, floated the idea of a national minimum with temporary lower wages for the coal-exporting districts that were struggling (primarily South Wales, Durham, and Northumberland). The TUC Committee was open to this proposal, providing it could get definite statements from both the government and the employers about measures to reorganise and rationalise the industry as recommended in the Samuel report. The government, though, had told the miners that they must accept the principle of wage cuts before any reorganisation would be contemplated.[18]

***

Amidst this confusion, the TUC's special conference of trade union executives met on 29 April to decide a common approach to the situation. Eight hundred delegates from 141 unions convened in Memorial Hall, Farringdon. The delegates discussed the Samuel Commission's report and supported the miners' opposition to wage cuts, despite disquiet from some at the top of the TUC who were sceptical about what they saw as the MFGB's obduracy. The TUC's Special Industrial Committee was rebranded as the Negotiating Committee and given a mandate to continue discussions with the government, but the mood seemed to be shifting towards confrontation. Bevin told the assembled trade unionists what would happen if the issue was not settled: 'Twenty-four hours from now you have to cease being separate unions. You will have to become one union with no autonomy.'[19] In this spirit, albeit reluctantly and not entirely genuinely, the MFGB agreed to give the TUC full control of the final negotiations. It was the price for securing the TUC's full backing if an agreement could not be reached.

Herbert Smith and Arthur Cook accompanied the Negotiating Committee for further talks in the prime minister's room at the House of Commons. Baldwin summed up respectable opinion in the country to Jimmy Thomas:

> There has been a curious spirit about among many people who perhaps do not know as much about it as we do of that peculiar kind of optimism that all English people suffer from of thinking that the thing that they all rather dread and don't want will not come about. I do not know what it arises from. It may be partly from a feeling that we shall not make fools of ourselves and I think it may be partly from a feeling that there may be some kind of conjuring trick at the eleventh hour that is going to save the situation.[20]

Thomas blamed this feeling on the press 'deliberately deceiving the public' by not acknowledging the complexities of the situation. Baldwin floated a proposal for a temporary extension in working hours, which Smith and Cook forcefully rebuffed. He appealed to the trade unionists to avoid a stoppage because the country would not forgive either them or his government for it. Thomas, despite his differences with the miners' leaders, was furious that there was still no definitive offer of a settlement from the coalowners' side. But Baldwin refused to go over their heads and table his own proposals. He inclined towards a *laissez faire* approach to industrial relations and lacked understanding of the details of the industry. Perhaps more critically, he was increasingly confident that the state was well prepared to see out a general strike successfully.

Throughout 30 April, a series of frenetic meetings between the different parties took place. Ramsay MacDonald and Arthur Henderson joined the talks alongside the Negotiating Committee. These Labour Party leaders were, if anything, keener to avoid a strike than the TUC or the government. Their immediate concern was to get the coalowners' lockout notices suspended in order to create more time for further talks. The government, it appeared, had other ideas. Jimmy Thomas had obtained a copy of a poster already produced by the Organisation for the Maintenance of Supplies announcing a state of emergency and asking for volunteers to enrol, and confronted Baldwin with it. The poster, Thomas said, had been brought to the General Council by the head of the National Society of Operative Printers and Assistants (NATSOPA) after some of his members had refused to print it. Thomas explained that, in the interests of keeping cool heads, it had not been shown to the assembled executives or to the miners. Confronted with this, Baldwin admitted that the government was making preparations for a strike. This did much to destroy any remaining trust that the TUC had in the government's ability to find a settlement in good faith. Alonzo Swales, a left-leaning member of the Negotiating Committee, wondered aloud 'whether we are not unfaithful to our people in keeping them back when you have set forth this declaration'. Thomas issued a vivid warning of irrepressible social chaos to the government:

> If a vote in this country were taken on an issue of a revolution I do not believe one per cent of the people would vote for it. That is my firm view… my engine driver, my guard, my signalman, my platelayer, the most decent, most loyal, the most conservative minded of men, feels that his duty is to help the miners and out he comes, and he is on strike. You, sitting there, feel that your duty is to feed the people, to run the mails and run the hospitals, all of which I know, and in the exercise of that function of State what do you do? You perhaps have to put troops on the trains, or signalmen in the boxes or whatever it may be, and you do it. You have your motor transport and you use that. The man who votes anti-revolution; the man in his soul who thinks of his children and his wife, in the midst of a revolution forgets consequences, forgets results… That is why I am striving, that is why I feel that it is a desperate state and if we are a bit over anxious do remember the knowledge of our own people, realise that our love of our country and our anxiety for the future of our country, not our politics, is at least the driving force, the impelling motive that makes us plead perhaps and appear to plead more than we otherwise would.[21]

Outside the negotiating room Thomas pulled Walter Citrine to one side and told him, from his own experience as a minister in the short-lived 1924 Labour administration, just how well prepared the government would be. During a train drivers' strike that year, he explained, 'I had on my desk every morning full details, photographs of letters that had passed, speeches made at private meetings.' He could only see one outcome if the full force of the state was mobilised against the trade union movement. 'It won't last more than a few days,' he told Citrine, gesturing to his fellow General Council members. 'A few of these people will get shot, of course. Many more will be arrested.'[22]

The negotiations were stuck in a loop. The miners would not consider any wage reduction until concrete steps were taken towards industry reorganisation. The government offered an Advisory Committee to look at reorganisation with union representation on it, but would not commit to maintaining existing wages while that committee sat. Baldwin protested that this would take months, and he was not prepared to extend the subsidy.

***

The TUC General Council may not have wanted a strike but they were, at last, preparing for one. Late in the evening of 30 April at Memorial Hall, a *Proposal for Co-ordinated Action* was distributed to the assembled delegates. Drafted largely by Ernest Bevin and Alf Purcell, the document sketched out the TUC's plans for a national stoppage of work. Purcell had a long career on the radical left wing of the trade union movement behind him, steeped in the rhetoric of the general strike as a revolutionary weapon. But he had also risen to be a senior TUC official, somewhat tempering his syndicalist leanings. In 1921 he had opined that 'the threat of a general strike would be more powerful than the operation of one.'[23] Bevin, for his part, was hardly a radical. Nevertheless, both men were determined that if a general strike had to happen, it should happen under the firm direction of the TUC's central leadership, and it should be successful. Threatening an embargo of coal had forced the government to back down on Red Friday, but it would no longer suffice. The government was now ready for it. The only feasible alternative was a widespread withdrawal of labour in support of the miners.

Initially, only a 'first line' of workers would be called out: those in transport, printing, metal and chemical manufacture, construction, and power generation. A general stoppage in transport would affect not only national rail and road haulage services, but also buses and trams within towns and cities. This choice of industries was, at first glance, somewhat arbitrary. Bevin wanted a broad front to ensure that it was not only transport workers – his members – bearing the burden of the strike. Some speculate that he chose some industries, like construction, primarily to test the resolve of their unions' leaderships whom he disliked for being all bark and no bite.[24] Everyone knew that a transport strike would be paralysing for the country, but it was not clear what immediate effects a withdrawal of labour in these other industries would have.

Even within the earmarked industries, the planned strike was not necessarily 'general'. Construction on hospitals and housing was to carry on as normal, and the power workers' unions were given the task of somehow keeping domestic power and streetlights going while shutting off power to industrial enterprises. Committees were set up to deal with these thorny questions and, most importantly, the issue of how to permit the movement of food and other essential supplies. The TUC itself used the term 'national strike' rather than 'general strike' to describe its action. It wanted to be clear that it wasn't a strike of every worker. A 'general strike', the TUC thought, would spark fervid accusations of Bolshevik subversion and revolutionary plots by the press. Of course, the press paid far less attention to the fine distinctions between 'national' and 'general' than the TUC might have liked.

The decision to mount the general strike was taken on 1 May, International Workers' Day. As they waited for news of the talks, the trade unionist congregation at Memorial Hall sang popular hymns, the melody of the socialist anthem 'England Arise!' complementing the Welsh delegates' rendition of 'Guide Me O Thou Great Redeemer'.

The vote, to adopt the Bevin-Purcell proposals for united action, was taken by roll-call in alphabetical order, with the Asylum Workers' Union being the first to vote in favour. The final result was that delegates representing 3,653,526 workers voted in favour, with just 49,911 against. The only significant union to oppose the strike was the National Sailors' and Firemen's Union, led by the maverick Havelock Wilson, which ironically had benefited from sympathetic strike action by other workers during its national conflict with the ship owners in 1911. 'We look upon your "Yes"', said Bevin to the delegates, 'as meaning that you have placed your all upon the altar for this great Movement, and having placed it there, even if every penny goes, if every asset goes, history will ultimately write up that it was a magnificent generation that was prepared to do it rather than see the miners down like slaves.'[25] Not everyone was impressed by Bevin's grandiloquence. Charlie Cramp of the railwaymen's union was heard to mutter 'pure fatalism' under his breath as the vote passed.

Bevin was under no illusion about the challenges of maintaining public support for the strike. He pointedly reminded the assembled trade unionists that they had no quarrel with the public but only with 'the government, pushed on by sordid capitalism'. In line with the plans he and Purcell had drawn up, he stated that the TUC was prepared to move and distribute vital supplies like food and milk around the country, and that they would approach the government with this offer so as to render the OMS unnecessary. Walter Citrine communicated this to Baldwin, but was rebuffed. The government could not face legitimising union control of the economy while decrying the strike as unconstitutional.

In the country, the mood hardened. Since the 1880s, May Day had been an annual day of demonstrations celebrating the strength of the labour movement and heralding a socialist future. Trade unions and socialist groups would march in processions behind their banners and hear speeches about the coming of the New Jerusalem, before relaxing with games and entertainment. With class confrontation now seeming inevitable, May Day 1926 provided a morale boost for the rank and file of an ill-prepared movement. Thousands filled the streets as cities like Leeds and Bradford saw their largest ever May Day marches.[26]

It was a platform for those on the left to make their feelings known. In Derby a speaker effused: 'We are ready, every one of us. I don't think we will have a man who will remain at work.' In the Nottingham procession, a hearse labelled 'Death of Capitalism' was followed by a carriage proclaiming the 'Birth of Socialism'.[27] At Wolverhampton two First World War veterans adorned their military attire with red armbands and were arrested and fined for wearing the uniform 'in such a way as to bring it into contempt'.[28] May Day marchers from East London to Trafalgar Square passed members of the TUC General Council on Kingsway who assured them: 'The General Strike is on... All out from Monday night!'²⁹

Returning to their offices from the demonstrations, union officials around the country found they had received telegrams instructing them to be ready for the strike:

> By decision of the General Council and ratified by Conference of Executive Delegates our Members must cease work at expiry of Monday night's shift. ARTHUR PUGH. IRON & STEEL TRADES.

> Our Executive Committee request you make all arrangements for members to cease work with other Railway Employees when called upon by announcement from Trades Union Congress General Council in support of miners. WALKDEN. RAILWAY CLERKS ASSOCIATION.

> Trades Union Congress decide to support Miners. Executive Council direct all tram and bus workers not to commence work Tuesday morning next. Make arrangements accordingly. Letter follows. All instructions will be issued over my name. BEVIN. TRANSUNION.³⁰

The TUC's Negotiating Committee again spoke with government ministers late into the evening. Both sides in principle agreed that any settlement would have to be based on the Samuel report's recommendations. A subcommittee of four representatives from each side retired to a private room to discuss further, the atmosphere almost that of a gentlemen's club. Jimmy Thomas, who enjoyed hobnobbing with his social betters, a characteristic that sometimes made him a figure of fun in both the labour and mainstream press, approached Lord Birkenhead 'in the tone of an old college friend', according to Citrine.31 Despite this cordiality, the discussion again foundered as the TUC men explained that they were mandated not to enter into further negotiations unless the lockout notices were withdrawn, and asked for an extension of the coal subsidy to cover the negotiating period. For its part, the government again stressed that the miners must accept the principle of wage cuts before any progress could be made.

The miners' delegates and executive had dispersed in order to organise their activity in the districts, therefore neither Cook nor Smith was still in

London by the time talks broke up in the early hours of 2 May. Cook was none too happy that the TUC had continued negotiations without him, despite having formally agreed to this, and he and Smith returned to London as quickly as they could. They, and their members, had a deep distrust of Jimmy Thomas due to the latter's role in holding back the NUR from backing the miners on Black Friday in 1921. Although there was no suggestion this time that the NUR would stand aside, the bad blood from five years ago remained.

From the government's point of view, the miners' leaders leaving London was the final proof that they were not interested in coming to an agreement. Over the afternoon of 2 May, the hardline faction in the Cabinet – Birkenhead, Chamberlain, Joynson-Hicks, and Churchill – had won out, and the government demanded an acceptance of wage cuts and longer working hours as well as 'an immediate and unconditional withdrawal of the instructions for a general strike' as a precursor to any further negotiations.[32] Had Cook and Smith been available, of course, the miners' answer would have been a resounding 'No'. The TUC's exhausted negotiators were minded to make concessions on the wages issue, but they knew they were now too far down the road.

***

It was in the print room of the *Daily Mail*, of all places, where events conspired to give the government a pretext to break off negotiations. Early on 3 May the printers, mostly members of the NATSOPA union, had been handed the text of an anti-strike editorial entitled 'For King and Country'. The editorial asserted: 'A General Strike is not an industrial dispute. It is a revolutionary movement which can only succeed by destroying the Government and subverting the rights and liberties of the people.'[33] Appalled by what they saw as an attack on legitimate trade unionism, the printers went against their own union leadership and refused to set the type. The editor rang the home secretary, Joynson-Hicks, at Downing Street to inform him of this unofficial action. For the hardliners this was the ideal excuse to bring the conflict to a head.

Baldwin acquiesced. He called Citrine, Thomas, Swales, and Pugh into a side room and rather sheepishly handed them a note stating that the government could not continue negotiations as 'overt acts' had occurred 'including interfering with the freedom of the Press'. The TUC leaders, unaware of the printers' action, were bewildered. They could scarcely believe that the government would dash negotiations on the rocks of such an apparently trivial incident. Exasperated, Baldwin had aligned himself with the hardline faction in his Cabinet. He thanked the trade unionists for the manner in which they had conducted the talks and said to Citrine: 'I believe if we live we shall meet again to settle it…if we live.'[34]

It was decided that the king, who was in residence at Windsor Castle, should be informed that the *Mail* would not be appearing and that a strike now seemed inevitable. Baldwin's private secretary Sir Ronald Waterhouse was dispatched to make the call. On answering the phone the monarch's assistant secretary told Waterhouse, 'That's alright my dear fellow. We don't take the *Daily Mail* – or the *Daily Express*.'[35]

The TUC negotiators retired next door to break the news to the rest of the General Council and launch one last push for a resumption of talks. An unsigned contemporary account, probably penned by TUC research officer Walter Milne-Bailey, sets the scene of those Downing Street negotiations in the early hours:[36]

> One o'clock strike[s]. Everyone is tired out, but we are too near to some tangible result for anyone to think of giving up. Then comes a message from the Premier… The message is read out by our coolly unemotional Chairman, Arthur Pugh. This is the dramatic moment. In the dim light one sees through the haze of tobacco smoke the circle of white, thrust-forward faces, tensely focussed on the speaker's lips, until out comes the verbal bombshell that negotiations are broken off – pouf! – like that, without any warning. A few make exclamations and spring to their feet. The Chairman imperturbably reads on. At the demand for unconditional surrender, derisive laughter mingles with a menacing growl from some of the sterner spirits.[37]

The negotiators drafted a reply to Baldwin, only to be informed that the prime minister had gone to bed. By the time a final proposal for a negotiating framework was submitted to the government the next morning, it was too late. That afternoon in the House of Commons, Baldwin read the proclamation of a state of emergency as signed by the king. He defended his government's decision to end the subsidy as looking out for the welfare of the general taxpayer, and justified his decision to end negotiations based on the *Daily Mail* incident. He then went on the offensive against the General Council, accusing it of pushing forward with a general strike without having consulted the members of their unions:

> I do not believe that there has been anything like a thorough-going consultation with the rank and file before this despotic power was put into the hands of a small executive in London. This irresponsible power is a gross travesty of any democratic principle. In most of these industries the unions have solemn agreements which were understood to safeguard these industries from sudden and paralysing stoppage. These are to be broken ruthlessly and the sanctity of contracts repudiated. When you extend an ordinary trade dispute in this way, from one industry into a score of the most vital industries in the country, you change its character.[38]

Speaking for the Labour benches, Thomas – who was also the MP for the railway town of Derby – opined that the dispute was still at heart an industrial one, and that there was still time to avert the strike. There was nothing any opposition MPs could say, however, to change the course of events. The House adjourned at 11 p.m. Outside the chamber the Labour Party's chief whip Arthur Henderson accosted Churchill and reminded him of his role, as home secretary, in mobilising hundreds of soldiers to violently dislodge an anarchist gang from an East London house in 1911: 'It seems to me, Winston, that you are trying to give us a dose of Sidney Street.'[39]

As the clock ticked down, the TUC issued a public statement explaining which workers would be called out at midnight. They placed the blame for the impending strike squarely on their opponents: 'The trade unions disclaim all responsibility for the calamity that now threatens. Their action is not directed at the public. Responsibility for the consequences that must inevitably follow a general cessation of work lies with the mine-owners and the Government entirely.'[40]

Both sides understood how important the battle for public opinion would be in the event of a strike. This accounts for the TUC's decision to call out printworkers as part of the 'first line', a deliberate attempt to curtail the power of the Fleet Street newspapers that were largely anti-union. But including the printers in the 'first line' was a double-edged sword, because it also hobbled the pro-labour press. At the time, newspapers closely associated with the trade union and socialist movements had a significant readership, especially the *Daily Herald*. Had they been able to keep printing during the strike, this would have been to the TUC's advantage in a country that was desperate for the latest news. The printers' unions, however, interpreted the TUC's instructions to mean a full stoppage, whatever the newspaper. This may have stifled some voices potentially critical of the General Council from within the labour movement, but it also gave the government dominance over print media when, from the second day of the strike, it was able to produce its own propaganda sheet, the *British Gazette*, on a large scale.

Around the country, people made their preparations for the now-expected stoppage. Tourists at West Country beaches cut their holidays short for fear of being stranded. In Torquay, the trains back to London were crowded with worried travellers and the stationmaster ordered extra coaches to be put on.[41] The Cunard liner *Mauretania*, travelling from New York and due to berth at Plymouth, was diverted to Cherbourg in France. There had been serious strikes across the country in the years since 1910, including in the mines and on the railways, but nothing approaching the scale of what was to come. No one could be certain what the country would look like the next day. As the Westminster correspondent of one regional newspaper observed: 'Outwardly the seven millions of London's community practised their lawful occupations. But behind the humdrum normality strange shadows flittered and the pulse of the Metropolis seemed to beat excitedly. Not even in those memorable August days and nights of 1914 was one more conscious of the deceitful hush before the storm.'[42]

PART 2

The Strike

The *Daily Herald* announces the beginning of the general strike.

5

THE FIRST DAY

In giving effect to this decision it must be clearly understood that the executive committee is still the only determining body and authority so far as our members are concerned, and instructions must not be taken from any other body.

- National Union of Railwaymen circular to branches,
1 May 1926

On the first day of the strike I went around to the Trades Council offices – and I saw to my amazement that there was quite a crowd of people wanting advice. Nobody knew what they had to do.

- Bert Edwards, Southwark Trades Council

The General Council's order for the 'first line' to strike came into force at the close of final shifts on Monday 3 May. Within a few hours, more than one and a half million workers had walked out in support of the million or so miners who were now locked out of their pits. The strength of the response shocked both the government and the General Council. Remarkably, among NUR members, perhaps more answered the call than had walked out during their own national strike in 1919. This solidity was no mean feat, since any worker who joined the strike was technically in breach of their contract, and had no guarantee that they would have a job to go back to when the strike ended. In Edinburgh, the city council warned that it would consider any bus or tram worker who struck to have resigned from their jobs. Despite this, a mass meeting voted almost unanimously to observe the midnight stoppage, to cheers from supporters outside.[1]

In Westminster, as Big Ben tolled midnight, a group of protesters gathered at Downing Street for a march through the West End, led by a marcher carrying a red flag. Police forcibly confiscated this offending item and the protesters were scattered. Outside King's Cross station two thousand railway workers held a mass meeting to mark the beginning of the strike, addressed by local Communist activists, which ended with three cheers for the miners and a rendition of 'The Red Flag'.[2]

The TUC's head office was located in a house in Eccleston Square formerly owned by its great enemy, Winston Churchill. Jimmy Thomas remarked with dry irony that the General Council met throughout the strike 'in a room that Winston had used as a dining room'.[3] The BBC's lunchtime bulletin on 4 May reported: 'Great privacy was observed about the proceedings of the Council, the outer door was closed and the press men were not allowed inside.'[4] On the first day, the office was inundated with reports from across the country attesting to the strength of the strike on the ground. From Tredegar in South Wales, a young union militant called Nye Bevan telegrammed: 'The whole of the trade unions are on stop. Everyone surprised at the response to the call of the TUC.'[5] A call-out from Eccleston Square asked for willing dispatch riders or anyone who could place their car at the movement's disposal to come forward.[6] Eager volunteers, comprising trade unionists, their family members, and left-wing students, thronged the square seeking to help the cause, somewhat overwhelming the TUC's relatively tiny administrative staff apparatus.

Solidarity was also quick to come from international quarters, especially but by no means exclusively from communist-affiliated unions around the world. The All-Indian Trade Union Congress expressed the sympathy of Indian workers with their British counterparts' 'great fight for the maintenance of their standard of life'.[7] Transport workers' unions in the Netherlands instructed their members not to book on to British ships lest they be used to take the place of striking workers.

Across the country on 4 May, the 'first line' industries more or less ground to a halt. The printing unions were so concerned not to be seen blacklegging that many local strike committees initially found it difficult to get their daily bulletins produced.[8] Few papers appeared in London on Monday evening, although non-union labour ensured that most of the nationals were able to publish throughout the strike, albeit in reduced and irregular editions. The National Union of Journalists remained at work but instructed its members 'not to do work of other departments nor their own work if non-union labour is introduced in other departments'.[9]

On the railways, the stoppage was even more complete than was first envisaged. The General Council's initial instruction that food should be moved had been challenged and overturned by the rail unions. John Bromley of the train drivers' union ASLEF had warned the TUC that, if volunteers or troops were used to drive trains, his members would likely not cooperate, even if the cargo in question was food or other vital supplies. The NUR concurred that it would be simpler to engage in a complete stoppage, and the Railway Clerks' Association (RCA) – the union for white-collar railway workers – agreed.[10] Therefore these three moderate-led unions pushed the TUC into the more radical position of ordering a stoppage of all rail traffic. Evidently this order took some time to reach the grassroots in all locations; the Durham and Northumberland Strike Committee spent much of the first day arbitrating between one union that had stopped moving food but was still moving construction materials, and another that refused to move construction materials but was still moving food.[11]

The RCA was traditionally the weakest union; it had little instinctive solidarity with workers in other industries. One member from Bradford remembered hearing disquiet in his office in the run-up to the strike: 'Strike for the miners? Not bloody likely! Why, we'll be striking next for the bricklayers and dustmen and God knows who else – we'll never be working!'[12] Nevertheless, in the event, the vast majority of Bradford RCA members obeyed the call, with 360 of 400 out on the first day. In Sunderland the local RCA first resolved not to join the strike, but reversed its decision at a later meeting. The national union's position shifted the attitudes of the membership on the ground. This caused a huge problem for the government's plans for volunteer labour on the railways, which relied on the managerial grades to train, oversee, and organise the strikebreaking effort. It was an unprecedented display of unity between the rail unions. Joint meetings were held, breaking down long-established barriers between grades. At one such meeting in Nottingham the local NUR organiser told the crowd: 'It is a day we have hoped for and prayed for and looked forward to...we ought to be delighted.'[13]

The NUR's instruction to its members that no trains should be moved contained a corollary betraying the union leaders' concerns that the situation could escalate out of their control: 'Allow no disorderly elements to interfere in any way. Maintain perfect order and have confidence in your own representatives. Perfect loyalty will ensure success.'[14] When midnight came and the strike formally began, some engine drivers simply stopped their trains on the tracks, climbed down the footplate, and went home. Signalmen locked their signal boxes and walked away with the keys.[15]

Only three London, Midland and Scottish Railway trains ran from Edinburgh's Princes Street station on the first day of the strike.[16] At Paddington, three station staff reported to work, and only one Oxford-bound passenger service was able to run.[17] Nationally, fewer than five percent of passenger services operated, and almost no freight. In Swindon, where the economic life of the town was dominated by the Great Western Railway Company, pickets turned up to the gates at all the main yards, only to find out that they were barely needed as everyone had stopped work. They allowed the apprentices to clock in, to save their jobs, but once inside there was nothing for them to do. The young men held a meeting and decided to join the strike. A manager who tried to keep them at work by turning a water hose on them found himself flat on the ground as the boys rushed out of the gate.[18]

Train companies faced a rotten problem. Loads of perishable goods – milk and food – sat on abandoned trains on the strike's first day. Without immediate attention, the food would spoil and the milk would curdle. It would be up to the growing commercial road haulage industry to pick up the slack. This was the weak point in the transport unions' organisation. The government's emergency plans would rely heavily on this industry in the coming days. In Northumberland, the newly formed joint strike committee met at 7 p.m. to determine its strategy for the current struggle. 'The meeting terminated', according to its report, 'with the first hint of the difficulties of a general strike in the shape of a complaint that the Miners' Clubs faced with a drink shortage were sending in motors for beer whilst Transport Workers were out on strike.'[19]

As the railways were paralysed, so were the ports. Traffic on the Manchester Ship Canal ground to a halt and the Salford docks lay silent. Internal water transport was stopped, but the decision of Havelock Wilson's National Sailors' and Firemen's Union (NSFU) to go against the strike meant that ships could keep sailing, if the government could find any labour with which to load and unload them in the docks. Local members and even regional officials of the NSFU broke ranks and joined the strike, at least in Merseyside and the North-East, in a bold move that, as we will see, would have significant consequences for them.

Municipal transport – trams and buses in towns and cities, as well as the London Underground – was crucial to keeping Britain running. From the turn of the century, many cities had rapidly expanded through slum clearances and the construction of suburbs, where a growing number of white-collar workers and skilled manual workers could afford to live. Private car ownership though was still a rarity. Tram networks and local buses were the crucial means by which millions of the country's urban workforce reached their factories and offices every day. If transport shut down, many factories and offices would find themselves unable to function.

Union organisation on urban tram networks was uneven. In many places, such as Bradford, no trams ran on the first day. In neighbouring Leeds, a lone tram returned to the depot under police protection after being attacked by a crowd. Other cities like Liverpool and Portsmouth were able to keep their tram services running as enough workers reported to work as normal, sometimes under threat of the sack. At Hull, the local council gave its tram workers two days to return or else hand in their uniforms.[20] Buses showed a similarly mixed picture, although even in weaker towns the response of the busmen tended to be firm on the first couple of days. Oxford and Bristol, which managed to run services more or less uninterrupted throughout the strike, were the exception rather than the rule.[21] Areas that had not traditionally been bastions of industrial militancy still saw a huge response to the strike call. In Birmingham, a city unused to strikes where disputes were often solved by conciliation, some ninety percent of the six thousand tram, waterways, and bus workers came out. Most of the remainder stayed at work with union permission to move food supplies, including feed for the horses at the city's goods depots.[22]

In manufacturing, the response was solid in the iron and steel works, but patchier in the newer chemical industry. In the steelmaking district of Teesside, thirty thousand workers were reportedly out. Buses carrying workers to a shipyard in Sunderland were surrounded by a crowd of a few hundred local men, women, and children, and pelted with stones. Two passengers required medical treatment and the buses ploughed on knocking down some of the strikers.[23] This happened even though shipbuilding had not been included by the TUC in the 'first line'. In contrast, Glasgow's Clyde shipyards, famous for their militancy and Communist influence, remained working. In the East End of Sheffield, a mass of huge steel factories, engineering shops, and hundreds of miles of railway lines, there were thousands of men on strike, although most of the big firms managed to keep some workshops open, and had some weeks of coal supplies in reserve. In Derby, members of the engineering unions and foundry workers walked out on the first day, swelling the number of strikers in the town to more than twenty thousand.[24]

Engineering unions had members across all manufacturing industries, comprising a minority of the workforce, but a highly skilled one. Without engineers, most factories would find it very difficult to operate. On the first day of the strike, there was confusion on the ground as to whether the engineers should be working or not. The Amalgamated Engineering Union (AEU) members had a strong Communist influence, albeit one that had been diminished by post-war unemployment – during which many companies took the opportunity to cast out troublemaking activists – and a bitter national lockout in 1922. The AEU's instruction to members was that those whose colleagues were striking should themselves walk out, but other members were to remain at work. Across Greater Manchester, engineers and electricians at tram depots, railway yards, and newspaper offices walked out solidly, swelling the total number on strike by some thousands.[25] At the Milner Safe Works in Liverpool, about a quarter of the workforce, members of the Electrical Trades Union (ETU), walked out. The whole works had to shut down – these workers were the only ones who could set up and maintain the machinery. When the works manager tried to start the machinery himself, he ended up hospitalised.[26]

Around the country, local branches of the engineering unions held disordered mass meetings to determine who should be on strike and who should be at work. It was a dilemma also faced by those in the building trade, where many expressed the preference that either all should be out or none. In Wolverhampton, when the TUC's instructions that building workers engaged on housing, hospital, and sanitation projects should remain at work were received, 'this caused a great deal of dissatisfaction... The whole of the workers were determined to stand by the miners, and it was with the utmost difficulty that [the Trades and Labour Council] was able to keep within instructions laid down by the TUC.'[27] One bricklayers' union told its officials: 'If in doubt, come out.'

In other industries, too, unions interpreted the TUC's instructions in a way that allowed them to join the strike. The National Amalgamated Furnishing Trades Association, the left-wing leadership of which included Purcell, called out all its members in car and carriage factories, who upholstered vehicles' seats, on the grounds that their work was connected to the transport industry.[28] The National Union of Vehicle Builders took the same attitude, which crippled the motor manufacturing industry in the West Midlands. Such was the response to the call on the first day that, for many union officials on the ground, their biggest problem was convincing workers to stay at work. As the General Council acknowledged in its first daily strike bulletin to local trade unionists:

> The General Council of the Trades Union Congress is delighted with the magnificent and whole hearted response to the instructions which became effective this morning. This response has exceeded all expectations. Everything is proceeding in accordance with the plan. The enthusiasm of the Trade Union members has been so marked that the difficulty has not been to persuade them to leave their work, but rather to keep them at it in those cases where the policy of the General Council required this course to be adopted.[29]

At the grassroots, many pushed the TUC to go further. Some did not agree with Bevin's strategy of calling workers out in stages. A mass meeting of TGWU members in Sheffield early in the morning of 4 May called on the TUC to call out all members of all affiliated unions.[30] In Wolverhampton 'an impression existed among some members of the [Trades and Labour Council's] Emergency Committee that they had full power to call out all workers irrespective of official instructions', but the majority opinion – that the local organisation should await the TUC's orders – won out.[31]

Today we might wonder why over a million people would give up their pay, risk their jobs, and go out on strike at the command of the TUC. But a worker in the 1920s knew the value of discipline and unity. The decades of struggle to establish trade unions as permanent organisations that could survive large strikes or lockouts were in living memory. Once a decision was made, adhering to it was a matter of course. Moreover, miners were the pride of the broader working-class movement. Everyone knew that the job was dangerous, arduous, and underpaid. And coal was indispensable. Harry Watson, an apprentice lighterman on the River Thames who had likely never been near a coalfield in his life at that point, recalled: 'They were an important section of the community and we depended on them for everything. Take the river alone, we used to transport hundreds of thousands of tons of coal a week to the power stations up and down the rivers and canals. Dockworkers felt a kind of bond with the miners.'[32]

Workers also feared that if employers could get away with cutting miners' wages, they would be next. This had been a key plank of Communist and Minority Movement propaganda since Red Friday, strengthened by the government's own frequent exhortations that sacrifices and belt-tightening would be necessary for the good of the nation. A local councillor expressed this sentiment at a mass meeting in Sunderland on the first day of the strike, appealing to railwaymen to show support to the miners' cause because 'if they went down the turn of the rest of the organised trade union workers would follow'.[33]

***

For those who were not striking or whose families were not directly affected, 4 May 1926 was a strange day. In Britain's industrial districts the air was clear of the sulphur and pollution that usually suffused it, staining curtains and laundry, when factories worked around the clock. An eerie silence prevailed as the hammers of the foundries slowed to a halt. As one St Helens trade unionist remembered, 'these were everyday noises that one had never noticed normally, but now they were not there it was very noticeable'.[34]

In London the quiet did not last long. Office workers, as well as factory workers not on strike, still had to get to work. On the first day, none of the LGOC, the London General Omnibus Company's four thousand buses could be moved, and only fifteen trains were running on the underground network. With the capital's transport structure completely paralysed, bicycles soon thronged the streets. Among those not on strike, who were attempting to navigate the stoppage and live as close to a normal day as possible, a spontaneous camaraderie developed. Those with access to a private car offered ride shares to their fellow suburbanites. Some even hung destination boards from the front of their cars as if they were driving a bus.[35] Any form of transport, whether motorised or horse-drawn, was seized upon by those eager to get to work. By mid-morning, the streets of the capital from Regent's Park through the West End to the Thames Embankment were choked with traffic, far more than they would have been on a normal day. In Sheffield 'from the early hours of the morning steady streams of humanity flowed towards the city, and more bicycles were seen in the streets than has been the case for some years'.[36] The *Yorkshire Evening Post* described how 'at least one Bradford businessman packed a kit-bag, and taking advantage of a friendly lift in a car, resolved once he reached business premises in Bradford to stay there, even if his bed had to be a "shake down" in the office'.[37]

The postmaster general appealed to the public to only send mail and telegrams if absolutely necessary. No packets weighing more than eight ounces would be accepted, nor any international mail. Some companies, anticipating either transport issues or a lack of necessary supplies, put their workers on short-time or only required some of their staff to come in. Those whose workplaces were shut, and in many cases strikers themselves, took the opportunity – if they were not on picket duty – to escape to public parks or, if they had access to a motor car, the countryside. Football and bowling matches proliferated.

Away from these more genteel pursuits came the first signs of a fraying social fabric. While reports across the country were overwhelmingly of a peaceful and orderly walkout, there were exceptions. At Blackwall in East London, strikers set up impromptu roadblocks and attempted to stop and turn around commuters' cars and inspect the loads carried by lorries and other vehicles. Police intervened with baton charges to clear the roads.[38] In

Hammersmith, a group of strikers surrounded the local National Fascisti office, as it had been distributing an anti-strike leaflet. Police were mobilised to prevent the workers from storming the building.[39] Two high-profile arrests were made on the first day of the strike. Shapurji Saklatvala, the Labour MP for Battersea North who was a prominent member of the Communist Party, was arrested on a sedition charge for a speech he had made on May Day. In Manchester, business-owner and Communist Party member William Stoker was pulled over by police outside the Socialist Hall at Openshaw and found to have 1,600 of the party's strike bulletins in the boot of his car. Two days later, Stoker received two months in prison for 'having attempted to do an act calculated to cause disaffection amongst His Majesty's Forces and civilian population'.[40]

Few though the disturbances on the first day were, they were indicative of the dangers the circumstances posed to those on all sides who wanted to treat the events as if they were just another 'normal' strike. In its 5 May bulletin, the General Council reminded strikers that they should maintain exemplary conduct and that 'in particular, pickets are instructed to avoid obstruction and to confine themselves strictly to their legitimate duties'.[41]

By the end of day one, the country had been thrown into a novel situation it had not quite come to terms with. No one could be sure how long it would last, or how it would end. Harold Croft was a Labour Party organiser who, after volunteering his services at Eccleston Square, was tasked by the TUC's Press and Publicity Committee to accompany the South African journalist William Bolitho Ryall, on assignment with the *New York World*, around the country's major industrial centres. In a Bristol hotel room, Croft thought of his experiences of the strike's beginnings:

> I quickly relapse into an inert but reflective mood – fortuitous impressions of Croydon, Streatham, London, Reading, Swindon and Bristol crowd into my mind and rapidly culminate to a tangible idea of the massive reality of the power and magnitude of the great Strike. Every town and city isolated – seemingly autonomous – yet all indivisibly and indissolubly one in unity and purpose – A vast phalanx of workers still – serious – silent – waiting for the victory of their immense passivity. This massing of toilers to demand a living wage for miners is an epic of Labour. The strain will

become awful if it has to continue, but one feels that the strike may not disintegrate as easily or so soon as some would expect.[42]

As the country came to terms with the 'immense passivity' of 4 May, the government ramped up the emergency machinery it had been putting into place during the last nine months. It would constitute, over the next nine days, the biggest state-directed strikebreaking operation in British history.

SOCIETY CATERERS FOR VOLUNTEERS IN HYDE PARK : LADY QUILTER (WITH TRAY) Mrs. CAUSTON (AT BOILER), LADY MARY ASHLEY COOPER AND LADY CARMICHAEL-ANSTRUTHER PEELING POTATOES

Volunteers at work in the government's Hyde Park depot.

6

VOLUNTEERS

Neither Marx nor any other social anatomist had spotted that it was the day-dream of almost every middle-class English boy to drive a train or a bus, to do something which his social position normally forbade.

- W. H. Auden, 1965

'Name?'
'Jellicoe.'
'Ever done anything?'
'I commanded the Grand Fleet.'
'Fleet of what?'

- Admiral of the Fleet the Right Honourable The Earl Jellicoe interviewed upon volunteering as a Special Constable, May 1926

As soon as negotiations to avert the strike broke down on the evening of 2 May, Whitehall sent a one-word telegram to civil commissioners' offices and the chairmen of the Voluntary Service Committees (VSCs) around the country: 'Action'. This was the signal to set the emergency plans in motion.

The breadth of the strike had taken the government by surprise. The Cabinet did not know which sections of workers had been called out until the morning of 2 May, when the postmaster general notified them of the content of the instructional telegrams that had been sent out by the unions.[1] In previous large-scale strikes, at least the government could count on white-collar and supervisory staff, who usually kept on working. This time, many of them were out of office, having joined their manual worker comrades in the walkout.

Months of government preparation ensured that the Supply and Transport Organisation and the VSCs were able to swing into action right away. The government's first essential task was to ensure the continued supply of power to key industries and to households. Beyond this, they were concerned with ensuring that crucial supplies of food and milk could be moved in the face of the total stoppage of rail transport. They also aimed to break the strike's effectiveness by ensuring that those who wanted to remain at work, or had signed up to volunteer, could do so. This meant dealing with pickets or groups of strike supporters who gathered at workplaces, depots, and major transport routes.

As the strike dawned, however, the organisation was only a skeleton structure; in order to function it would require large numbers of willing volunteers to step forward and keep the country going. Until the outbreak of the strike, the government had kept the active recruitment of volunteers at arm's length or outsourced it to groups like the OMS, reasoning they would have no shortage of willing patriotic citizens when the time came. They were right. Once the VSC offices opened, in many places they were inundated with offers of help.

There were volunteers from an array of social backgrounds. A number of high-profile aristocratic volunteers grabbed headlines by stooping to involve themselves in the world of work for a few days. In Northampton the Earl Spencer fronted the volunteer effort in the town nearest to his ancestral seat along with a posse of other local lords and ladies.[2] There were society women with experience of 'mucking in' with charity work through churches or philanthropic groups. Some had served in hospitals in 1914–18 and saw an opportunity to revive that wartime spirit. Society's upper crust and their children often volunteered in groups; there were bands of volunteer workers from each Oxbridge college and units of special constables from each of the gentlemen's clubs of Piccadilly.

While the aristocrats brought notoriety, the backbone of the volunteer movement was formed from the middle class and white-collar working class. Local organisations representing the business community, like Rotary Clubs and Chambers of Commerce, drew up volunteer lists, opened goods depots, and helped provide details of available vehicle transport. In Sheffield, the Chamber of Commerce cooperated closely with the OMS to organise volunteer labour, but in most places the established organisations of the local business class were more than comfortable taking the lead, in close cooperation with the VSCs and civil commissioners.

Most individuals who volunteered, however, did so on their own initiative. Their motivations were a mix of the political and social. They were keen to uphold English constitutional government against the perceived threat of a labour movement that they had little to do with, and little knowledge of. Fears of revolution and the usurpation of democratic rule by tyrannical trade unions certainly drove many of these volunteers. This was the constituency Baldwin had so successfully appealed to in the 1924 election, desperate to defend their calm, genteel England from socialists of any stripe from Zinoviev to Jimmy Thomas. Oxford graduate Nancy Burton remembered that 'the solid middle class regarded Arthur Cook, the miners' leader, as a devil incarnate – talked of him in terms like the ones we later used of Hitler. He seemed such an enormous threat to the peace and security of our lives.'[3]

There were political groups, on the right wing of conservatism but not quite fascist, who were keen to join the fray. The Middle Class Union, which had rebranded as the National Citizens' Union (NCU) in 1921, was obsessively anti-communist and anti-trade union and claimed some three hundred branches and tens of thousands of members across the country. They had been volunteering to break strikes, which they predictably saw as part of an all-encompassing Judeo-Bolshevik plot against the Empire, since 1919.[4] Likening the TUC General Council to the Prussian militarists who had led Germany during the war, the NCU exhorted its members during the strike: 'Every member – man or woman – should be up and doing. It is no time for talk, but, in small ways or in big, it is a duty to aid or be ready to aid the efforts of the Government to maintain and protect government, law, and order, and to prevent the slow throttling of the people.'[5]

There were many who were not so explicitly politically motivated and signed up to 'help the community' rather than 'break the strike'. Many would even have been offended at the suggestion. They came forward, as one historian of the volunteers has put it, 'because it was what one did in a crisis'.[6] There were those who, being too young to have served their king and country in the trenches, saw the strike as an opportunity to fulfil some sort of national service, and to prove to their elders that they, too, possessed the mettle that was needed to keep the Empire safe. The British Legion urged its members, veterans of the Great War, to volunteer to 'uphold law and order' and 'ensure the interests of the community as a whole'.[7]

For some the strike simply served long-forgotten boyhood dreams to work on the footplate of a steam engine or behind the wheel of a bus. The writer Julian Symons, who sourced testimonies from hundreds of volunteers, described this as a kind of 'strike euphoria'.[8] They took pleasure in the harshness and dirtiness of the work, a temporary proletarian cosplay. Strikers watching on joked that there was no way these tourists could stick at the job for long, nor would they want to. Of course, for the dirtiest job of all, there were no volunteers. The pits lay idle with every single miner out except for the safety men needed to stop the mines from flooding. There was no attempt, no discussion, no thought to even attempting to cut coal with volunteer labour. Even the most enthusiastic Knightsbridge gentleman would have baulked at that.

Volunteers' experiences varied depending on which industry they were allotted to and where in the country they worked, but there were some broad similarities. Training for temporary transport workers, such as it was, was short and basic. Volunteer bus drivers recalled being given just a medical and a test drive of a few hundred yards on a practice road before being sent out. On the London Underground, drivers were put on the job after a few hours' work on a dummy controller.

In urban industrial districts, where mass pickets targeted bus and tram depots, many volunteers were billeted in the depots themselves for safety, and to avoid any trouble that would arise from attempting to cross picket lines. At the London General Omnibus Company's major Chiswick depot, which was beset by mass pickets for much of the strike, an irreverent bulletin was produced by office staff to keep up the morale of the volunteers. Unfortunately only its farewell number has survived, with a wry volunteer's lamentation:

> *I don't want to go home!*
> *I don't want to go home!!*
> *Please keep me at Chiswick*
> *I'll sleep on your floor*
> *And never be naughty*
> *No, never no more!*
> *Dear Mr Ell-gee-oh-cee*
> *Please don't try to get shot of me*
> *I'll sigh, then fade out and die,*
> *Should I be sent home!!*[9]

On the railways, too, some volunteers faced uncomfortable digs, sleeping on benches in the stations themselves. Those in Glasgow's Princes Dock, who were housed on a luxury ocean liner and given three meals a day, could count themselves lucky.[10]

In London, upper-class families hosted volunteers in their townhouses, giving them the rather incongruous experience of ending their day of manual labour and returning to their lodgings in their soot or grease-covered overalls to be greeted with sumptuous meals and expensive wine, and feted for their hard work – forms of courtesy that had never been extended to the workers whom they had replaced. Others ate their evening meals in large canteens at Hyde Park and at Earl's Court where the food had been prepared by aristocratic ladies and society debutantes.

Hyde Park in particular was a magnet for well-heeled volunteers and press photographers eager to document their heroic deeds. Here, as part of the government's plans to feed the capital, a massive logistics camp for food and milk had been thrown up overnight on the eve of the strike. Everyone who was anyone was photographed at Hyde Park. The king's cousin Princess Helena Victoria visited the YMCA-run canteen where Lady Carmichael-Anstruther was among the aristocratic battalion of potato-peelers. Here they provided 'ten cups of tea, three buns, and three-and-a-half eggs' every minute of every day to feed the volunteers.[11]

A columnist in society magazine *The Tatler* was typically effusive in its praise for the generous spirit of its readers:

> Many hostesses who had been preparing for big entertainments during the season are cooking and handing out food in the many canteens or doing special welfare work among the women and children hit by the strike, and others with big houses have been turning them into dormitories for the Oxford and Cambridge graduates who have come up to do volunteer work… The strike didn't prevent the house from being well filled for the opening of the Opera Season, but it had a distinct effect on our garments. Many men just off duty were in ordinary day suits, and the women in warm coats over afternoon dresses and thick shoes were quite prepared for a walk home in the rain.[12]

In contrast to other industries, the railway companies were more or less left to their own devices to recruit volunteer labour. This could have been because they had some experience from the 1919 national railway strike, or because neither the government nor the companies expected the walk-out on the railways to be so complete, especially among the white-collar staff, whom they would normally have relied upon to run some services. On the Great Western Railway, enrolment of volunteers in the first couple of days was chaotic, but despite this there was still no shortage, and by the end of the strike, fewer than half those who came forward had actually been deployed on the railway.[13]

The role and effectiveness of the OMS have been matters of historical dispute. The government's decision in the autumn of 1925 to keep the enrolment of most volunteers 'contracted out' to external organisations like the OMS certainly brought the organisation to the fore of public consciousness and debate. In trade union parlance, 'OMS' inaccurately became a shorthand term for any volunteer workers. The ETU reported on the strength of the OMS in the power stations, although, as we have seen, these were men recruited centrally by the government long in advance. They were mostly made fun of – the 'Organisation of Mugs and Scabs', the 'Order of Mugs and Saps'. On the strike's first day the London area of the TGWU reported to its members that twenty volunteers had been introduced to Nelson's Wharf but there was no need for alarm as 'the personnel of the OMS are not gifted with exceptional mental or physical abilities.'[14]

This elision of the OMS with all volunteers has given the organisation a notoriety ever since that it never really deserved. It had always been the government's intention for the OMS to effectively dissolve itself into the state's formal emergency organisation upon the outbreak of the strike. The chief civil commissioner William Mitchell-Thomson and his deputy J. C. C. Davidson had met OMS representatives in December and made it clear that their volunteers should be pledging allegiance to the government and not the OMS itself. On 3 May, the organisation turned over its list of about 85,000 volunteers to the government. The total volunteer workforce during the strike has been estimated at between 300,000 and 500,000.[15] Therefore, OMS volunteers actually comprised a minority, albeit a sizeable one, of the total strikebreaking force.

OMS volunteers were disproportionately based in the south and east of England. Where the City of Westminster provided over seven thousand OMS volunteers, Manchester and Liverpool could not muster a single one between them.[16] Aside from training up a not insignificant number of lorry drivers – about 1,300 – at special 'schools', few of the volunteers possessed specific skills necessary to do the jobs of strikers. Across the country only 640 railway personnel and 91 tramwaymen signed the OMS pledge.[17] Such low numbers can perhaps be accounted for by the fact that transport workers who wanted to break the strike could do so simply by turning up to work without making any prior commitment to an external organisation. But they demonstrate that the OMS volunteers came overwhelmingly from white-collar and middle-class backgrounds.

After the strike, many government figures were scathing about the OMS's role. Senior Home Office official Sir John Anderson claimed the organisation was 'a useful lightning conductor before the strike but apart from the fact that it trained a few drivers its practical utility was almost nil'.[18] Mitchell-Thomson's post-strike report into the emergency organisation noted: 'Generally speaking the OMS is not thought by the Commissioner to have justified its existence…in fact some reports state that it did positive harm as tending to confuse the Government arrangement with what was considered a "class" organisation.'[19]

This is a marked difference to Joynson-Hicks's warm words to OMS leaders in the run-up to the strike. In retrospect, the government found it was able to substantially rely on its own volunteer organisation, with the overly partisan army of privately recruited strikebreakers coming to be seen as an embarrassment. On 30 June, just a few weeks after the strike, Jix himself wrote to Lord Hardinge advising him to wind up the OMS as the government's own organisation had shown it was not necessary.[20]

Students provided a relatively small, but high-profile, pool of volunteer labour. At the time, a tiny proportion of young people went to university and they were almost exclusively from privileged sections of the population.[21] Some university authorities, including the majority of Oxford colleges, actively encouraged students to volunteer, opened recruiting offices on campus, and granted leaves of absence with promises that any service would be taken into consideration when assessing performance in the forthcoming exam season.

Around 1,300 Cambridge undergraduates were employed as volunteers and 700 enrolled as special constables.[22] Most of the 1,300 worked in London, and the largest contingent, around a third of them, worked on the docks. Women students, who were forbidden from leaving college during term time, were formally shut out of the volunteer movement, although some still managed to help by, for example, delivering copies of the *British Gazette*. In Scotland, almost all of the student population of St Andrews and around half of Edinburgh University students volunteered, many of whom were also put to work as dockers. The Edinburgh students were at pains to point out that they had no links with the OMS or Fascists and were officially sanctioned by the civil commissioner.[23]

There was a desire to escape studies for more exciting pastimes. This was the case for the Cambridge undergraduate who wanted to sign up for the Special Constabulary's high-speed motor patrol but, since his car was not fast enough, ended up with the decidedly less glamorous job of unloading bacon at the Grimsby docks.[24]

Many students had no particular feelings about trade unions or understanding of the industrial working class. Sylvia Makower, a Cambridge student, remembered seeing those of her contemporaries who were on the side of the government and those on the side of the strikers driving off together cheerfully in the same car: 'the strikers' struggle was not the point, the escape to 'real' work was the big thrill.[25]

Those few students who supported the strike conscientiously were almost all activists of the political left. They included Hugh Gaitskell, the future leader of the Labour Party who was in his second year at Oxford at the time, and Jennie Lee, the future Labour minister who rushed from her Edinburgh University accommodation to a local trade union office to offer her services. At Cambridge a group influenced by the Communist Party unsuccessfully tried to convince power station workers to walk out. The Labour Club at Oxford, which was of course home to the unions' own Ruskin College, was the most organised, raising money for the strikers' hardship fund and distributing leaflets to their peers discouraging volunteering:

DON'T BE A DOCKER!
You are being asked to go to places like Hull and Bristol and work as Dockers during the strike.

Ought you to go?

Even if you feel that you ought to help in maintaining food supplies, there are sound reasons why you should not go. If you want to serve, go as an individual to your own home and offer your services among your own people.

Don't join a special corps of University Strike-breakers. Don't drag the University as a collective body into this dispute… If you give your labour to the Government for essential services, it will only release others to do work which is not essential. That is how you will be helping to break the strike.[26]

Even if they failed to achieve much, the strike was a formative political experience for these young activists.

The effectiveness of volunteers is the subject of contradictory anecdotal evidence. Some dock employers noted that once their port was staffed with volunteer labour, they were able to unload ships at a normal rate. Trams, if they could get past the hostile crowds and had enough police protection, could be run just as quickly with a volunteer driver.

Buses and trains were another matter. Volunteer bus drivers, unfamiliar with their routes, took unauthorised detours. Some struggled to restart the engines when their bus stopped and therefore skipped several stops. Buses did not go out after dark and often ran on curtailed routes. Many stories recount student bus drivers taking attractive women to specific destinations regardless of their route, and one possibly apocryphal tale tells of a gentleman driver who diverted his bus to his own house so that his butler could hand him a cup of tea.[27]

Volunteer train drivers found they could make the engines stop and go relatively easily, but that was often the limit of their skill. One self-effacing volunteer Great Western Railway clerk recalled being sent to a shunting yard for a day, 'but after that we returned to the office, probably because there was no traffic to deal with, or because we were useless'.[28]

An inability to read and operate signals led to many trains ending up in the wrong location. There were stories of services taking hours or even days to reach their destination. The normal rules of safe operating were completely ignored. For instance a passenger train that erroneously ended up at Saltmarshe in Yorkshire was reversed down several miles of track to the previous station.[29]

Unfamiliarity with the engines led to explosions and other accidents. Three passengers were killed near Edinburgh on 10 May when their volunteer-driven service collided with a goods train. On the same day, another goods train was shunted into the back of a passenger service at Bishop's Stortford, claiming another life.[30] A volunteer fireman was killed instantly at Diss when his train passed under a bridge and, he being unfamiliar with the lack of clearance room, his head struck the structure.[31] The longer the strike went on, the greater was the possibility of a major catastrophe on the railways due to the incompetence of a poorly trained volunteer workforce.

Authorities turned a blind eye to the role of volunteers in these incidents, with no attempt to hold them responsible. Volunteer-driven buses also proved deadly. On 7 May in South London a Tilling's bus was attacked by some strikers and, in an effort to get away, mounted the pavement and fatally hit a bystander. One of the strikers was arraigned for preventing the proper use of a public vehicle but nothing happened to the driver.[32]

Despite all the difficulties, as the days went by, the rail companies gradually managed to run an improved service. On the first day of the strike all the big four companies were running fewer than one percent of their usual number of goods trains. This had increased to eight percent on the Great Western by 12 May, although the other companies lagged far behind. The improvement in passenger services, although less crucial to the country, was more marked, with both the Great Western and Southern Railways running just over a fifth of their usual number of services during the strike, but the two companies serving the North, LMS and LNER, could still only manage 13.4%.[33] Well into the second week of the strike, it was the road operation, rather than the railway volunteers, that was instrumental in the movement of goods around the country.

By far the most effective use of volunteers was in power stations where critical specialised staff were necessary. Due to their importance, the volunteer lists here were meticulously worked out beforehand and each individual was given a specific job. The government had been keeping lists of relevant individuals since at least 1922. These volunteers were highly skilled workers or students provided by the engineering institutes. The Electrical Power Engineers' Association (EPEA), a union representing skilled and managerial staff in power stations that was not affiliated to the TUC, on paper denounced the use of voluntary labour but in practice allowed its members to work alongside volunteers and naval personnel throughout the strike. Had the EPEA and its members walked out, the far greater military intervention would have been needed.

While the impetus for the volunteer movement came from forces outside the industrial working class, not all its adherents were from society's upper echelons. A relatively small but significant layer of industrial workers themselves played a role in undermining the strike. On the railways, where the companies had been left to their own devices to secure labour, a tiny number of train drivers and a slightly larger proportion of signalmen remained at work and, along with managers, enabled the volunteer staff to be trained and supervised. Retired drivers and signalmen were brought back to work to subvert the action of their erstwhile union colleagues.

Companies in other sectors also drew from the well of 'loyal' retired workers or took back workers they had previously fired or rejected. The fact that, at the end of the strike, so many companies would try to sack strikers and retain volunteer workers is itself proof that many of those volunteers came from the working class; it is unlikely that the Oxbridge undergraduates or Mayfair gentlemen would want to throw in their day-to-day lives for a permanent job on the waterfront or in an engine shed.

Overall, just as the trade unions had cause to be pleased with the rank-and-file response to the strike call, so could the government be more than satisfied with its volunteer organisation. By the end of the strike there were, in most places, more volunteers than jobs that could be found for them, and generally speaking, the operation that successive governments had meticulously planned since 1919 worked smoothly when its major test came in May 1926.

***

One very much untested aspect of the government's strikebreaking plan – and a key one – was the use of road transport. The railway strike of 1919 provided the first chance for road haulage to be used as an alternative to rail in a national strike, and a scheme was piloted by the government with some success. As in 1926, Hyde Park had been used as a central distribution centre to ensure London was fed.[34]

In 1919 Lloyd George had the advantage of wartime government controls over the food supply still being in place. With these having been dispensed with, Baldwin had to rely on voluntary cooperation. Although the emergency regulations gave the government the power to requisition private vehicles to keep food moving, this proved unnecessary. Road haulage companies and self-employed drivers organised into 150 local committees under the Supply and Transport Organisation (STO), jumped at the chance to serve the government, whether out of patriotic duty or simply seeing a ripe business opportunity. The AA and the RAC helped to recruit private drivers, almost all of whom would have been drawn from the middle and upper classes since car ownership among workers was negligible at the time. This scheme had its genesis in the 1911 strikes when Joynson-Hicks, an avid car enthusiast who was himself the founding chairman of the AA, had proposed something similar to the Home Office of which he was now in charge.[35] Those recruited through the drivers' organisations were often given specific roles, such as the two hundred motorcyclists organised by the RAC to act as scouts for the Metropolitan Police.[36] The strike was a lark for private motorists; one of the first measures the government had taken was to suspend the speed limit or the need to hold a licence for the duration of the emergency.

Senior civil servants and the all-important power station volunteers had their own private chauffeur services directed by Lord Curzon from Horse Guards Parade.[37] Many others, however, simply turned their cars into commuter transport outside of any of the formal volunteer structures. Cars became makeshift buses as office workers blagged lifts into the centre of London and other cities. The drivers improvised wooden signs to show potential passengers their destinations, or just pulled up and asked people where they wanted to go. The experience of this neighbourly bonhomie lingered long in many people's memories of the strike, and provided the press with some of its more colourful tales. 'I wonder how many romances the "lifting" business has given birth to,' mused the aforementioned *Tatler* columnist. 'I saw one car the other day, driven by a real charmer in the way of young men, which bore the placard "For Flappers Only" and he had certainly gathered an attractive collection.'[38]

The major benefit of road transport, however, was to be in the movement of freight. Once it was clear that all the railway unions were joining the general strike, an effective road transport system became paramount to the government's plans. Mass road transport was a relatively new phenomenon, one that had figured little in previous disputes. There were unionised lorry drivers, members of Bevin's TGWU and several smaller unions, but their level of organisation was nowhere near that of the railwaymen. Through local Haulage Committees, private firms and self-employed drivers could come together to provide a relatively reliable source of strikebreaking labour.

There had been some debate about the exact nature of a road-based strikebreaking operation in the event of a general stoppage of rail traffic. Early in the new year, a convoy system was mooted both by civil servants with an eye for efficiency and by private hauliers worried about attacks on their drivers and damage to their vehicles. Many police chiefs protested that their men would be too busy keeping order to escort convoys, and that in any case the spectacle of private lorries under heavy police or military protection would be more likely to provoke resentment and attacks from strikers and their supporters.[39] There was a further question of jurisdiction – whether escorts should be provided in a 'shuttle' system whereby one police force went only as far as their town or county boundary, or a 'through' system whereby the same escort stayed with the convoy all the way to its destination. In April the chief constable of the West Riding expressed his and many of his colleagues' view that the through system was better as 'the accumulation of a body of police at one spot would only be likely to gather a crowd of loafers and malcontents'.[40] It was only a matter of days before the strike, though, that the Home Office brought together local police forces to pool their manpower so that the escort system could be made to work.

The nerve centre of the government's road transport operation was the Hyde Park depot. Based at this encampment, over the course of the strike, convoys of lorries would move food and milk from docks and wharves to locations around the country. Large camps were more the exception than the rule, and elsewhere in the country the scheme of simply allowing private hauliers to move necessary goods around with little government direction initially worked remarkably well. This meant there was little cost to the government and only two areas where government officers had to step in to instruct the companies to prioritise food over other cargoes.[41]

There was of course an initial shock to the food distribution system caused by the calling of the strike, but many firms had been working overtime in the preceding days to ensure food stocks were high enough, and Bevin, keen to demonstrate that the unions were not out to starve the nation, chose not to implement an overtime ban. By the third day, the road transport system was working pretty much smoothly across the country – a major success story for the government.

***

The emergency machinery came into operation impressively quickly, but there were instances where it ran into trouble. On 6 May the Labour MP Martin Connolly made a sensational claim about the situation in the North-East:

> The position in Newcastle is that the OMS has entirely broken down, that the authorities have approached the trade unions, and asked them to take over the vital services, and that the trade unions have consented to do so on condition that all extra police, all troops, and all OMS services shall be withdrawn. That has been done, and the city is going on all right.[42]

His revelation alarmed the House. Attorney-General Douglas Hogg went scrambling for a phone line to Newcastle and, on his return, reassured the honourable members that the chief constable had told him that the supply and transport organisation in the city was intact.

What was going on? The civil commissioner for the North-East was Sir Kingsley Wood, who had no connection to the area and had been subbed in only at the last minute on 28 April, which may explain why his actions were somewhat less confident than those of his peers.[43]

On 5 May, the port authority introduced volunteer labour to the docks. At this point, dockers were unloading food cargoes under union permit. Now they flatly refused to work alongside volunteers they considered to be strikebreakers, and walked out. Making matters worse, they could see the ominous presence of two warships and a submarine on the River Tyne and feared that military personnel were going to be landed.

Later that night a meeting was set up by a Labour alderman at the local Miners' Federation headquarters. Wood professed to the strikers that voluntary labour had been introduced without his knowledge or permission, and that he was opposed to it as long as the trade unionist dockers were content to keep handling food cargo. For their part, the strike committee's representatives stated that ships with non-food cargo should be anchored in the middle of the river to be discharged after the dispute had ended, and that the naval vessels should return downriver to Jarrow 'as it was impossible for us to agree that our men should be forced to work under the shadow of their guns'.[44]

They reconvened the following afternoon along with the local food officer and Major-General Sir Kerr Montgomery. At this meeting, according to the strikers, Wood proposed a system of 'dual control' whereby his officers and the unions would jointly supervise work on the docks to make sure only foodstuffs were being handled, but rejected the principle of union-issued permits. After some discussion among themselves, the strike committee rejected this proposal as it would have still involved trade unionists working alongside non-union volunteers. Further to this, and because of regular reports of abuses of the permit system that they had been made aware of, the strike committee resolved to withdraw all permits for the movement of food.

The morning after Connolly's sensational claim it was privately confirmed to the Cabinet that the unions had refused the offer of dual control and as a result 'the transfer of food supplies from boats at the quayside at Newcastle has practically ceased'. Three days later, the docks were still at a standstill except for a small amount of food being unloaded, and bunkered coal being taken aboard working fishing trawlers.[45]

By 8 May Wood was backtracking, stating to the local press that the unions had simply misconstrued his 'friendly visit' to their office, and no dual control system had been proposed.[46] After the strike, he denied again in the House of Commons that he had done this, admitting only to telling the trade unionists 'that if they found there was any difficulty at the quay in relation to the employment of labour, they were to report it to my officer or to me, and I would immediately deal with it'. The reason for this, he claimed, was that due to the presence of naval vessels, rumours were being circulated that military personnel were about to be used on the docks, which was not the case.[47]

Wood's proposal to cede some control of the port to the unions landed him immediately in hot water with some on his own side who regarded him as lacking nerve. In Mitchell-Thomson's post-strike report he delivered a not-so-veiled rebuke to Sir Kingsley Wood in his conclusion that no civil commissioner should hold any discussions or negotiations with strikers at all in future emergencies.[48]

It was, however, a rare failure of the machinery that had been tested in crises since 1919 and perfected in the months since Red Friday. By and large, the anti-socialist and anti-labour opinion so carefully courted by Baldwin in the 1924 election was successfully mobilised. Volunteers flocked to the colours with an enthusiasm akin to those who had mobbed recruiting offices in 1914. Unlike during the war, however, there were more of them than the state knew what to do with. Most were, in fact, idle throughout the great strike, although their escapades have lived long in the national memory.

TROUBLE IN HAMMERSMITH BROADWAY DURING THE PASSAGE OF A MILK-LORRY : AN ARRESTED MAN BETWEN BETWEEN TWO CONSTABLES AND A MOUNTED POLICEMAN (IN BACKGROUND).

Police clear crowds in Hammersmith to allow a lorry through.

7

THE STATE RESPONDS

The side which is organized wins the fence-sitters in the battle between the loyalists and the revolutionaries.

- C. E. Penney, Government Food Controller, 1919

The time is not very far distant when you WILL be called upon to help the employers to bludgeon the Workers into still Lower depths of misery. Now, in what way will it benefit you if the employers succeed in their nefarious task?

- Communist pamphlet, 'To the men of His Majesty's forces', April 1926

With its volunteer machinery up and running, the government had to contend with controlling the flow of the information. The presses had stopped. Even if the vast majority of newspapers, local and national, longed to denounce the general strike, they couldn't.

Many in the establishment railed against their impotence, denouncing the TUC's decision to call out printworkers as an all-out attack on press freedom. While the National Union of Journalists had not joined the strike, it did instruct its members not to carry out the work of striking colleagues. Enough journalists ignored this and applied their limited technical knowledge to production that many newspapers were able to appear intermittently as crudely put-together single-sheet bulletins. Only around

40 of the country's 1,870 local papers continued to appear as normal throughout the strike. Compounding this were difficulties in distribution due to the transport strike.[1]

Most people in 1926 relied for their news on a daily paper or two. This was just as true of the king as it was of any of his subjects; he asked to be personally briefed every day by a member of the Cabinet in light of the failure of the papers to appear.[2] Without a supportive press, the country would be in the dark as to the government's actions and the justification for them. Half-truths and rumours would spread easily in the fraught situation. Even worse, alternative narratives of events would emerge.

The solution was simple: a government newspaper. The main driving force behind the idea was J. C. C. Davidson, the deputy civil commissioner. On 2 May the illustrious members of the Newspaper Proprietors' Association, many of whom were bitter commercial and political rivals, informed Davidson that they would not pool their resources to produce a joint newspaper if the printers went on strike. So he approached the editor of the *Morning Post*, an ultra-conservative newspaper owned by the Duke of Northumberland and edited by the antisemite Howell Arthur Gwynne. Expecting his staff to remain loyal and not strike, Gwynne agreed to turn his presses over to the production of a government daily newspaper, to be called the *British Gazette*.

As the *Gazette* was to be such a crucial political instrument, the *Post*'s offices were essentially fortified with the help of the police and military detachments. Every night, heavily guarded vans carrying copies of the paper were dispatched around the country, as well as to Biggin Hill and Northolt airfields from which military planes couriered them to the further-flung regions.

Nevertheless, the *Gazette* encountered a rocky start. Gwynne's assumption that his workers would remain loyal proved wishful when, on the afternoon of 4 May with only five columns of type set, the *Post*'s compositors contacted their union about the paper and were promptly instructed to stop work. They did so, breaking the type as they left, and so did the workers at the print shop Davidson had commandeered to produce a duplicate as a plan B. A veteran typesetter had to be drafted in from the *Daily Express* to single-handedly set most of the first issue, while editorial and journalistic staff had to man the presses to get it out on time.[3] Crowds of strike sympathisers attacked the lorries that left the *Post*'s offices with the first *Gazette*, and the police presence there had to be bolstered.[4]

Despite these early obstacles, by 6 May the *Gazette* was up and running as a full operation, and successfully produced a four-page paper every day until the strike ended. With all but one or two of the *Post*'s staff on strike, replacements were drafted in from the *Mail* and *Express* and assisted by student volunteers.[5]

With the *Gazette* constituting the government's only direct physical means of communicating to the public, the question of its editorial line was a crucial one. Winston Churchill has gone down in history as its editor and driving force, but this is contested in J. C. C. Davidson's memoirs. Davidson recalled a conversation with Baldwin at the outset of the strike where he had confided: 'I'm terrified of what Winston is going to be like'; he decided to put him in charge of the *Gazette* to 'keep him busy and stop him doing worse things'. Davidson reminded Baldwin that Churchill had 'no power except the power of a personality that is very difficult to deal with'. He installed a direct line between the *Post*'s office and his own in the Admiralty building, and claimed to have censored or heavily edited about a dozen articles that Churchill wrote during the strike, to tone down their content.[6]

Each day the *Gazette* reported, often with exaggerated figures, the increased numbers of trains and buses running. Its repeated refrain that services were 'improving' was technically true but elided the fact that they were still a small fraction of the usual. Its main purpose was to delegitimise the strike altogether by hammering home the idea that it was a revolutionary plot.[7] Each day, the *Gazette* reprinted Baldwin's message to the country:

> Constitutional government is being attacked. Let all good citizens whose livelihood and labour have thus been put in peril bear with fortitude and patience the hardships with which they have been suddenly confronted. Stand behind the Government, who are doing their part, confident that you will co-operate in the measures they have undertaken to preserve the liberties and privileges of the people of these islands. The laws of England are the people's birthright. The laws are in your keeping. You have made Parliament their guardian. The General Strike is a challenge to Parliament and is the road to anarchy and ruin.

Despite Davidson's efforts, Churchill's hardline came across consistently in the *Gazette*. One theme was his admiration for labour relations in fascist Italy, from where the *Gazette*'s own correspondent reported approvingly that agricultural workers had settled their differences without resorting to a strike.[8]

Churchill's brusque manner and desire to micromanage the paper did not endear him to its volunteer staff. His tendency to turn up at all hours and demand minor changes to wording and punctuation did not go down well. One undated memo stated: 'He rattled them [the staff] very badly last night. He thinks he is Napoleon, but curiously enough the men who have been printing all their life in the various processes happen to know more about their job than he does.'[9] Davidson attempted to prevent Churchill from frequenting the *Post*'s office to avoid a potentially catastrophic breakdown in relationships.

In later years, Baldwin described his decision to 'put Winston in a corner' by giving him the *Gazette* as 'the cleverest thing I ever did'.[10] Putting the government's regular propaganda tool in the hands of such a hardliner, however, was no small matter. If Davidson is to be believed, an unfettered Churchill editorship would have been a disaster for the government's efforts to win over moderate opinion.

The TUC's answer to the *Gazette* was already in the works before the first issue of the government paper hit the streets. The General Council's Publicity Committee discussed with the print unions and the *Daily Herald*'s editor Hamilton Fyfe the possibility of producing a pro-TUC news sheet. This was not easy, as the print unions were loath to exempt any of their members from the strike, even those working on labour-friendly papers. The printworkers' intransigent attitude prompted Fenner Brockway of the Independent Labour Party to ask: 'Was this a general strike or a general do-as-you please?'[11] Fyfe was adamant in explaining to the printers that this was no ordinary strike; there was a war on: 'These people want everything to be done as it is done in normal times… On the day the Last Trump sounds they will complain that their shaving water hasn't been heated for them as usual.'[12]

The print unions eventually agreed to issue exemptions after the General Council issued a direct order, and the *British Worker* was born. The *Worker* and the *Gazette* would engage in a propaganda war over the nine days of the strike.

Like that of its government counterpart, production of the *British Worker* was arranged impressively quickly. It would be printed at the *Herald*'s offices at Victoria House, overseen by Fyfe but with strict control over content exercised by the General Council. It faced an immediate crisis when, while the first issue was on the presses, the police raided Victoria House. On the evening of 5 May, around one hundred police officers with a warrant from Joynson-Hicks surrounded the building. As the paper was plunged into jeopardy, one staff member managed to get through the police cordon and notify the General Council. Labour MPs were contacted and told to raise the issue in the House, but before they could do so, the police informed the staff that they could find nothing objectionable in the content of the paper. Printing went ahead as planned.

It may have been the large crowd that had quickly gathered outside that changed the mind of the officer in charge, or it may have simply been the paper's ultra-moderate tone. The first issue praised the 'workers' quiet dignity' and reminded its readers to do nothing that might provoke the authorities. There was no question, the paper emphasised, of an attack on constitutional government; this was merely an industrial dispute.[13] Further issues followed in the same vein. Strikers were urged not to congregate in public and pickets were told not to obstruct roads. Instead, they were to busy themselves with educational classes, cricket matches, and other forms of enrichment. There was no discussion of the strategy and tactics of the strike in the pages of the *Worker*, but constant exhortations to trust the leadership. It bore little resemblance to the more boisterous editorial culture of the *Herald*, which remained pluralist in the perspectives to which it gave column inches, even after the TUC took over ownership.[14]

Behind the scenes the TUC's Publicity Committee did argue about the content of the *Worker*. Fyfe wanted it to be closer to a regular newspaper, including updates on sports and world events. TUC publicity officer Herbert Tracey icily commented 'he does not yet understand that a strike bulletin is not a newspaper' and 'readers of the *British Worker* are so anxious to get news about the strike that they won't feel the absence of the cricket scores and other general news Fyfe seems to think important'.[15] Ultimately, Tracey's view won out.

Demand for the two newspapers soon outstripped supply as the public was hungry for news from both sides of the divide. The government and

TUC attempted to ratchet up production, although of course the former had the huge advantage of state power and the emergency regulations. With paper workers having been called out alongside the printers, Churchill seized the *Daily Herald*'s entire stock of paper for use by the *British Gazette*. There was a daily struggle to source paper, and by 10 May there was only four or five days' worth left on the government's presses. Churchill took decisive action in commandeering a paper mill at Northfleet, with a volunteer workforce under the guard of the Royal Engineers and a naval detachment. Volunteers slept on site and produced fifty tonnes of paper every day, which was enough to print 1.5 million copies of the *Gazette*.[16]

Demand for the *British Worker* was far in excess of what could be printed and distributed from London. Trade unionists did not trust what they read in the 'capitalist press' or heard on the wireless, and union officials wanted a source of reliable news to stop the spread of rumours. Plans were made to print in other locations with the typed copy couriered from Victoria House in the early hours, but the negotiations with various local printers' unions and cooperative printing houses were so torturous that locally produced issues did not hit the streets in Manchester and Cardiff until 10 May. On the final day before the strike was called off some 700,000 copies were printed in all.

No doubt the *Worker*'s coverage was patchy. Supply was insufficient in many cities, especially in the South, and some remote localities probably did not see a single copy during the strike. On the other hand, one exasperated military intelligence report from 8 May noted that there were districts where the *Gazette* was unobtainable and the population entirely reliant on the TUC's paper.[17] People weren't getting the same news. The pro-strike and anti-strike populations were inhabiting parallel universes.

Alongside print media, the government was keen to utilise newer technology to reach the public. Founded in 1922, the British Broadcasting Company (BBC) was still a young organisation run by a young man, the thirty-six-year-old John Reith. Reith ardently professed the importance of political impartiality to the BBC but, as the future reorganisation of the company was being discussed in Whitehall in the months leading up to the strike, he was susceptible to government pressure. The company was not entirely independent of government and the postmaster general

Mitchell-Thomson, who had responsibility for broadcast media, was also, perhaps not entirely coincidentally, the chief civil commissioner of the government's emergency organisation. On top of this, Reith's next-door neighbour was none other than Mitchell-Thomson's deputy, J. C. C. Davidson.[18]

Government sources, at the time and afterwards, maintained that the independence of the BBC was respected during the strike, but this does not tell the whole story. On the first day of the strike, Reith had lunch with Baldwin at the Travellers' Club on Pall Mall and agreed to broadcast five daily news bulletins, the bulk of the source material for which would come through Davidson's office. He warned the prime minister that if the government were to take formal control of the BBC, as was being pushed for by Churchill, it would lose its credibility and be seen as a partisan organ like the *Gazette*. Even worse, the unions could respond by extending the strike to the BBC and paralysing broadcasting altogether.[19]

In return for retaining formal editorial control, Reith acceded to every government request during the strike. On 7 May, he denied both Ramsay MacDonald's and the Archbishop of Canterbury's requests to be allowed national radio broadcasts. In both cases he discussed the matter with Davidson beforehand, with the government fixer somewhat wryly noting in his memoir that when Reith rang Lambeth Palace to inform the archbishop of his decision he 'made it clear that he was acting on his own responsibility'.[20] The archbishop's proposed statement, drafted in conjunction with clergy from other denominations, called for a swift resumption of negotiations to end the strike but was privately denounced in government quarters as a lily-livered plea for peace at any price. By contrast, the BBC and the *British Gazette* – which had refused to print the archbishop's appeal – gave prominence to a sermon given by Cardinal Bourne, head of the Roman Catholic Church in England and Wales, at Westminster Cathedral, in which he described the strike as 'a sin against the obedience which we owe to God'.[21]

On 11 May the Cabinet discussed both Ramsay MacDonald's and Lloyd George's requests, as leaders of the Opposition parties, for a public broadcast slot and reaffirmed that no politician except the prime minister should be allowed to address the nation until the crisis was over.[22] Message discipline and censorship at the heart of government were such that even other Cabinet ministers were barred from giving interviews to British or foreign journalists.[23]

All this editorial acquiescence just about sufficed to stop the government taking full control of the BBC. Tory backbenchers daily bombarded the Cabinet with complaints that the company's daily bulletins did occasionally report the strike's strength and successes. Lord Birkenhead and Churchill argued forcefully that broadcasting should be commandeered by the state, but Baldwin and Joynson-Hicks both opposed the move as an unnecessary risk. The prime minister's view won the day.

Baldwin was, however, just as keen to wield this new propaganda weapon as were his belligerent ministers. The previous election campaign had taught him of its power to reach those fence-sitters who were not yet sure what they really thought of the strike. At 9.30 p.m. on the evening of 8 May the prime minister addressed the nation from Reith's personal study. He employed the same affable and informal style as he had during the election. Then, his fireside chat-style broadcast, addressing voters directly in their own homes, had been compared favourably with a more raucous recording of Labour leader Ramsay MacDonald addressing a public meeting. Baldwin drew on this experience to once again address the public in a measured and steady tone, lighting his pipe before beginning to speak. He denied that his government was attempting to lower the living standards of the people. Rather, he said, it was the strike itself that was bound to increase unemployment and place a burden on the taxpayer. The government was willing to negotiate a settlement but could not do so until the general strike was called off. He concluded:

> I am a man of peace. I am longing, and working, and praying for peace, but I will not surrender the safety and security of the British Constitution. You placed me in power 18 months ago, by the largest majority accorded to any Party for many, many years. Have I done anything to forfeit that confidence? Cannot you trust me to ensure a square deal for the parties? To secure even justice between man and man?[24]

This was in keeping with Baldwin's carefully cultivated image but at odds with the reality of the weeks leading up to the strike in which he had singularly failed to secure such a deal. Nevertheless, the broadcast was a great morale boost to the suburban white-collar workers undertaking the 'Great Trek' to the office every morning, to the volunteers and the Special Constables who were surer than ever that they were on the side of right.

The BBC was a powerful weapon for the government, especially as the labour movement simply could not compete. It's an open question whether Reith would have been knighted at the end of the year, and appointed the first director-general of the newly reorganised British Broadcasting Corporation in 1927, had he stood up to government pressure during the strike.

***

Underpinning the apparatus of volunteer labour, government decision-making, and propaganda were the state's coercive agencies: the police and the Armed Forces. We have seen how both the police and the military had been consistently used during industrial disputes since the start of the Great Unrest. During the strike, both the civilian and military authorities were keen to avoid the scenes of soldiers on the streets of Britain. But that meant placing more strain on the regular police force, requiring rapid expansion of the supplemental special constabulary.

There were, at least initially, some signs of good and even friendly relationships between strikers and the police. At Luton there were cricket matches arranged between them (it is not recorded who won), and at Merthyr Tydfil the strike committee was 'in daily consultation with Chief Constable and assisted in organisation of sports and concerts, thus keeping strikers off streets'.[25] In Sussex, the Mayor of Lewes arranged a billiards match between the two sides and put up the prize money himself, while at Seaford a mass meeting of strikers passed a vote of thanks, halfway through the strike, to the police for how they had conducted themselves.[26]

Stories like this have entered the mythology of the strike as characterised by a British sense of moderation. For instance, the football match at Plymouth, kicked off by the chief constable's wife, when the strikers beat the police 2–1, is a tale told time and again. But not everyone in government even thought it was a good news story. Churchill attempted to prevent the *British Gazette* from reporting it, condemning it as unacceptable 'fraternisation' between police and strikers. On this occasion, he was overruled by cooler heads, who clearly saw the propaganda value. Needless to say, a riot in Plymouth earlier on the same day, involving several thousand workers attempting to stop the running of trams, has received rather less attention.

The inadequate number of regular police meant they would have to be supplemented by a force of volunteer special constables. Specials had been raised at various points throughout the previous century during times of potential unrest and mass demonstrations for electoral reform. This had included industrial disputes, for example three thousand specials were sworn in during the 1911 transport strike in Liverpool.[27] Widespread recruitment of special constables had also been a feature of the 1921 coal dispute. In 1923, when a new law was debated that put the special constabulary on surer footing, the Labour MP Charles Trevelyan – himself of aristocratic stock – urged that an anti-strikebreaking clause should be included or else workers would shun the specials 'and this new Force will be composed only of enthusiasts for the mine-owning and property-owning view of industrial disputes, people who, from their side, believe in class war'.[28]

The feel-good stories about strikers and police being on the same page don't capture the very real pressure put on the police forces. Almost from the outset of the strike, regular police forces in some areas were operating at capacity and needed the help. In Cardiff, for example, more than twice as many special constables were sworn in as there were regular officers. But outside the city, in the South Wales coalfield, 'the numbers compared to the size of the [regular] forces were infinitesimal and wholly insufficient to relieve the duty policemen'.[29]

In many working-class areas, enrolling as a special constable was seen as tantamount to scabbing. And because of the social background of many specials, and their willingness to knock trade unionists' heads, working-class communities hated them even more than strikebreakers. Many came from the upper echelons of society, like the two hundred 'ex-cavalry men and polo players' enrolled as mounted police in London under Major-General John Vaughan.[30] They took pride in being up for a fight and willing to mete out violence, such as the Putney rugby team who volunteered *en masse* and 'asked to be sent to where they could find the roughest house possible'. At Nine Elms in South London, a NUR official complained of police harassment of his members when they were queueing up to collect their strike pay: 'what grieves the men most is the sudden arrival of irresponsible youths called "Specials" in motor cars, who jump out and commence slashing about with their batons without using any discretion whatever... Unfortunately women have also been injured during these charges.'[31]

The eighty-five-year-old Earl of Meath, founder of the Empire Day Movement, enrolled as a special towards the end of the strike, affirming that he was still able to tackle a man and boxed every morning.[32] Of course such aristocratic recruits comprised a minority; the majority were shopkeepers, white-collar professionals, students, and a number of workers in domestic service.[33] The latter may have enrolled at the instigation of their masters or out of a genuine affinity with the more privileged classes to whom, unlike industrial workers, they were in close proximity. Certainly some more patriotically minded employers, or those who just recognised the need for the government to beat the strike in their own class interest, released, encouraged, and in some cases cajoled employees to sign up. The London furnishing company that threatened its workers with wage cuts or even dismissal if they did not enrol was, however, almost certainly an aberration.[34]

Just as the civil servants had to contend with the thorny question of volunteers recruited by the OMS, so did the police chief constables grapple with how to respond to offers of special constables from dubious sources. The British Fascists, their forces small but motivated, were keen to both demonstrate their patriotism and to receive official sanction for violent attacks on trade unionists. In the run-up to Red Friday in July 1925 Fascist representatives had met with several chief constables, despite a Home Office warning that 'the police should certainly proceed warily in any relations with the BFs [British Fascists], some of their activities are not such as police should have any sort of connection with'.[35] Chief constables took a variety of views. In Manchester the Fascist offer was firmly rebuffed. Wolverhampton's Fascists though, who claimed they could enrol six hundred men, were invited by the police to turn up for their annual inspection subdivided into companies of fifty. They were assured that they would remain in command of their own men provided no Fascist uniforms or insignia were worn. After this came to light in the *Daily Herald*, the plan was abandoned on the day in the face of a mass protest at the town hall.

Liverpool police similarly abandoned plans to enrol Fascists in the face of public hostility.[36]

The Fascist question had still not been satisfactorily resolved on the eve of the strike when Birmingham's Chief Constable Rafter asked for a Home Office circular to be issued. Rafter had been approached by the management of the Birmingham Small Arms Company works who had mooted the possibility of swearing some of their own employees who were Fascists in as specials to protect the factory. Rafter was opposed to Fascists serving as police even in individual capacities, but advised the use of an obscure local law that enabled anyone committing an offence to be 'apprehended by the owner of the property on or with respect to which the offence shall be committed, or by his servant, or any person authorised by him, and may be detained until he can be delivered into the custody of a constable'.[37] The Home Office maintained its position that Fascists should not be enrolled *en bloc* but would be eligible to serve individually. Upon the outbreak of the strike, many Fascists duly signed up but were essentially indistinguishable from their colleagues from more respectable walks of life during the dispute.

For the vast majority of trade unionists the specials, wearing their armbands over their smart civilian clothes and swinging their truncheons with apparent impunity, were decidedly the class enemy. Those who would have thought twice about attacking a regular police patrol or a uniformed soldier often had no such reservations about letting the specials know how they felt. They were jeered and jostled by working-class men and women in many areas. In places like Ipswich, for their own safety, the specials could only be deployed in large groups and in the company of uniformed officers.[38]

Nevertheless, a small number of trade unionists did enrol as specials, some as individuals and some as part of a deliberate attempt by local strike committees to be seen helping to uphold public order. On 7 May Sam Moss, the president of the National Glass Bottle Makers' Society, wrote to the TUC asking for guidance regarding some of his members who had signed up. 'It appears to me', he lamented, 'that they are assisting the Government to feed the children while their parents are being crucified.'[39] Police at Doncaster refused the Council of Action's offer to enrol specials and instead recruited from local officer and non-commissioned officer veterans of the Great War.⁴⁰ It appears a similar offer from the unions in Lincoln, where the chief constable was a Labour supporter, may have been accepted and there was little trouble in the city during the strike.

Workers' conflicting views on the matter of serving in the special constabulary are illustrated by the case of Birmingham. Here, a number of tramwaymen were pre-existing members of the special constabulary and, when they went on strike, were called up to their police duties. One of them, John Leedham, was himself arrested and fined £5 for holding up traffic as a picket. Birmingham Labour councillor Alfred James Gilmore, a member of the National Union of General and Municipal Workers (NUGMW), had been a special constable since 1911. After the strike he was summoned to a meeting of the Trades and Labour Council and informed that they considered him to be a blackleg: 'You cannot be a trade unionist and a Special Constable' were the words of one committee member. Gilmore protested that his actions were no different to the many trade unionists who served as magistrates.

One of Gilmore's fellow Labour councillors was George Sawyer, a striking railway guard. He came closer to expressing the view of the majority of the labour movement when, during a speech at an open-air meeting on 7 May, he proclaimed: 'The Special Constabulary is nothing more than a body of traitors, and each member should be locked up as a suspicious person. I mustn't say too much about them because I'm a member of the Watch Committee, and they serve under me.'⁴¹ Sawyer was arrested under the emergency regulations but released on giving an undertaking not to make similar statements in the future.

In the clash between the labour movement and the state, many trade unionists found themselves in a tricky position. As the labour movement had advanced politically, they had become local councillors, magistrates, pillars of respectability. The argument over serving in the specials was therefore not just a matter of bad blood within the labour movement, but in microcosm a debate between two conflicting views of the labour movement's purpose – was it aiming for a seat at the table, to take its place among Britain's great institutions, or was it engaged in a conflict with the state to build a new type of society?

In the event, specials were used to break the strike. Among their key tasks was to provide 'flying squads' that would patrol routes along which buses or lorries were travelling, especially in areas where they had met stiff resistance from pickets. These mobile squads were instrumental in enabling the London General Omnibus Company (LGOC) to get some buses out of its Chiswick depot by 6 May, along with uniformed officers who rode with the driver on each bus. They also enabled the stretched regular police forces to operate the road convoy system with extra manpower where necessary. Many other specials, though, spent the nine days in more mundane service, directing traffic or going on routine patrols to free up regular police for public order duties.

Behind the police stood the Empire's Armed Forces. By mid-April, when the prospect of a coal lockout was becoming very real, military preparations were stepped up. It was assumed troops would have to be deployed to the coalfield districts in a similar manner as had happened in 1921, but such movements were fraught with risk before an emergency had actually been declared. In South Wales, the hardline chief constable of Monmouthshire Victor Bosanquet urged the government to move military units into the area as soon as possible to serve as a warning to the unions, whereas his Cardiff counterpart was convinced that such a provocation would make a strike inevitable.[42]

There was obvious tension between military commanders and senior police officers. The former, by and large, were very reluctant for the Army to be drawn into what they saw as a political squabble and fervently wished that the civil authorities were prepared to meet the challenge themselves. The latter were sceptical that their numerically weak thin blue line would be able to hold out in the event of widespread disorder. Meeting the head of the Army's Western Command a week before the strike, the chief constables of North-West England urged the early movement of a full twelve battalions of infantry to the region, instead of the planned four. Fearing the worst, one pointed out: 'We might all be wiped away before the military reached here. If there were a general strike, how were the military going to get here?'[43]

This plea fell on deaf ears; on 29 April the War Office ordered two battalions to Bury, one to Cardiff, and one to Edinburgh, but stressed that the movement should only take place after a state of emergency had been proclaimed. These movements duly took place on 1 May and were followed two days later by the movement of a full brigade from Aldershot to

Yorkshire, to be nearer to both the northern coalfields and the key ports of Hull and Newcastle. This latter movement was done by sea as the authorities feared that the civilian drivers of the military transport were on the verge of joining the strike. Finally, on the eve of the strike, military guards were sent to explosive factories, for fear that subversive elements might attempt to liberate some useful materials.[44]

The Army Council met daily during the course of the strike to consider the unfolding situation. Its main concern was not to scatter its forces too thinly. It was reluctant to deploy soldiers at all, but if it had to, they should not be in units any smaller than a platoon. This was to avoid inviting attacks on isolated soldiers, and to make any potential fraternisation between soldiers and strikers more difficult.

Draconian though they were, the emergency regulations did not constitute martial law, and the military could only act upon requests from the civil authorities. Requests soon rolled in, often at the urging of employers who wanted military guards to scare pickets away from their premises. By and large, authorisation for such guards was restricted to locations that were deemed strategically crucial. Petrol stations, which were often relatively remote and therefore vulnerable to vandalism, were one such point. Key workplaces were another. The LGOC bus depot in Chiswick hosted two platoons of grenadier guards from 4 May for the duration of the strike.[45] The Army was reluctant even to provide these guards because they found that, once committed, it was impossible to withdraw this protection without affecting the morale of the volunteer workers, who would feel abandoned.

Some authorities placed consistent demands on the military for more support. The Lord Advocate of Scotland, for example, spent the strike convinced that the radical elements of Red Clydeside were on the verge of insurrection and asked numerous times for a larger military presence. His fears appeared confirmed when rioting took hold in the city's East End, which shaded into Lanarkshire's coal country. When miners from Cambuslang marched into town to stop buses and trams there were fierce battles with police billeted at the Ruby Street tram depot. It took three days and over one hundred arrests before a semblance of control was restored by the police.[46] From 7 May military convoys were provided between Edinburgh, Glasgow, and Stirling due to lorries being systematically stopped by miners on the roads. Royal Scots were also posted at LNER railway sites in Scotland. The lord advocate requested the use of armoured cars for convoys, and the local Army commander cabled the War Office for advice. The response reveals the worries the military authorities had about the potential for a flashpoint that could lead to civilian casualties: 'We leave to your discretion the question of escort but dispersal of troops should be avoided. Would point out only method of attack of armoured cars is by firing. Egress is difficult and tactically less than a section is unsound. Generally troops in lorry are more suitable.'[47] In the event, the armoured cars were not deployed.

The Navy's role in the strike was better defined and, in many ways, more crucial to the strikebreaking operation. Since the end of the war, the Admiralty had developed various 'UC' – standing for 'Unrest, Civil' – schemes. These included well-worked-out arrangements for shipping yeast from Ireland to supply bakeries. Under UC11, warships were dispatched to all the country's major ports. Their function was mainly intimidatory although they did also land naval ratings – sailors below officer rank – to assist with unloading ships in some ports.

It was in London and the Thames Estuary where the Navy was most prominent. Here, it maintained and ran the Tilbury ferry, provided transport for Thames river pilots, and protected oil and petrol terminals to ensure the vital fuel supplies for road transport were kept intact. On the docks, submarines were brought in to provide power for cold storage warehouses when left-wing borough councils in the East End threatened to cut off the power supply.

Relations between the Navy and the Port of London Authority (PLA), which seems to have been woefully unprepared for the strike despite the relatively common industrial strife on the docks throughout the 1920s, were somewhat strained. Naval personnel arrived at the docks to find themselves faced with insufficient and uncomfortable accommodation and no reliable supply of food. 'The arrangements made with the Port of London Authority for the feeding and accommodation of the parties from Chatham [Dockyard] broke down completely,' noted the Admiralty.[48]

The Navy's most important role, however, was not in the docks but in the power stations. The local electrical power scheme provided for ratings to take over duties where workers had walked out. Naval stokers, used to shovelling coal into warships' vast furnaces, were redeployed to do the same job on land. The exact number of ratings that would be required at each station was worked out well before the strike and, alongside the working engineers of the EPEA, the Navy was able to keep the lights on.

The authorities were acutely sensitive to any efforts to get the rank and file of the forces to show sympathy with the strikers and perhaps even disobey orders. After the arrest and trial of the twelve Communist leaders in October 1925 the CPGB's attempted agitation in the military did not abate. It produced a pamphlet by the barrister Robert Dunstan, 'The Soldier's Conscience', putting forward a legal argument that soldiers had a moral right and duty not to carry out orders with which they disagreed. Dunstan drew on the speeches of Conservatives and unionists during the Ulster crisis of 1914 to back up his point. Then, prominent politicians had solemnly intoned that British officers and soldiers who were ordered to disarm loyalist militias would be justified in refusing to obey. Embarrassingly for the government, this included Lord Birkenhead who had warned that if the Liberal government ordered the Army against the Ulster Loyalists it would 'break in their hands'.

CPGB activists also distributed the 'Soldiers', Sailors' and Airmen's Charter' at military barracks in early 1926, a political programme demanding increased pay for soldiers, increased pensions for widows, and trade union rights for servicemen. Joynson-Hicks's nephew Phil Bower, a serving soldier, sent his uncle a copy of the 'Conscience' pamphlet that had been thrown over the wall of his barracks. 'I have been considering what action, if any, I can take,' wrote the home secretary in reply, 'but the pamphlet is very skilfully worded and I am anything but hopeful.'[49] As well as this leafleting, slogans were chalked on walls and anonymous letters were sent to fictitious soldiers in the Manchester Regiment's barracks at Hartshead.

This agitation cut through to at least some soldiers. One Aldershot NCO reported on the outbreak of the strike the low morale of his unit was due to the CPGB's propaganda campaign of the preceding months. Nonetheless, military intelligence agents who acted as *agent provocateurs* by staging arguments in the town's pubs noted: 'In most cases, when political arguments were started the soldiers finished their beer and left at once.'[50]

The Communist campaign continued once the strike was underway, during which time any attempt to instil disaffection in the forces was a clear offence under the emergency regulations. On 6 May two party members were arrested attempting to distribute literature to naval ratings billeted at a Territorial Army building in Chelsea. The same day 1,500 pamphlets aimed at soldiers were seized from the Communist James Clarke at Euston on his way north. This provoked a row between the police and the security services, as Clarke's driver was an MI5 agent. Furious at what he saw as the police's premature arrest of Clarke and the driver, the agent's handler argued that he had been prevented from identifying the address in Clerkenwell where the remainder of the offending pamphlets were stored.[51]

Although many soldiers were reticent to get involved in the dispute, there are only a handful of isolated examples of actual mutinous feeling. A War Office intelligence report of 11 May acknowledged that soldiers suspected of communist sympathies had been under surveillance but the only serious issue among these was a private who had expressed his support for rioters in Newcastle.[52] One member of the RAF at Upavon was given two months' hard labour under the emergency regulations for causing disaffection among the civilian population. More worryingly for the authorities, soldiers of the Royal Tank Corps at Aldershot were heard saying that they would not fire on strikers 'unless it was a case of one or the other'.[53]

This latter issue may have been the spark for various rumours of mutiny that persisted throughout the strike, as it was repeated in some strikers' news sheets and, to the consternation of the War Office, 'discussed by people who should be in a position to know better'.[54] The Communist Party seized on the rumours to pursue a deliberate and consistent campaign of misinformation. The most-repeated was that the Welsh Guards had been confined to barracks after refusing to entrain for a coal-field area. There were other rumours that troops in the government's huge temporary logistics depot in Hyde Park had disobeyed orders. Several arrests, mainly of Communists, were made for republishing or verbally repeating these statements.

In the second issue of the Communist *Birmingham Worker* newsletter, an Aldershot-based soldier apparently wrote: 'We have all discussed the strike and we are for the Miners and we don't want to be used as strike breakers, we are willing to refuse to do anything despite the consequences. Will you please tell us what we ought to do through your paper.'⁵⁵ This clumsily worded letter was almost certainly fabricated. In general soldiers were willing to follow what they saw as innocuous orders, such as guarding a petrol station from vandalism. And their superiors didn't try to push their luck too far. Had soldiers been ordered to fire on working-class crowds, their attitudes may well have dramatically shifted. As the author of the London Army Command's post-strike report noted: 'One young soldier…with one shot, can upset the whole apple cart.'⁵⁶

***

For many in the security services, the strike provided an opportunity for the showdown with communism they had been waiting for. We have seen how those in the apparatus of the secret state were convinced of the possibility of a Moscow-funded Bolshevik insurrection being carried out by a small group of hardened revolutionaries given the right conditions. The dramatic nature of the strike and its significant early success in paralysing the economic life of the country appeared to these agents to create those conditions perfectly.

Once again the security services' unfamiliarity with their subjects led to some overblown descriptions to their superiors of basic labour movement activity. The Portsmouth branch of the Independent Labour Party (ILP), which organised activists to take street collections for the strikers, was described as running 'a sort of mild campaign of extorting money by threat…with the object of intimidating ladies etc into contributing'.⁵⁷ The need to find Reds around every corner led to an agent improbably describing the town of Hitchin in Hertfordshire as 'though extremely quiet, [harbouring] a large number of avowed revolutionaries'. One informant in the market town of Stratford-upon-Avon, hardly known for its militancy, tailed a left-wing railwayman, R. H. Webb, throughout 5 May. Webb was noted as taking part in such nefarious activities as speaking 'in whispers to a gentlewoman' outside the local NUR office and attending a meeting in a hut on an allotment. Quite what was supposed to be achieved by such activity is not made clear.

The endemic prejudices of the security services are betrayed in their notes on those who were being surveilled. Antisemitism was never far from the surface; it was noted pointedly that the partners of a Birmingham company making red rosettes were Jewish. Fulham activist Ben Franks was described: 'Greyish hair, prominent red Jewish nose... Black brilliant eyes with that peculiar epileptic burn in them, so characteristic of the enflamed extreme communist who has suffered a great deal from extreme inactivity. Very dirty in his appearance.' Names taken in Portsmouth included 'Mullins. HM Dockyard. Coloured electrician. Communist agitator' and 'Blitz. Electrician in the Dockyard. German Jew. communist.' A spy identifying Communist meeting places in East London noted one on Mile End Road where to his apparent horror 'girls with bobbed hair, evidently of loose character' were in attendance.[58]

More sober assessments of Communist activity from Scotland Yard noted the party's limited influence on the events of the strike. This did not stop the CPGB from being regularly targeted by the police during the nine days. From 7 May onwards a series of raids on local Communist Party offices and meeting rooms occurred around the country, with party members arrested and duplicating machines seized. In Sheffield, after a first raid resulted in seven arrests, the local Communist bulletin reappeared the next day, printed from a different house, and a second address was raided and three more arrests made. Party leaders in London were said to be leading a 'hole and corner existence' and sleeping in different houses every night.

The leaders of the Miners' Federation, and senior members of the TUC General Council, were spied on throughout the strike. At the National Hotel, where Cook, Smith, Arthur Pugh, and many other trade union officials were based during the strike, room numbers were taken and a chambermaid kept a close eye on any comings and goings. Not much useful information appears to have been gleaned from this, except regarding a curious incident where Cook's room was broken into after which the miners' leader 'would not enter his room until he had got one of the porters to search it thoroughly for bombs etc'. The identity of the intruder remains a mystery although the chambermaid thought she recognised him as a lawyer.[59]

Britain's security apparatus spent most of the strike attempting to paint a picture of a Communist conspiracy, and colouring the facts to fit. However, no matter how important the military intelligence services saw themselves, their actual role in the strike was incidental. Tailing a man going about his daily business hardly made a dent in getting Britain working again. The police, Army, Navy, and hundreds of thousands of volunteers were what the government needed. On these pillars the government had successfully built its strikebreaking operation, against which the General Council and trade union rank and file around the country were on a collision course.

A massive open air meeting of strikers in Doncaster.

8

WHO RUNS THE STRIKE?

Workers – do not join OMS. If you do you are a blackleg. The workers are winning. The bosses are on the run. Now is the time for mass picketing.

- Placard hung outside the Labour Exchange in Newcastle-upon-Tyne

Pleased to say everything in Midlands solid. No wavering of any description. <u>Our trouble is to keep the men at work. In a number of instances it is impossible.</u> The whole Area is solid for the miners.

- TGWU area officer to Ernest Bevin, 6 May 1926

The General Council's call for workers to down their tools threw the trade union movement into battle across the length of the country. If the strike was to have any hope of success in the face of the government's carefully laid preparations, it would need the active participation of thousands of branch officers, shop stewards, and members. Workers who had experienced the turbulent years since 1910 knew that just obeying the order to stop work would not be enough. The strike would require a mammoth organisational effort, the likes of which they had never undertaken before.

Unlike the General Council, many workers had been wrestling with these questions for months. The Minority Movement's campaigning had cut through, but even without that it was patently obvious to most trade unionists that the fight of their lives was just around the corner. In many localities including Merseyside and parts of Scotland, meetings began to be held from the summer of 1925 with a view to strengthening cooperation between different unions.[1] These meetings would form the nucleus of the strike committees and Councils of Action that would run the strike on the ground during 'the nine days' in May. It is impossible to tell exactly how many workers involved themselves in the organisation of the strike, but at the very least tens of thousands joined picket lines, sat on committees, relayed messages, wrote and printed leaflets, gave speeches, and attended meetings.

At the outset of the strike, however, this large and enthusiastic army of labour, by and large, patiently awaited instructions from above. For those who had argued for the TUC General Council to assume a central authority over the movement, the general strike was the litmus test for this strategy. Having learned the importance of discipline and unity in winning industrial disputes from bitter experience, most trade unionists began the strike determined that the orders of their leaders, whatever they might be, should be faithfully carried out.

These leaders sat in continuous session in the three Victorian terraced houses in Eccleston Square, Pimlico, that housed the central offices of the TUC and the Labour Party. As soon as the strike machinery was put in train Eccleston Square whirred with activity. Union officials came and went, journalists began to crowd the entrance hoping for a comment from one of the drama's big players, and sympathetic volunteers turned up to offer their services to the movement.

Inside, the TUC's small coterie of staff and officials were meeting around the clock. 'Everyone on the General Council wanted to be on a subcommittee of some kind,' remembered Ernest Bevin.[2] Not wanting to rely on official wireless news, the TUC tasked the Intelligence Committee with gathering information from across the country. Speakers were sent to address meetings in the provinces with instructions to report back on troop movements, strikebreaking, public opinion, and the state of food supplies.

The TUC's General Purposes Committee got to work on a much more solid and structured system of communications. As early as 2 p.m. on 4 May, it had established a daily service of dispatch riders to convey TUC instructions and gather information from the country's major industrial centres by car and motorbike. Just before the strike, the TUC purchased 2,500 gallons of petrol, anticipating the government might commandeer supplies. Seventeen routes were set up to cover the country along with additional routes for Greater London, overseen by the Labour Party's Herbert Morrison.[3] Riders were provided with TUC credentials so that the local trade unionists would know they were legitimate. From their agreed stopping points they would phone or telegraph messages back to the centre, giving the TUC leadership vital information as to how the strike was progressing on the ground. The riders knew their telegrams were likely being intercepted by the government and, part way through the strike, the TUC's General Purposes Committee attempted to develop a system of codewords including 'beauty' for police, 'beautify' for baton charges, 'beautifully' for troops opening fire on crowds.[4] It seems, however, that these codes were little used. They would have been unlikely to tax the brains of the government's intelligence officers too much.

Cars and bikes became indispensable tools for the unions, and the TUC desperately sought both vehicles and anyone who could drive them. It was time for middle-class sympathisers to step up. When the theatre director Lewis Casson turned up in his motor at TUC headquarters, he swiftly became A. J. Cook's and Herbert Smith's driver.[5] General Council member Margaret Bondfield was lent a car and driver by Lady de la Warr, the wife of the first lord to join the Labour Party. Between 5 and 11 May they traversed the industrial towns of the south coast and south-west of England relaying reports back to Eccleston Square.[6]

Many working-class helpers were much less experienced motorists. Liverpudlian ILP activist Bob Edwards, despite never having driven before, careened from Merseyside to the capital in a borrowed car, where he spoke at meetings packed with Londoners eager for news from the provinces. On his way back, he dropped off communications from the General Council in several places along with a Labour MP who had been isolated from his Midlands constituency upon the strike's outbreak.[7] This lack of experience may have led to several couriers suffering accidents, including an ASLEF member, E. J. Judge, who came off a bike and broke his legs. Judge was still in hospital over Christmas 1926 and was so badly injured he was unable to return to work, with the TUC still paying him a maintenance grant over two years after the strike in recognition of his service.[8]

The system of overlapping subcommittees risked giving rise to conflicting jurisdictions and disputes within the General Council. The Food and Essential Services Committee (FESC) under Margaret Bondfield and Mary Quaile initially attempted to deal with the question of what essential supplies ought to be moved with union permission. When, however, the government rejected the TUC's offer to help with food distribution and the railway unions stuck to their line of not moving anything by rail, this committee effectively fell into abeyance and was succeeded by a National Transport Committee of the rail unions and the TGWU. Bondfield was sent out into the country as a touring speaker and Quaile dispatched to her hometown of Manchester to be the General Council's eyes and ears there.

Similarly, a Public Services Committee, under the chairmanship of the veteran gasworkers' union leader Will Thorne, was initially tasked with determining how essential services could be maintained. On the second day of the strike, though, the Electricity and Gas Advisory Committee took over, dominated by representatives of the skilled unions in the power industry under Jimmy Rowan of the ETU.[9]

Amid this chaotic jockeying for position, Bevin took decisive action on 5 May. His Powers and Orders Committee was rebranded as the Strike Organisation Committee (SOC) and given hour-to-hour decision-making power over the dispute. Bevin was the dominant character on the SOC and exerted by far the greatest influence of any one individual over the actual industrial conduct of the strike. He was far from a revolutionary. His perspective was simple: strikes should be a weapon of last resort, but if one had to happen, he wanted to win it. And to win, centralisation was necessary. For him, and many other moderates, the General Council's new powers were a logical extension of the amalgamations that had given rise to the TGWU and of the Triple Alliance, to ensure different groups of industrial workers did not unwittingly undermine one another's strikes. During the strike itself, Bevin was primarily concerned with keeping decision-making in the hands of the central machinery, specifically the SOC, and making sure the TUC's constituent unions were following its orders.

Communications from London at the outset of the strike betray the union leaders' nervousness about maintaining control of the strike. Under the heading 'Trust your leaders', the *Daily Herald* opined on 3 May: 'Any who sow distrust are the worst foes of Labour, worse than any Capitalist.' It went on to imply that such individuals must be *agents provocateurs* in the pay of the state. The NUR's eve-of-strike telegram to its branches instructed them: 'Allow no disorderly or subversive elements to interfere in any way. Maintain perfect order and have confidence in your representatives. Perfect loyalty will ensure success.'[10] Union members were to act strictly within the bounds of the law and not provoke the police into any reaction.

The leadership also obsessed about discipline because they worried that they would become incapable of reining in radical elements as the strike went on. Producing the *British Worker* gave the General Council control of the messaging coming from their own side. In its post-strike report, the General Council's Publicity Committee noted:

> The closing down of the Labour Press along with the general press of the country, regrettable as it appeared to those who wished to assist in the influencing public opinion during the Strike, permitted the General Council through the Committee to exercise a genuine measure of control over the presentation of the Council's case and prevented the raising of extraneous political and economic issues…it would have been unwise to allow any but the official version of the Trade Unions' case to obtain currency during the stoppage.[11]

For this same reason, the General Council refused requests from prominent socialist George Lansbury and the ILP for permits to continue producing their own papers. What it had not reckoned with was the importance of local bulletins by strike committees. In the context of a struck or hostile press and shortages of the *British Worker*, trade unionists were in need of news on the dispute. Bulletins could also include useful local information that would go under the *Worker*'s radar, such as which major workplaces needed to be picketed, and when and where mass meetings would be held.

The local bulletins that survive give an indication of strikers' experiences on the ground, and the spectrum of their political views. Some faithfully followed the General Council's lead. 'Keep smiling, and the victory is ours!' proclaimed the daily *Preston Strike News*.[12] The Cardiff Strike Committee similarly instructed readers: 'Keep smiling. Refuse to be provoked. Get into the garden. Look after the wife and kiddies. If you have not got a garden, get into the country, the parks and the playgrounds.'[13] These condescending messages were hardly likely to enthuse the strikers.

At the more radical end, local committees went much further than the *British Worker*. Merseyside Council of Action's bulletin urged all strikers to present themselves to local committees in order to build the most comprehensive picketing system possible. Spen and District Trades Council likewise advised this and for any instance of blacklegging to be reported to Council of Action officials. Some bulletins, like that of the ETU's London District Committee, even published the names of known strikebreakers.[14]

Even the most moderate of local bulletin editors, to make themselves useful, inevitably included items on the course of the strike in their area or appeals to specific action. The Oxford Council of Action's bulletin mostly reproduced official items but also printed the text of a letter sent to the vice-chancellor of the university urging that students should not be used as volunteer labour locally, in case this created bad feeling in the town.[15] In Coventry and other centres where large engineering and manufacturing firms were based, the local bulletin kept workers up to date with which factories had come out on strike.

Bulletins also helped keep up the morale of strikers. A favourite topic was the ineffectiveness of middle-class volunteers:

> The volunteer drivers no doubt had to use many tins of vaseline on their poor hands because, as any bus driver will tell you, there is a vast difference between tooling a bus over London streets and running a little two-seater sports model to Brighton and back on Sunday. Ah well! Let them have their little 'rag', they'll be all the better for it when the stiffness wears off, and are likely to have a great deal more respect for the honest working bloke after this little 'war' has been won by us.[16]

Middle-class commuters and leisure-seekers more broadly were the butt of many jokes. Strikers called them the 'Plus Force' – a pun on plus fours, the sports trousers that were fashionable with the well-to-do set. When London cabbies voted to join the strike on 6 May the TGWU Area Committee's bulletin remarked that 'all the flunkeys in the whole of the West End of London could today blow out all their teeth without getting a ghost of a response from a taxi-cab driver'.[17]

Commenting on the length of time it was taking volunteer-driven trains to complete short journeys, the *Westminster Worker* joked that 'luncheon cars are to be put on trains running between Westminster and Blackfriars'. Satirising the mainstream press, Grimsby's bulletin was given the grandiose title of *The Grimsby Chronicle and Strike Bulletin (Incorporating the Lock-out Review)* and the tagline 'Free Insurance Against Rumours – Priceless'.[18]

With the printers' unions out on strike, most strike bulletins were produced using rudimentary equipment. Basic duplicators were sourced, often from local trade union branches or supportive political groups like branches of the ILP. The use of non-professional volunteers often caused friction with the striking and male-dominated printers' unions. In Edinburgh, the bulletin was put together at the National Council of Labour Colleges office where some striking printworkers had been reluctantly persuaded to help. When they arrived and found that a woman was operating the duplicator, they left and did not return, their places being taken by other women volunteers.[19]

The existence of local strike bulletins was regarded as, at best, a necessary evil by Eccleston Square. Initially the General Council attempted to compromise, issuing a circular instructing local bodies to only reproduce material supplied by the centre 'and to add nothing in the way of comment and interpretation'. Although some committees did their best to adhere to this, it was unreasonable to expect them not to offer any opinion on the momentous events surrounding them. The Publicity Committee turned a blind eye to some local strike committees producing bulletins in places that the *British Worker* had not reached, and perhaps hoped by the end of the strike that the regionally printed editions of the *Worker* would plug these gaps and render local news sheets unnecessary. But by the time, on 10 May, the TUC ordered all local bulletins to cease production altogether it was far too late. Trade unionists starved of information save for that from government channels were unlikely to adhere to such an order, and it appears to have been widely ignored. The grassroots initiative unleashed by the strike was not to be so easily curtailed.

***

It was not just in the field of propaganda that the unions had to contend with choices between centralisation and local initiative. The day-to-day organisation of the strike itself threw up similar problems. The two men most responsible for drawing up the strike plans, Bevin and Citrine, initially disagreed with how the strike should be run on the ground. Bevin was keen to keep the strike under centralised control and issue instructions through the national leaderships of the TUC's affiliated unions. Citrine, however, realised that the realities of a cross-industry strike and the problems that would be thrown up by the attempt to coordinate so many different unions would require local oversight. For Citrine, the only bodies capable of fulfilling this role were the hundreds of trades councils that existed in most cities, towns, and districts around the country.[20]

This disagreement was reflected in a TUC document of 30 April recommending that 'instructions should only be issued by accredited representatives of the unions participating in the dispute' but that 'the responsibility of organising the Trade Unionists in dispute in the most effective manner for the preservation of peace and order' would rest with local trades councils.[21]

Trades Councils were local umbrella bodies of the trade union movement. While they varied in strength and size, their basic structure was similar. Local branches of any trade union would be entitled to send a number of delegates based on their size. These delegates would elect an executive committee. Trades Councils were campaigning organisations as well as industrial ones. In many towns they were at the centre of efforts to organise the unemployed and push for greater welfare and pension rights.[22] They were also, mostly, explicitly political bodies, running trade unionists for election to local Boards of Education, Boards of Guardians, and borough councils as Labour candidates. Indeed, in many places, the local trades council and the local Labour Party were still essentially the same organisation by 1926. The Labour Party, initially founded as an alliance of trade unions and socialist groups, did not allow individual membership until 1918 and retained its essentially federal structure. So a trades council could reflect all the shades of opinion in the movement from moderate Labour (or even Liberal and Tory) members through to revolutionary socialists and communists.

This inclusion of radical-left elements was partly why the relationship between the movement's local bodies and its central leadership had never been particularly rosy. The democratic nature of the councils meant that those unlikely to attain national leadership roles, including communists, could get a hearing at local level. The union and Labour Party leaderships often regarded them as troublesome bodies full of ranting revolutionaries and derided them as talking shops. But grassroots pressure led to something of a rapprochement in 1924 when a Joint Consultative Committee of representatives from the trades councils and the General Council was established.[23] This was partly done to mend the growing rift between the centre and the localities, and partly to prevent trades councils becoming, in Herbert Tracey's words, 'centres of disaffection'.[24] Nonetheless the fault lines in the relationship would become exposed over the course of the strike. The TUC wanted trades councils to loyally carry out their policy. But many in the grassroots saw the trades councils as forums to change policy.

Most trades councils set up a strike committee on hearing of the TUC's instructions for the stoppage of work. They went by various names, with at least fifty-four reviving the 'Council of Action' label that had been used during the 'Hands Off Russia' campaign of 1919–20.[25] These pre-existing organisations could put strike machinery in the field far more quickly than individual unions with their many jealousies and rivalries. Citrine recognised this reality, however much he may have wished the General Council to be fully in charge of things, while Bevin tried to ignore it.

Some of these committees sat in continuous session, twenty-four hours a day. They were most often based out of a local union or Labour Party office. Local discretion dictated who was allowed to be involved. Unions previously unaffiliated to the trades council might nevertheless be co-opted on to the strike committee. Some opened their membership to representatives of left-wing political groups and co-operative societies. For example, the Oxford Council of Action included representatives of the Labour Party, including its Women's Section, the University Labour Club, and students from Ruskin College, which had strong ties to the trade union movement.²⁶ Other areas like Glasgow kept committee affiliation strictly to unions. This meant that political organisations could only wield influence insofar as their members were delegated from bona fide trade union branches. Nevertheless, at least at the outset of the strike, there was a tremendous sense of unity. One member of the Glasgow committee, himself a prominent Communist, later recalled that despite political differences 'the feeling that it was our job to do all in our power to make the strike solid was an overriding one, that united us – left, right, and centre: it was the theme running through the whole conduct of the work'.²⁷

The composition of strike committees was of course also shaped by the local economy. Where one industry dominated, this was reflected in who ran the strike on the ground. There were coalfield villages where the miners' union looked after affairs more or less single-handedly. In towns where the railwaymen comprised the bulk of the strikers, like Dorking, Llandudno, and Chesterfield, the NUR and ASLEF, and to a lesser extent the RCA, ran the show without feeling the need to consult unions in other industries.²⁸ This meant that, in a handful of places, the wider union movement was cut out of strike organisation on the ground. Remarkably, in the vast majority of cases trade union unity won out. Reps and officials from unions that were not, initially, directly party to the dispute could still contribute and in many cases threw their energies behind the strike without hesitation. Officers of the National Union of Distributive and Allied Workers (NUDAW), whose members worked directly alongside transport workers in warehouses and depots, took particularly prominent roles in many committees.²⁹ White-collar trade unionists who had not been called out often lent material help in the form of volunteers bringing typewriters and Roneo machines.

The area covered by each trades council was small, usually just a single city or town. Since the government had divided the country up into large regions for the purposes of the emergency, the TUC General Council had to contend with the headache of communicating with over five hundred local bodies during the course of the strike. The dispatch rider system was designed to tackle this problem as far as possible, but in cases where more immediate communication was required, Eccleston Square was bombarded with telegrams and phone calls. Precisely which building workers should be on strike? Should beer be regarded as food? What should workers with exemptions from the strike call do if volunteer labour was introduced alongside them? At this time, many union branches still had no access to their own phone and, in Leeds, three rival strike committees fought over the use of one landline.

The most developed local organisation emerged in the North-East, strongly influenced by the Communist activist Robin Page Arnot. A conscientious objector during the war, Page Arnot was one of the twelve CPGB leaders who had been arrested and imprisoned after the raid on the party's headquarters in 1925. Released a matter of days before the strike, he headed to the Great Northern Coalfield where the Communists had some influence and where miners at Chopwell had been engaged in a local dispute with their bosses since the autumn.

Page Arnot appears to have been more concerned with the government's emergency operation than many other activists and realised the unions would have to compete with it. He convinced Ebby Edwards, an important figure in the Northumberland Miners' Association, that 'he who feeds the people wins the strike'. On 3 May, together with NUDAW regional officer Charles Flynn, they started to put together an organisation that, it was hoped, would cover the whole of Newcastle, Gateshead, County Durham, and Northumberland, matching the area overseen by the government's Civil Commissioner Sir Kingsley Wood. This organisation first met on 4 May with representatives from unions and trades councils across the region, with the significant notable absence of the Durham Miners' Association which, to the organisers' exasperation, stood aloof from their committee until the strike had practically ended.[30] This meeting elected a regional General Council that would be responsible for producing propaganda and organising demonstrations and entertainment, and a joint strike committee that would oversee picketing, food supplies, and the issuing of permits. By 8 May the organisation was in a position to bring together a conference of eighty-seven local committees held at Gateshead Town Hall.[31]

A further example of sophisticated local organisation can be found at Merthyr Tydfil in Wales. Here, the executive of the trades council co-opted members of various unions and local co-operative societies in April in preparation for the dispute. This meant they were able to extend organisation across the borough rapidly: 'The Sub-Committees and the District

Strike Committees were functioning so effectively that Headquarters met in the evening only to receive reports.'[32]

***

Regardless of how well organised they were, all strike committees and Councils of Action confronted the question of the movement of essential goods during the strike. Many strikers did not want to totally paralyse the movement of food and milk, upon which they and their families relied as much as anyone else. This was particularly true of goods provided by the Co-operative Wholesale Society to which more than four million working-class people belonged.[33] Pre-strike approaches to the labour movement's 'third pillar' had been limited and marked by a certain mutual distrust. Communists had agitated among Co-op members for closer ties to the trade unions without much success. For Arthur Cook, the Co-ops could potentially be key to helping feed the miners in the event of a long struggle. But many Co-op societies were still owed money for credit that they had advanced to the miners during the brutal 1921 dispute, and were disinclined to offer much more than lukewarm support. The Co-op were also mindful that their workforce was much more heavily unionised than that of other wholesalers, and a general withdrawal of transport, warehouse, and shop labour would put them at a commercial and competitive disadvantage.

Accounting for all these complexities could give any logistics coordinator a headache. But the unions wrestled with an even more contentious question – should they attempt to block all movement of goods, or try to institute a system of workers' control whereby essential goods could be provided to working-class communities under union supervision? Local committees were close to the households in their communities that would suffer acutely if any food shortages occurred. They were also, in many cases, keen to exercise some power over economic life to demonstrate that necessities could not be provided without the work of the labouring class. Trade union committees of all kinds almost immediately began to accept applications from businesses, traders, and shopkeepers for permits to move food, milk, building materials and other things that might be deemed essential.

In theory, the permit system should have been simple. Those in possession of an official TUC permit would be able to transport their goods through union picket lines without any hassle by producing the correct paperwork. To obtain a permit, they would have to apply to the local unions who would adjudicate as to whether their proposed cargo counted as essential goods. This gave rise to a sense of the world turned upside down. Businessmen went cap in hand to plead with the unions for permits. A sheet metal worker who sat on the Ashton Strike Committee recalled that 'one and all were put through stern questioning, just to make them realise that we and not they were the salt of the earth'.[34] In Edinburgh, where a football pitch on the outskirts of the city soon filled with lorries waiting on a permit decision, a business owner asked the strike committee for a permit to visit his ill son. When it informed him that he did not need its permission to run this private errand, he insisted on being given one anyway for fear that pickets would not believe his story.[35] On the first couple of days of the strike the London area secretary of the TGWU, Tom Scoulding, claimed to have received hundreds of applications for permits of which an 'infinitesimal' number were granted, including pleas from the German and Japanese embassies for some personal effects of their staff to be removed from boats stranded in the docks.[36]

However, the permit system couldn't withstand the onslaught of employers and hauliers determined to beat the strike. The decentralised nature of road transport meant it was impossible for pickets to stop and check every vehicle, and many were prepared to chance their arm by simply chalking 'FOOD ONLY' or 'TUC' on the side of their lorries. Reports soon reached Eccleston Square of widespread abuses of the system. Some complained that the unions were being too liberal in their interpretation. Matt Pringle of the Bakers' Union wrote to the Newcastle *Workers' Chronicle*: 'It's all very well from a publicity point of view to see all vehicles being marked food supplies, but in all my experience as Organiser in one of the main Food Trades I never knew Dainty Toffees, Ice Cream etc could be called food, unless there was a surplus of labels to use up.'[37]

Even scab labour was being moved under the guise of essential supplies. A 'Food Only' van that broke down in Sheffield town centre was found to be carrying ten engineers on their way to work. Similar activity was reported by a NUR picket in Holloway, where the LNER's managing engineer was allegedly being ferried around in a van labelled for food.[38] The *Westminster Worker* wryly noted that 'people are often found masquerading as loaves of bread'.

At Eccleston Square, Margaret Bondfield's FESC had attempted to come up with a consistent line on this, producing and distributing a template permit to local bodies, but in the meantime the railway unions, meeting separately, resolved that nothing whatsoever, not even food, should be moved by train.[39] They reasoned that so many workers would have to be issued permits to work food trains that it would fatally weaken the strike. The TGWU, representing workers in less labour-intensive road transport, was more amenable to issuing permits but recognised that a system whereby their members were permitted to work goods that had been 'blacked' by the railwaymen would likewise prove disastrous to unity. A National Transport Committee operating out of the NUR's headquarters and initially composed of just the railway unions and the TGWU took over from the FESC, immediately paused the issuing of permits, and ordered local committees – also of just the transport unions – to review any existing ones that had been granted.

By 7 May the permit system's inadequacies were made clear to the SOC. It was agreed that the granting of all permits should cease. Despite discussions with co-operative societies, some of which did not want to rely on government transport to move their food, and MPs, no agreement could be reached exempting Co-op supplies. However, workers ancillary to transport, taking food from warehouse to shop or from shop to customer, including Co-op milkmen, would remain at work.[40] That evening the TUC sent a telegram to local bodies requiring that 'all local transport committees review all permits which have been issued' and the next day drove home the point: 'No Trades Council, Labour Party, Council of Action, Strike Committee, or Trade Union Branch has authority to deal with permits.'[41] As we will see, shop assistants and warehouse workers were placed in an almost impossible position by this messy compromise.

By this point, some local strike committees had already come to the conclusion that the system was self-defeating and unilaterally discontinued it. The Durham and Northumberland Joint Strike Committee revoked permits for building materials as early as the evening of 4 May, and withdrew all permits two days later. 'The mere rumble of wheels', noted

NUDAW organiser Charles Flynn, 'was something that weakened the morale of our men and correspondingly cheered the other side.'[42]

On the other hand, much to the annoyance of Bevin and the officials of the TGWU, many local bodies kept issuing permits in defiance of the new arrangements. The *British Worker*, the TUC's dispatch riders, and the transport unions themselves reiterated daily that the sole authority to issue any permits rested with the Transport Committees. Officials of some individual unions also flouted the new system, such as the Drug and Chemical Workers who issued their own permits for the movement of medical supplies. TGWU officers, who had come to be in lockstep with the rail unions on the question of holding up the food supply, complained that other, smaller unions were in Bevin's words 'handing out permits ad lib' to their members and undermining the strike.[43]

There were many reasons why local strike committees continued with their permit systems despite orders. Stan Hutchins of the Shop Assistants Union in Southwark recalled how Council of Action pickets wearing red armbands would stop high street traffic and ask for paperwork: 'Of course, we did not want to starve ourselves out, so we would let food lorries through. Unfortunately, the authorities tried to get through by pretending that they were carrying food when they weren't, and this would sometimes lead to angry scenes and violence.'[44]

Inadequate communications meant the instructions to rescind all permits took time to filter through in some places. Meanwhile, those requiring permits may not have been aware of the existence of a local Transport Committee and would have applied to the local trades council, a familiar body, by default. Some strike committees used the permit system to demarcate the boundaries of the dispute where the TUC's instructions were vague or hard to interpret. The permit system could also be used by strikers to bring pressure on errant employers. Cadbury's, at its famous Birmingham factory, had initially been allowed to move cocoa and chocolate with the strike committee's assent, but when it emerged that the company was using administrative staff to cover the work of striking ETU members, the permits were swiftly withdrawn.[45] Similarly, when it was discovered that the Great Western Railway's approved safety men were moving goods other than food, permits were withdrawn and picket numbers doubled at Paddington station.[46]

By the end of the strike's first week, however, the message was getting through. Most food permits had been withdrawn and exemptions clamped down on. The government's Supply and Transport Organisation was ramping up. There now came a clamour from strike committees and union branches to extend the strike. The General Council could either accede to this, or risk losing control.

The aftermath of an altercation with a working bus driver in Glasgow.

9

ALL OUT?

The Committee places on record its regret that the [TUC] should deliver a rebuke because of our endeavours to put into operation the first instructions of the General Council with regard to the 'so-called' General Strike.

- Electrical Trades Union London District Committee to Walter Citrine, 10 May 1926

I replied that we did not take our instructions from the TUC but were loyal subjects who only recognised the authority of the government… He then asked if we still wanted the light and I replied that as we had managed so far without it, we would rather use candles than electric light by permission of the TUC.

- S. T. Ellice-Clark, Managing Director of Barrett & Elers Ltd, 20 May 1926

The general strike was not a general strike, or so the General Council said. They preferred the term 'national strike', to emphasise that not all workers had been withdrawn. After all, they did not want to starve the nation. Had they not offered to keep food supplies moving for the government? But with permits withdrawn and volunteer labour rapidly appearing in workplaces, the strike was taking on a more serious dimension.

On the ground, more and more striking workers took to picketing, preventing strikebreakers from going into work. The legal status of picketing remained an open question in 1926. The 1906 Trade Disputes Act had defined 'peaceful picketing', but for many Tories and the right-wing press, any attempt to picket a workplace was, by default, a form of intimidation. The 1920 Emergency Powers Act threw up more hurdles to picketing, casting a wide net when it came to industrial action. Of the emergency regulations brought into force on 30 April, Regulation 21 made it an offence to 'cause civil disaffection'. Regulation 20 targeted any act 'calculated to injure, or to prevent the proper use or working of' factories, mines, railways, canals, power stations, and the transport of food. These could be, and were, interpreted as rendering pickets illegal.

This did not dissuade trade unionists from standing on the picket lines. They knew picketing was a vital tool in maintaining the strike – and extending it. These pickets were a mammoth effort, requiring coordination across different unions to an unprecedented extent. Local committees took up the mantle of targeting workplaces for pickets. This wasn't a straightforward affair. In certain factories and workshops some workers had been called out and others had not. Would they be comfortable crossing their colleagues' picket lines? Should they be picketed out regardless of the instructions of their own unions or the TUC? What attitude should be taken to non-union workers, apprentices, and women workers who may not be eligible for union membership? Local committees spent countless hours considering these questions.

Initially, in many locations, picketing was left to the individual unions to organise, as they were technically the only bodies who had the authority to instruct their members. In practice, however, strike committees soon found it necessary to establish greater coordination. In Manchester the transport unions joined together to enforce a round-the-clock eight-hour shift system of pickets. Among the best-organised was Bolton, where a force of 2,280 picketed four hours on, twenty hours off. It is perhaps not coincidental that, with such a high level of discipline, no arrests were made in Bolton during the strike.[1] In other areas a hybrid system was used whereby union branches organised their own pickets but could draw on a central reserve if they needed extra strength. Where this reserve came from reflected the lie of the land in a particular place. St Helens was close enough to mining country for the MFGB to supply the manpower. In

Battersea a Special Picket Corps was formed from all participating unions, and in Hackney pickets were supplemented by volunteers from the National Unemployed Workers' Committee Movement.[2] Some unions joined together on an industry-wide basis, such as in Sheffield where a Metal Trades Joint Picketing Committee attempted, with mixed success, to bring out all factory workers who were working on machinery that was powered by 'black' coal.[3]

There were places where the strike was so solid, with so few men going into work, that picketing was quickly abandoned as an unnecessary waste of time. This was the case in Airdrie and Coatbridge near Glasgow after the second day of the strike. Carmarthenshire police reported that no pickets were out but still warned that any attempt to start running transport services would likely meet with a violent reaction. Picketing was needed more in places where the union movement was weaker, where the power of persuasion, backed up by a large body of workers, could be used to spread the strike. This might mean a group visiting the box of a working railway signalman or, in the case of a large factory, workers from better-organised departments talking to their fellows elsewhere. The Newcastle *Workers' Chronicle* of 8 May summed up the local Council of Action's approach: 'ENORMOUS MASS PICKETS ARE THE ORDER OF THE DAY. That's the stuff to give 'em. In spite of the fact that there (sic) EC has ordered a stoppage, there are still 500 men scabbing at the Alkali Chemical Co. It appears that they only require gentle persuasion. What about a Mass Picket?'[4]

More inventive means of picketing were pioneered during the strike. Where transport services could not be totally stopped, strikers would ride motorbikes deliberately slowly in front of scab buses or lorries, forcing them to slow down and enabling groups of pickets to board them and persuade the passengers – gently or not – to disembark.[5] Similar 'boarding' tactics were used a few days later when local authorities attempted to restart their tram services. Supportive women would also gather at tram stops to urge commuters away.[6]

In areas where strikers and their supporters felt strong enough and could muster large crowds at short notice, roads and highways were picketed rather than workplaces. This was the case in Yorkshire coalfields where the miners, locked out of their own workplaces, had the time and inclination to help bring transport to a standstill. Mobile pickets were a headache for the police, especially in more remote areas, as they could disperse when law enforcement arrived and easily gather again somewhere else. 'Had the strike gone into another week,' one historian of the dispute in Durham and Northumberland has noted, 'the grip of the pickets on the roads through the mining areas would have tightened and led to even more determined attempts by the authorities to break it.'[7]

In the railway town of Swindon, nine ASLEF members did not initially strike, including one member of the branch committee. Two of his colleagues poured a gallon of tar through his letterbox. Then the branch arranged a mock funeral procession for the strikebreakers, gathering hundreds of people and taking mock coffins to the rubbish dump. They knocked at the house of each blackleg on the way. Engine driver Roy Green later remembered explaining to one – 'Timber' Higgins – that if he did not join the strike he would be buried. At the tip, a mock funeral service was held where a driver using a tablecloth as a surplice set the coffins alight and said: 'May the wind blow their remains to the four corners of the earth, and to hell with them all.' Green recalled that when he was at Higgins' real funeral, as an ASLEF representative, many years later, 'I found myself muttering the committal words of his first funeral.'[8] Pickets and supporters at the Horwich Locomotive Works in Lancashire followed a working employee home at the end of their shift; the worker had to be taken into police custody for their own protection and the crowd outside the police station dispersed by force.[9]

To avoid clashes with pickets, across the country's docklands and in many major bus and tram depots, volunteers were billeted and settled down in somewhat uncomfortable accommodation for an uncertain length of time. In Leicestershire, a railway volunteer later recalled 'sleeping happily on 3rd class carriage seats and [being] jeered at by the bloody minded mutineers…we were a naval train with a Lieut. Commander as driver, a naval chief stoker and myself (a reserve officer) to assist him. Our driver carried a revolver which he said he would use if we were attacked.'[10]

It would be impossible to construct a comprehensive picture of how effective picketing was during the strike. Eighty men were kept out of the Surrey Docks in Deptford as they refused to cross a mass picket without police protection. For the rest of the strike, volunteers had to be brought down the river by boat instead.¹¹ On the other side of the Thames in Hackney, OMS volunteers successfully broke through a picket line into the tram depot, but a mass mobilisation trapped them in the building and they were unable to take any vehicles out. When a police superintendent arrived and appealed to the trade unionists for help he was met with the response: 'You bloody took them in, now you bloody get them out!' They eventually escaped by climbing over a wall into a churchyard but were caught by pickets and dunked in a water trough.¹² These incidents undoubtedly served as morale boosts for strikers. But the real prize of picketing came in successfully shutting down or severely restricting access to workplaces. Perhaps the best marker of its effectiveness lies in the fact that by the end of the strike, relatively few regular workers had gone back. Where volunteers were introduced, significant police and state resources often had to be deployed.

There were, however, risks associated with the tactic of mass picketing. Large crowds of pickets and supporters attracted the attention of the police. For this reason, it was predictably discouraged by the more cautious union officials, but opposition to the tactic also occasionally came from unexpected quarters. After a mass picket outside the Sun Flour Mills in Poplar resulted in the arrest of a seventeen-year-old supporter, George Lansbury, perhaps the most respected figure on the Labour Party's left wing, told the party's national women's officer Dr Marion Phillips he disagreed with the tactic:

> Lansbury's view is that mass picketing is inadvisable, but it is an old custom there [in East London]. He is convinced that no matter what kind of picketing is done the police will disperse pickets. The strike leaders, however, are impressing in the men the necessity of giving way at once before the police, and not entering into any struggle with them, and since Tuesday this has been carried out admirably.¹³

***

Not everyone was so committed to peaceful methods. Despite the trade union movement's constant appeals for order, strikers and supporters sometimes took matters into their own hands when picketing alone could not ensure adherence to the strike. The tactic of choice was industrial sabotage: acts of targeted property damage were carried out to render vehicles or machinery useless. This seems to have been most common on the railways. Using their expert knowledge of where there were imperceptible gradients on the track, strikers would coat rails with wagon grease, confounding volunteer drivers who could not get their engines to move. Bolts were removed from railway points and signal boxes were tampered with. In Middlesbrough crowds went further, chaining lorries to railway tracks.[14]

South London in particular was a hotbed of sabotage and vandalism. TGWU pickets thwarted volunteers' attempt to bring trams out of New Cross depot by jamming objects into the rails. In Battersea, striker Charles Whitely was jailed for a month for spreading nails on the road to puncture bus tyres. Food lorries in the borough were immobilised by strikers removing engine parts.[15] A *Guardian* story, which may have been exaggerated, claimed that mothers in Camberwell were laying their young children down in the road to stop vehicles which would then be set upon and smashed up by gangs of men.[16]

Buses and trams, and their drivers, bore the brunt of working-class anger when companies and local authorities attempted to take them out of depots. This was the biggest cause of large-scale disturbances during the strike. The depots were situated in urban areas. Each bus or tram on the road was a visible crack in the strike's united front, and large groups of strikers and working-class supporters could gather quickly to remedy the situation. In West London, Chiswick Bus Depot was practically besieged in the first days of the strike and attempts to run buses invariably resulted in smashed windows and other damage, until more police protection was provided. It was common for volunteer drivers to arrive at depots to discover that the magneto wiring in their bus engine had been removed or cut. Nottingham busworkers removed the carburettors before walking off the job to immobilise the buses. London tramworkers removed crucial switches from section boxes throughout the network.[17]

Not even the quieter areas were totally immune to sabotage; in the village of Saltcoats in Scotland, dockers sank the dinghy taking mail to the Isle of Arran by throwing stones into it until it went under in the harbour.[18] In Lancashire, colliers and their wives stretched wire and rope across roads to block or delay vehicles.[19] The moral code that held volunteers and strikebreakers in contempt meant that, for many working-class people, it was worth the risk of potentially causing injury to a 'scab' in pursuit of making the stoppage more effective.

Trains were frequent targets for attack and sabotage. Working-class children would gather on railway bridges and attempt to stone volunteer drivers as they passed, or place obstructions on the line. In the northern coalfield, locked-out miners were prepared to go a step further to prevent the removal of coal trains by deliberately removing lengths of rail from the line. On the night of 8 May, they succeeded in this at Killingworth, Northumberland.[20] Other similar attempts were foiled by the railway companies' security patrols.

However, by far the most serious instance of sabotage occurred at Cramlington in Northumberland on 10 May, when the *Flying Scotsman* passenger train was derailed.[21]

That morning, William Golightly of the Northumberland Miners' Association addressed a meeting at West Cramlington, urging the miners to redouble their efforts: 'If you can't stop them at the stations,' he reportedly said, 'stop them between the stations.' These words seemed to galvanise a group of younger miners. At lunchtime a group of LNER workers who were patrolling the railway looking for signs of damage were set upon by a gang of twenty to thirty miners who hurled abuse, and stones, at them until they retreated to the nearest station. The miners then broke into the nearby platelayers' hut and appropriated hammers and other tools. They knocked the wooden chocks out from underneath a rail before removing the rail itself and discarding their tools.

The trackside patrol, led by a working engineer's assistant but mainly composed of young volunteers, unaware that a rail had been removed, managed to warn the driver of the *Flying Scotsman* and his volunteer crew that a hostile crowd was waiting ahead. They advised the passengers to pull down window blinds and stay in the aisle seats, in case the train came under attack. The driver then pressed on, unable to notice the missing rail, and his engine careened to both sides before toppling from the track, followed by five of the train's passenger coaches. His volunteer fireman suffered a scalded foot and shaken passengers began to emerge from the wreckage. Considering the scale of the crash, there were remarkably few injuries among the five hundred on board and no one lost their life. Had the engine been travelling faster, it would have been worse. A group of the perpetrators was seen jeering at the passengers after the crash. Other locals rushed to help, but their offers were rejected by the travellers who insulted them and told them to go home.

It could not be denied that deliberate sabotage had taken place. The miners were not expecting a passenger train and intended to target coal trains. There were suggestions that some had attempted to warn the train crew of the missing rail by waving a red handkerchief from a bridge, but they were not seen. Golightly no doubt got the men's blood up with his speech, but in a memoir written many decades later one of them, Bill Muckle, claimed that he and three others had taken the tools from the railway shed before the morning meeting, having already made up their minds.[22]

No arrests were made straight away. Initially, a conspiracy of silence descended over the community. Despite extensive police questioning, no one spoke for three weeks until one of the miners involved, who was the younger brother of a local police constable, was prevailed upon to turn king's evidence and give names to the authorities. Eight miners were found guilty and handed sentences of between four and eight years in prison. No charges appear to have been brought against Golightly for incitement, and in fact he appears to have been sworn in as a Justice of the Peace in July.[23] He had gone from rabble-rouser to a pillar of law and order in just two months, perhaps a record even among trade union officials.

***

Pit villages saw many acts of self-organised militancy by miners and their families, who had no need to picket the mines. In the North-East and Scotland, mass pickets instead congregated on main roads in order to enforce a 'food only' policy over transport. The same activity happened around Doncaster where the Council of Action had initially apparently offered to enrol pickets as special constables and assist in the volunteer operation.[24] After being rebuffed, relations apparently deteriorated with groups of miners throwing up roadblocks.

At a meeting of the Hatfield Main branch of the Yorkshire Miners' Association on 12 May, a visiting speaker took to the stage claiming to have instructions from the TUC that all transport needed to be stopped. He urged the miners present to form a mass picket and block the main roads nearby. The man was William Squance, the district organising secretary of ASLEF. Despite warnings from their own branch officials, around a thousand miners and others from the village of Stainforth followed Squance's advice and marched to the road, where they held up vehicles and emptied the contents of a newspaper van. One miner's subsequent petition of appeal allows us to see why they did:

> During the period of the general strike we were ordered to obey the orders of the Trade Union Congress, this we did, believing at all times that anything we were ordered to do would be quite within our rights and that such a body as the Trade Union Congress composed in the main of loyal citizens would never attempt to issue orders that was either a challenge to or a menace to the state… We went out on that picket ignorant of the fact that we were performing an illegal act, we marched in procession some 1000 strong a distance of 2 ½ miles under police observation.[25]

Initially, heavily outnumbered, the police watched the march peaceably and did nothing to stop vehicles being held up. Once mounted reinforcements arrived, however, the crowd was forcibly dispersed and seventy-two miners arrested under the emergency regulations. Of these, sixty-nine were convicted in front of magistrates with no opportunity for legal assistance and sentenced to three months' hard labour. When the men appeared in front of the Leeds Quarter Sessions in August and their sentences were confirmed, one threw down his war medals on the prosecuting counsel's table in disgust.[26]

Squance also received, for incitement, three months' hard labour as well as a £50 fine, even though the prosecution admitted that he had stressed the term 'peaceful picketing' several times during his speech. There having been no police officer present during the incident, Squance was convicted on the evidence of two miners who his lawyer claimed had been 'got at' by the police.

The police and magistrates justified their actions at Hatfield on the basis that a failure to make an example of the miners would have had serious consequences. 'Had this situation not been promptly and firmly dealt with by the police,' stated Chief Constable Colonel Coke, 'I am satisfied that more serious outbreaks would have occurred, not only in the vicinity, but throughout the Riding within a very short period.'[27]

Earlier that morning, at nearby Edenthorpe, a separate group of two to three hundred men armed with hedge stakes had stopped traffic and attacked a driver, following allegations that he had been threatening pickets with revolvers. Police then charged and arrested fifteen of those men, who were dealt with *en masse* without any evidence of specific actions being brought against any of them. Likewise, when the Hatfield case reached Quarter Sessions, the prosecution admitted that they had no direct evidence against a large number of the prisoners, and many were bound over – released on a promise of maintaining good behaviour – in exchange for an undertaking not to submit any appeal.

Authorities saw the hand of the Communists behind the Hatfield disturbances and went searching for the local CPGB activist, miner Arthur Evans, whom they believed to have been responsible for the attack on the newspaper van. At 1 a.m. the night after the incident they raided the house of Evans' friend Thomas Purvis, who informed them bluntly that 'if I knew where he was now, which probably I do, I should not tell you' but would rather take up arms and shoot the police first. He ended: 'You are nothing but dirt. Bah. Beat it quick.' For this outburst, Purvis was given three months and a £100 fine for making statements likely to cause disaffection among the police.[28] They did eventually manage to arrest Evans. He denied that he was present when the van was overturned, saying only that he had helped to organise a 'moral picket' or demonstration. Nevertheless he got the three months' hard labour alongside his comrades. 'I care not for the sentence, that does not worry me,' said Evans in court, 'I am class-conscious.'[29]

***

These attacks on strikebreaking vehicles and their occupants undoubtedly bolstered the morale of those on strike. However, the strike's victory ultimately depended on how many workers would stay out, day after day. The TUC's initial strike call only called some sections of organised workers out, as the 'first line'. What about the others? From the very first day, many workers wanted to join in. And so from the ground up, workers and union officials debated if, how, and when the strike ought to be extended to other sectors of the working class.

Workers discussed and debated developments on street corners and on the shop floor. Jack Charlesworth was an Independent Labour Party member who worked at Weldon's & Wilkinson's hosiery factory in Nottingham. He later recalled: 'I remember at Weldon's ordinary people said "How is it we're not involved?" People who had never been interested in politics or industrial questions or even rates on the shop floor, they said "Why are we not involved?" to such an extent that the Union had to go to the TUC to which we weren't affiliated to ask if they wanted us to strike.'[30]

The Weldon's workers were annoyed to be told that they should remain at work as they were not part of the first line. Many Sheffield cutlery workers likewise walked out initially but were ordered back to work on 5 May by their moderate local union leadership. Members of the same union, NUGMW, who worked in Reading's biscuit factories were said to be 'straining at the leash' to join the strike and getting criticism from the local railwaymen for staying at work.[31] The TUC, having brought all authority to itself in the calling of the strike, deferred decisions in many of these matters to regional officials of the unions involved. They were not in the business of antagonising the full-time officers on behalf of the rank and file.

Labourers at Woolwich Arsenal, the huge government-run munitions works, who walked out at the onset of the strike against the advice of their union, the Workers' Union, were also disappointed to be ordered back to work by the TUC. Seven thousand had struck on 4 May, leaving only a couple of hundred at work. When the managers threatened to withdraw the strikers' pension rights, their shop stewards distributed a flyer urging them to stand firm: 'The workers are solid all over the country, and no settlement of this dispute would be tolerated by our Leaders which meant victimisation to any worker. The General Council of the Trades Union Congress have definitely decided that under no circumstances will the general strike be called off if one case of victimisation is reported.'[32]

On 10 May the shop stewards from the Arsenal, alongside their comrades from the Enfield Small Arms Factory in North London who had also walked out, were summoned to Eccleston Square and admonished by the Strike Organisation Committee for encouraging the workers to join the strike. They were told in no uncertain terms that they should not have made such a guarantee about victimisation, but Citrine was of the opinion that, as the men were already out, it would badly affect morale if they went back to work. The situation seemed to be resolved until the following day when the local strike committees received the General Council's instruction that the 'second line' of engineering and shipbuilding workers was to come out on strike, except those working in government establishments. This caused chaos, confusion, and bitter recrimination from local committees, one of which considered that 'it would have been better for the movement if the Arsenal men had not come out at all'.

The government had considered that it would have to deal with striking workers as an employer itself, but was mostly concerned with the possibility of Post Office staff joining the walkout along with telegraphists and telephonists.[33] The TUC kept these workers in, partly due to the patchy nature of union organisation and partly because it was relying on those means of communication during the strike as much as the other side.

Outside of Woolwich, where agitation had been going on prior to the strike, it seems to have been only skilled workers who initially answered the call in government establishments: printers at His Majesty's Stationery Office, skilled building and maintenance workers at the Office of Works, and civilian engineers at some RAF bases. By 7 May, other workers were joining the walkout and a majority at Woolwich and the Royal Small Arms Factory in Enfield were out.[34] At the Royal Navy's Victualling Yard in Deptford, thirty-three 'established' men – permanent employees – walked out. By doing so, they put their pension entitlements in jeopardy and the TGWU subsequently waged a long campaign for their restoration that was rebuffed by both Labour and Tory chancellors of the Exchequer.[35] These men were offered re-employment at a lower status after the strike, and it may have been only Baldwin's personal intervention that prevented the insertion of a no-strike clause into their new contracts.

While the strike only affected a minority of their workers, the experience of it shook the government as an employer. Behind the scenes a debate raged about trade union rights for civil servants. Churchill had advocated for the government employees to be banned from striking, if not from union membership altogether, but realised that would be practically impossible to carry out.[36] Instead, ministers encouraged them to leave the large unions and join 'domestic associations' – those unions that catered wholly for civil servants – on the grounds that membership of the former created a 'dual loyalty' in the workforce. It was noted that had any civil servants' unions been called out it would, in one official's words, 'have been necessary to impose extreme penalties… Fortunately no such calamity occurred, and steps are now being taken to ensure no such calamity could ever occur in consequence of affiliation to the Trades Union Congress of any association of Civil Servants.'[37]

The fiasco at the Arsenal was far from the only incident that arose out of the General Council's decision to call only a partial strike. Engineers and foundry workers in Glasgow cabled their unions' national executives asking for all members to be brought out. Building workers, who belonged to several different unions, held mass meetings in several major towns and cities pressing their leaders to issue an all-out strike to end any confusion and accusations of scabbing.[38] These meetings put pressure on the national leaderships as, on 11 May, the president of the National Federation of Building Trade Operatives wrote to the SOC complaining that the building unions, by following TUC instructions, were seen by their members as being 'chiefly concerned with finding excuses for keeping men at work'.[39] The 'Altogether', the builders' and labourers' union, under similar pressure, urged the TUC without success to sanction a full withdrawal.

We should bear in mind that this was a genuine sacrifice for builders to make. They were a poorly paid workforce, and their unions had little cash on hand. Sidney Taylor, general secretary of the 'Altogether', expressed this when he wrote to his members that the union was not in a position to pay strike pay: 'This is a dispute in which (in order to defend the miners and workers generally) every worker is expected to line up against the capitalists on principle, and to stand solidly together until justice is done.'[40] As with many other unions, the officials drew no salary for the duration of the strike.

Most union leaders, regardless of their personal opinions, showed discipline in sticking to the TUC's line in public. Behind the scenes, however, many were pressuring the SOC to bring more workers out. This did not only come from the usual suspects on the left who saw extending the strike as the best means of victory and a way of opening up a broader confrontation with the government and the capitalists. Many workers were appalled at having to work alongside strikebreakers and volunteers, and they were prepared to let the leaders know about it. Sheffield steelworkers demanded a more unified position in mass meetings. Nationally, many thousands of members of the National Union of General and Municipal Workers wanted permission to join their comrades who had come out, but their leadership was non-responsive during the first few days of the strike.[41] It seems likely that Will Thorne, the sixty-eight-year-old veteran of new unionism who still served as the union's general secretary, paled at the financial ruin it would spell if too many of his members put in for strike or unemployment pay.[42]

In engineering and shipbuilding, significant pressure was building from the ground up as early as 6 May to call a full stoppage due to the confusion being caused by the TUC's instructions. The following day the SOC met with representatives of the AEU who agreed to bring out the bulk of engineers who were not already striking, as long as they could give adequate notice to their members.[43] On 9 May the SOC formally decided to call out the 'second line' of workers, comprising everyone in engineering and shipbuilding. This further stoppage was to occur on 12 May. The AEU contacted its district secretaries and told them to prepare by forming strike committees with the other engineering unions.

***

Closely related to the engineers were those who worked in the power industry. Their initial instructions, that industrial power should be stopped but domestic power and street lighting should be continued, caused immediate practical problems for the unions. How easy was it to disentangle these different power supplies? Who should remain at work to maintain the domestic supply? And what would happen if volunteers or military personnel were introduced to keep industrial power switched on? Rather unhelpfully, having issued the instructions, the General Council then resolved: '[Unions] should carry them out in the best manner possible, and where it is impossible, it is left to them to deal with the matter as best they can.'[44]

On the evening of 4 May the TUC's Electricity Advisory Committee (EAC) decided, only by the chairman's casting vote, that all electrical power workers should be called out at any power station where management did not make a full attempt to stop industrial power.[45] They initially set a deadline of 3 p.m. on 7 May. Delegations were sent to managers at both public and private power stations. Eventually ten of the publicly owned ones, especially in Labour-controlled authorities, signed an undertaking that 'instructions will be given for electricity to be supplied from the Council for the purpose of public lighting (streets), shops (but not shop signs), social and domestic lighting…for food production but not for any other purpose'.[46]

Meanwhile, however, the London District Committee of the Electrical Trades Union (ETU) had called their members out on the afternoon of 5 May. The ETU men claimed that some local authorities had promised to cut off industrial power and then rowed back. There was also confusion as to whether the 7 May deadline was being adhered to. The TUC demanded that the ETU rescind its strike notices. At a meeting on 8 May the District Committee was 'mad over the complications which have ensued as a result of the varying decisions regarding electricity, power and lighting which have been given by the General Council's committee in this matter'.[47] The next day it sent a deputation to the SOC to argue that the EAC should be abolished and control of the dispute given over to the joint union committee for the industry; for this it was castigated by the TUC for its 'acts of indiscipline'.[48]

While in London the managers at both public and private power stations were visited by trade union delegations, the decision was not promptly communicated to the provinces so the picture outside the capital remained unclear. Only on 10 May, for example, did the sluggish NUGMW executive call out its members at power stations in Nottingham, Leeds, Birmingham, and Leicester. As volunteers began to be brought in, some local branches and strike committees began to ask the EAC for permission to escalate in response by calling out other blue-collar local authority workers, such as those in sanitary and health departments.[49] This pressure was consistently resisted by the SOC who considered that such a move would alienate public opinion.

Over the weekend of 8–9 May, many local authorities attempted to restart their tram services for the first time, further exacerbating the electrical power workers' quandary. These attempts were creating flashpoints of conflict in many major population centres. Where trams could be successfully run, there would be increased pressure for the regular tramwaymen to return to work or see their places filled permanently by volunteers. Therefore, at Bevin's urging, the National Transport Committee met and resolved that, where authorities were attempting to run a skeleton service, the electrical power workers should immediately join the strike.

For three days between 8 and 10 May, probably in protest at the treatment of their London District Committee, the ETU representatives did not attend the EAC despite their general secretary nominally being the chairman. They seemed to have resolved to go it alone, and by the end of the strike had effectively called out all their members in power generation, although there were towns like Southampton where the workers did not respond and the trams kept running. This was a rare example of a national union getting ahead of the General Council's orders, and had the strike continued, the TUC would have probably had no choice but to catch up.

The failure to stop all industrial power caused another problem for many factory workers. Once it was clear that power was being supplied in contravention of the TUC's orders, many did not want to work using what they called 'black juice' – to them it was comparable to handling 'black' goods that had been moved by strikebreakers. The TUC resisted pressure to call out all those factories that were still being supplied with power. To do so would have been a huge escalation and would have drawn the textile industry – at the time the second-biggest employer in the country after the mines – fully into the dispute. Curiously, however, when the Tobacco Workers' Union informed the EAC on 11 May that two of London's seven tobacco factories were still at work and supplied by 'black juice', they were asked to stop work. At the same time, permits were being issued for commercial laundries and other enterprises such as cinemas and music halls to carry on working.[50] These inconsistencies were never fully resolved before the strike was called off. Consequently the many local officials of the ETU, the AEU, and similar unions spent most of their energy during the nine days determining which of their members should be in or out, working from often contradictory and bewildering guidance.

***

The issue of what to do if strikebreakers were introduced did not only occupy power workers. It reared its head also in industries ancillary to the core transport functions that had been called out, not least in distribution. A significant number of distributive workers appear to have walked out on their own initiative. On the second day of the strike George Maurice Hann of the Shop Assistants' Union reported that his members at Army and Navy Stores (a department store chain run as a co-op for military families) were 'at this moment busily engaged in separating all the foodstuffs from other stuff on the banks ready for dispatch to customers' and asked if they should refuse to load vans with food if they were driven by government volunteers. On Merseyside there were five thousand NUDAW members on strike and the union's general secretary Joseph Hallsworth professed to have 'never known a response like it'.[51]

Nevertheless, most ancillary workers obeyed their instructions to stay at work. After the general withdrawal of transport permits for food, however, warehouse and shop workers knew that any transport workers who came to pick up or drop off goods would be doing so without union permission. This would inevitably mean having to work alongside strike-breakers. On the afternoon of 7 May, Hallsworth called Eccleston Square to inform them that he would not be able to hold back the tide: 'Mr Hallsworth says that if this is the General Council's instructions they are asking more than the Distributive Organisation will do. Our people, he says, will not receive goods from blacklegs or government services while their own men are on the streets. 70,000 people will refuse in this district [the North-West].'[52]

The following day Hallsworth travelled to London from his union's Manchester office. The SOC at first reiterated that his members should not refuse to handle foodstuffs on government lorries, but then relented slightly and advised him to visit the Transport Committee at Unity House 'and agree upon a formulae [sic] which would meet the national position, and whatever they agreed would be endorsed'.[53] Such vague instructions hardly sat well with the General Council's claim to have thrown the responsibility of food distribution over to the government when its initial offer to move food had been refused on the eve of the strike. It also rested uneasily against the situation in other ancillary sectors, such as in breweries where workers were being told to come out if they were made to work alongside strikebreakers.

Hallsworth railed at the Transport Committee about the 'ridiculous position' his members had been put in by the TUC, and it was agreed that all his members should be ordered out except those engaged in delivering bread and milk.⁵⁴ It was, however, another two days before NUDAW representatives were invited onto the National Transport Committee. A meeting of the five main unions representing staff ancillary to transport unanimously agreed that all their members should walk out as soon as voluntary labour was introduced into a workplace, or as soon as workers were told to handle goods transported by strikebreakers. They asked the General Council to consider a complete stoppage as the only way to reliably put this position into action. This meeting was on the evening of 11 May, the night before the strike was called off. Again it is likely that, had the strike continued, the TUC would sooner or later have given in to the pressure from its affiliated unions to unconditionally extend it across the sector.

The co-operative societies, with a much more unionised workforce than their competitors, would be affected the worst by such a blanket stoppage. As early as 6 May the Co-operative Wholesale Society complained that food permits were being withdrawn from its lorries. They informed the TUC that the government had offered to move its supplies, and while it did not wish to use the state's volunteer organisation, it would have to if not permitted by the unions to move its food and milk normally.

Ernest Rowlinson of the Sheffield Strike Committee summed up the situation there in a letter to Eccleston Square on 10 May. The Co-op's workforce, he explained, was one hundred percent unionised but the level of organisation among their competitors locally stood at just five percent. A general withdrawal of distributive workers would force the Co-ops to source volunteer labour and lead to shopworkers having to handle 'black' goods 'whilst fellow members of the same union, on the outside staff, are being blacklegged'.⁵⁵ The only alternative would be to shut down the Co-ops' operations totally, which would leave the field open to their private competitors and disproportionately adversely affect working-class households. Rowlinson's suggestion was for authority to be delegated to the local strike committee to deal with the issue alongside local NUDAW officials, but the TUC would not countenance this weakening of centralised decision-making. The same day, the Co-operative Wholesale Society implored the TUC to issue definitive instructions that Co-op food being moved by government labour should not be interfered with by pickets.⁵⁶

Just as with the power supply, the problem of whether to handle 'black' goods inevitably spread to the factories. By the end of the strike's first week, ten thousand Yorkshire textile workers in dyeing and finishing roles had been brought out where they had been instructed to handle wool brought in by non-union transport. 'It would appear that we cannot deal with the situation,' their leaders told the TUC, 'unless instructions are issued to close down the whole industry.' The textile unions were prepared to do this, but the TUC refused.[57]

***

In heated meetings, frantic telegrams, and unofficial action, unions felt the weight of their members' frustration behind the scenes as the strike went on. But the CPGB and its fellow travellers in the National Minority Movement levelled criticisms at the TUC's handling of the strike openly. The CPGB pushed for an 'all out' policy in their bulletins and leaflets, and reiterated its policy of forming Workers' Defence Forces to protect pickets from attacks by the police or Fascists. On 7 May the Birmingham-based Communist *Workers' Bulletin*, while also reprinting the TUC's message that the strike was an industrial dispute, urged that the resignation of the government and formation of a Labour government should be a key demand of the strike: 'The Communist Party warns the workers against the attempt being made to limit the struggle to its previous character of self-defence against the capitalist offensive.'[58]

Although the Communists made these demands of the TUC leadership, they did not have much of a strategy for translating these demands into action. Writing shortly after the strike, Communist militant Jack Murphy explained the party's approach:

> The Minority Movement and the Communist Party...have not yet sufficient leading positions in the unions to be able actually to control the unions even in the crisis without an accession of strength arising from sharp and big divisions in the existing leadership of the unions.
>
> Had the General Council been divided and the Left Wing leaders proved themselves to be fundamentally different from the Right Wing leaders, had they been bold enough to stand in a minority and fought their way on the straight issues of no wage reductions, the story of the strike and

its conclusion would have to be written in another way. But they were not different.[59]

In short, they were hoping for the leaders whose virtues they had extolled in the months leading up to the strike – Swales, Purcell, and George Hicks of the Operative Bricklayers – to show their mettle when the long-awaited battle arrived. In the event, although Purcell busied himself as Bevin's deputy on the SOC, Hicks and Swales were almost anonymous throughout the nine days, and the Communists had no means of building an alternative leadership. Although the party's first *Workers' Bulletin* actually hit the streets the day before the *British Worker*, constant state harassment made its distribution difficult. Some party branches were more or less cut off from communicating with headquarters for the duration of the strike, and of course important party leaders remained in prison from the previous November.[60]

Nonetheless, CPGB members played a significant role on the ground supporting the strike and urging its extension. Communist influence was most pronounced in the North-East where Page Arnot had pioneered his organisation of federated Councils of Action, in parts of South Wales, and, most worryingly for the authorities, in large parts of London. The East End docklands and Saklatvala's Battersea stronghold had a significant CPGB presence. Charles Ammon, a Labour MP acting as an intelligence-gatherer for the General Council, also reported from Camden that 'the movement has got into the hands of the Communists…the local Trades Council, which is under such influence, seems to be arrogating to itself certain authority which should be in the hands of the Executive Councils of the Trade Unions', which in turn was resulting in confusion in the factories as to who should be on strike and whose orders should be followed. Nevertheless, Ammon praised the Trades Council's Workers Vigilance Corps, set up at Communist instigation after a particularly brutal clash between police and workers on 8 May, as 'doing wonderful work'.[61]

Despite the hue and cry of the press denouncing the strike as a communist plot, there were only a few places where Communist influence, coupled with the preponderance of a single industry in the local economy, empowered local trade union committees essentially to run whole villages or towns. These were mainly in or near the coalfields of Scotland, the north-east of England, and South Wales. At Llanelli under the chairmanship of the Communist Enoch Collins, the strike committee immediately brought out all steel, gas, electricity, and brewery workers and stopped all essential services. All strikers got full poor relief from the Board of Guardians, and the police allegedly worked with the committee to turn back blackleg lorries.[62] Villages like Mardy and Bedlinog went down in folklore as 'little Moscows'. In the latter, some small businessmen were Communists and ran the Council of Action alongside miners, and in Mardy the strike committee set maximum prices on many goods.

By the weekend of 8 May, trade unionists had every reason, from their perspective, to be confident of victory. The response to the strike call had been like nothing anyone had ever seen. Workers across different industries came together in an unprecedented display of unity, many thousands participated in formidable pickets, and trades councils and other bodies were perfecting systems of local organisation. Hundreds of thousands more workers had been clamouring to join the dispute and the officials were assuring the rank and file that they still had many more trump cards to play. At Eccleston Square, though, those same leaders, the reluctant instigators of Britain's biggest ever strike, were getting nervous, and beginning to look for a way out.

| How the Strikers Fought the Bosses— | **Sunday Worker**
 SUNDAY, MAY 16, 1926 | And How the Bosses Fought the Strikers |

HISTORIC SCENES IN THE GREAT INDUSTRIAL STRUGGLE

Armoured cars and armed troops patrolled the streets. These were used in London to protect blackleg traffic.

Submarines were sent for the first time to the London Docks. Four were sent to the Victoria and Albert Docks as a result of the strike.

THE BALDWIN GOVERNMENT USES FULL POWER OF STATE AGAINST STRIKERS

Tanks and armed soldiers at Wellington Barracks, London.

Lady members of jolly class "taught" doing something useful in Hyde Park.

Welsh Guards in full war kit and tin hats at Hyde Park.

The Communist *Sunday Worker* shows examples of military intervention in the strike.

10

THE STATE'S OFFENSIVE

> *In regards to this affair in Lewes Road, the whole affair was Treacherous... women and children knocked about by those heroes on horseback... also some of the foot police were very insolent to the women who were looking for their children. My two children 5 & 7 have been under the doctor owing to fright and delirium caused through the men on horseback.*
>
> - Y.J. Harrison, eyewitness to a police riot in Brighton, 11 May 1926

> *All ranks of the Armed Forces of the Crown are hereby notified that any action that they may find it necessary to take in an honest endeavour to aid the Civil Power will receive, both now and afterwards, the full support of his Majesty's Government.*
>
> - *British Gazette*, 8 May 1926

The *Gazette*'s warning of Saturday 8 May startled many who read it. What action was the government referring to? To the strikers it appeared to presage something potentially dangerous, even deadly. Rumours were swirling among affluent London society that things were getting out of control: buses dumped into the Thames, policemen killed, Churchill assassinated.[1] The previous evening, the king had told the government of his concern about the level of intimidation coming from pickets and advised it to place all police activity under the control of a single executive officer.² In the morning, though, he eschewed the belligerent tone of 'this unfortunate announcement' and relayed his alarm to the chief of the imperial general staff.³

By Friday, there were reasons for the government to be concerned. Manchester only had enough flour for the weekend, and in parts of the North-East it was reported that food arrangements might break down without police reinforcements. Food stocks were running low in the capital, and a number of mills would cease to function in just a few days unless the situation at the ports in London, Liverpool, and Hull could be improved.⁴ With the food position in London becoming more serious, the Army moved from its initial 'defensive phase' to its 'offensive phase'. To secure the supply of essential goods without risking widespread riots, speed and surprise were crucial.

How could Britain teeter on the precipice of a food crisis when the government had prepared for a confrontation for months? Put simply, the Port of London Authority (PLA) had not anticipated, and was not prepared for, the completeness of the strike along the Thames. While safety-critical lock staff remained at work with union permission to prevent flooding, only a handful of regular dockers reported on the first day of the strike. There were seven at the India and Millwall docks, five at the London and St Katharine Docks, and another seven at the Surrey Docks in Rotherhithe. Even among white-collar staff, a traditional area of weakness for the dockers' unions, only fifteen to twenty percent were at work.⁵ This situation had not improved at all by 7 May when only nine dockers and two railwaymen of the Port of London's regular workforce had reported for duty.⁶

Most of the districts surrounding the docks on both sides of the river – Bermondsey and Deptford on the south side, Stepney and West Ham on the north – were solidly working class, and a strong radical left wing existed in the local labour movement. Mass pickets were quickly and effectively organised, resulting for example in many factories on either bank being closed regardless of whether the workers were covered by the TUC's instructions.⁷ In some boroughs the strike committees were operating out of public buildings. The docklands, in short, were surrounded by some of the 'reddest' neighbourhoods in the country.

Faced with this, the PLA informed the government on the first morning of the strike that it would be impossible to get any food out of the docks or bring any volunteers in. This was not good enough for the government, which wanted a show of force against what they regarded as the communist-infested areas of the East End and South London. The PLA warned that any attempt to bring volunteers in would likely prompt the unions to withdraw the safety-critical men, but the government was prepared to use the military if necessary. On 6 May, a scheme was finally drawn up to offload the food ships that were already berthed on the north side, which would require a volunteer workforce of 650 and an exclusion zone of a quarter of a mile placed around the docks' main entrance.[8]

Overnight on 7–8 May, preparations were made for the show of force that Churchill and others had been advocating. The entire 1st Guards Brigade was moved to Victoria Park. This was done not out of logistical necessity but as an attempt to intimidate and cow the local population. One battalion, fully armed, was deployed to the docks themselves and set up machine-gun posts along the outer wall. Simultaneously, five hundred volunteer workers were landed at the docks by boat under cover of darkness.[9] A number of these were Cambridge undergraduates, shipped downriver in barges towed by naval personnel. One recalled 'looking up from the bowels of the barge and seeing rows of policemen's helmets looking down at us as we passed under Waterloo and other bridges' before arriving to be billeted on an old P&O liner with little food or comfort to be had.[10] The volunteers set about unloading meat, grain, and flour as best they could with the help of naval ratings manning the dock cranes.

Meanwhile, in the early hours of Saturday 8 May, a mass convoy of over one hundred lorries set out from the Hyde Park camp escorted by twenty armoured cars. Crowds gathered along the route to watch the spectacle but mostly stayed silent and, in the face of the military might on display, made no attempts to interfere with the convoy. By midday it had returned to central London to a rapturous reception, laden with four hundred tonnes of flour to ease the worsening food situation in the capital. The Army described the massive food convoy of 8 May as its 'first definite offensive move'.[11] It was a symbolic and psychological victory for the government and opened the way for daily convoys to successfully break the strikers' blockade of the docks. It was a risky move, as soldiers may have had to use live ammunition if any workers attempted to stop the convoys, but it was the only way for the government to successfully break the strike in the docklands.

Over the following days, even larger convoys entered the docks, with even larger military escorts, without any significant violence occurring. To take on a platoon of fully armed soldiers was, after all, a different proposition from a fight with the police. The show of force had its desired effect. More lorry drivers felt confident to join convoys without fear of molestation, although much to the chagrin of the Army command, by the end of the strike many of the Hyde Park drivers were still flatly refusing to join any convoy without military protection.[12] Army officers found it was difficult to withdraw protection after it had been offered, which partly accounts for their general reluctance to commit troops.

Alongside the convoys, the port authority belatedly attempted to get the tugs and lighters running on the river under naval protection. Rumours of naval ratings manning tugs reached pickets like the young apprentice lighterman Harry Watson. Heading out to investigate, despite warnings from the river police, Watson and his workmates witnessed a tug inexpertly towing two barges, losing control, hitting stationary craft 'caus[ing] mooring ropes to tauten and break as if made of cotton instead of two-inch manilla', and setting a chaotic chain of collisions resulting in loose boats escaping downriver. On their way home they demanded of the police: 'What are you going to do about those blokes? You were going to tow us to your Police Station if we caused trouble?' 'The only reply we got', remembered Watson, 'was a dirty look.'[13]

As the PLA had predicted, the introduction of volunteer labour dramatically escalated the situation on the waterside. Labour-run local authorities in the boroughs around the docks began to discuss cutting off the power supplied from their municipal power stations, which had initially been left on for preserving food stocks in warehouses. This is probably what prompted a PLA representative to lie to the chief engineer of West Ham Borough on 8 May, denying that any volunteers had been brought in.[14] Unfortunately the delicacy of the situation didn't restrain the *British Gazette* from triumphantly gloating that the dock 'siege' had been broken, revealing the presence of volunteers to everyone. At 4 p.m. on 10 May, the municipal power station cut off its supply of electricity to the Royal Docks. By then, however, the Royal Navy was well prepared. It took them just twenty-three minutes to hook up a submarine as an alternative power source.[15]

As successful as the convoys and volunteers were at averting a general food shortage across the capital, their effect was still limited to the moving of food supplies. While the London and St Katharine Docks were effectively opened, the India Docks did not start working until the very end of the strike. South of the river, the effectiveness of picketing had seen off an attempt to introduce volunteers into the Surrey Docks on 7 May and, while volunteers and naval personnel were subsequently brought in by boat, there was no attempt to run road convoys in the same manner as had been done on the north side.[16] Goods other than food remained gathering dust for the duration.

A post-strike military intelligence report underlined the importance of the Port of London. It recommended that in future emergencies the entire area should be immediately declared a prohibited military zone and evacuated of residents.[17] This was an extreme attempt to save face, the government having been caught unprepared. It could only have been put into practice by committing large numbers of soldiers to the streets of the East End. The risk of violence in this scenario would have been immense.

***

Further downriver on the Thames estuary was another critical flashpoint of the strike that required hard intervention from the state. Although coal was still king in power generation in 1926, the early twentieth century had seen a growing demand for oil. With the railways ground to a halt and the government relying heavily on road transport, the movement of petrol was crucial. Much of this was unloaded by ocean tankers at the depots of Thameshaven and Shellhaven in Essex.

Workers here came out on strike on the morning of 6 May, after the end of the night shift. Despite joining belatedly, the Thameshaven workers immediately organised strong and militant pickets that were initially successful in turning many tankers away from the depot. A convoy system was mooted early on, but the manager of the Thameshaven site opined that the real problem would be protecting the men who had remained at work after they went home, as the feeling against strikebreakers in the surrounding villages was running so high.[18] A number of men came forward during the strike to say they would be happy to return to work if the police could provide security for their houses while they were out. This was considered by the authorities but not acted on.

There were only a few roads into Thameshaven, through the nearby town of Stanford-le-Hope. Pickets soon started gathering there in large numbers, stretching obstacles across the road and stopping vehicles. One police car was damaged when, refusing to stop for a line of pickets, it drove right at them and they scattered, revealing that behind them they had placed a telegraph pole on four barrels across the road.[19]

On the afternoon of 8 May, three hundred strikers gathered at the war memorial in Stanford-le-Hope, where they were told by an engine driver, James Partridge, that a detachment of special constables in motor cars from Ilford had jeered and waved their truncheons at pickets while entering the depot. Partridge later claimed in court that the specials had run their vehicles into and injured some pickets.[20] The incensed crowd marched the five miles to Thameshaven, cutting the telephone wires connecting the depot with the outside world. When another police convoy from London passed them a stone was thrown through the windscreen of the first car, cutting the face of Inspector Ede. Partridge was arrested for grievous bodily harm, but he denied being the stone-thrower. At court after the strike, where several witnesses including his own manager at the Shell Mex depot where he worked vouched for him, he was only convicted of the lesser charge under the emergency regulations of impeding the movement of fuel. The fact that Partridge was a Royal Navy veteran also worked in his favour. This charge, however, still carried a one-month sentence or a £25 fine.

The Metropolitan Police blamed its Essex counterparts for being too soft with the pickets and allowing the attack to happen, but the police liaison officer's report claimed that Ede had ignored the Essex Police's advice to take a route that would have avoided most of the pickets. The evening after the attack, an armed party of naval ratings was deployed in the countryside around the depot to fix the phone lines, and police patrols were stepped up in the area.

The troubles at Thameshaven were compounded by jealousies between the various petrol companies. The government's scheme to transport petrol upriver to the London wharves was overseen by the Royal Navy, specifically Douglas Forsyth, commander of the *HMS Marshal Soult*. He was infuriated by the rivalries and jealousies between the petrol companies, which were refusing to accept the other companies' petrol at their own wharves:

> It was understood that the Literage and Petrol Companies were pooling their resources, but when I arrived at Thames Haven, I found this to be far from correct, in fact, I found them to be working in most jealous opposition. They were oblivious to the fact that a National Crisis existed. A good deal of valuable time was wasted discussing the matter, and in the Managers having to telephone their London offices for definite instructions.[21]

Forsyth prevailed on the Port Authority to allow petrol to be landed further upriver at Purfleet but faced opposition from the companies because, he suspected, they did not want to lose trade at Thameshaven. It was not until 11 May that two ocean tankers were able to discharge their cargo at Purfleet, and it was only after the strike was formally called off that Forsyth, much to his relief, was told to hand over responsibility for the petrol transport scheme to the civilian authorities. Despite this, with the help of the Navy, many thousands of tonnes of petrol were successfully sent upriver to Silvertown and Fulham during the course of the strike.

A few miles upriver towards the end of the strike, Tilbury's massive commercial docks similarly saw serious violence between those supporting the strike and those attempting to break it. On the afternoon of 11 May, a convoy of lorries heading towards the docks to pick up international mail encountered a pro-strike march in the town. Most passed peacefully but a few began to throw objects at the vehicles, and a piece of concrete thrown by a woman broke the arm of one of the drivers. Once they were safely in the docks, the lorry drivers refused to return to London until an armed escort was provided.[22]

A detachment of thirty-two special constables was dispatched from London. Members of the Bath Club in Mayfair, they were the epitome of the hated upper-class strikebreaker. It was hardly surprising that, when they arrived at Tilbury, they faced a hostile reception, especially after the leading constable, who was riding a motorbike, ploughed straight into the crowd. In the ensuing riot, the cars carrying the specials were attacked and a basket filled with bricks dropped on them from an overlooking tenement block, but despite this they made it to the docks. The drivers were hardly pleased to see the specials either. 'They promised us a military escort and they've sent us thirty ------- Specials. We don't go till we have a proper escort,' said one.

To break the impasse, as the crowd outside the docks swelled to several thousand, Inspector Hurrell invited two members of the local strike committee inside, to check that the vans were loaded only with mail, with a view to getting their permission to let them leave. The trade unionists agreed to let the vans out with an escort of regular police. 'But God help the Specials' if they tried to leave, one added.

C. W. B. Tress, the officer in charge of the specials, was not impressed with Hurrell's attempt at mediation and phoned Scotland Yard. He received a direct command from the commissioner to hold everyone in the docks until reinforcements arrived. 'If any orders are to be given,' Tress told Hurrell, 'they will come from the police and not the mob.' After several more tense hours, a unit of armoured cars arrived and the mail drivers were able to leave under their protection without further incident at 4.30 a.m.

The Tilbury incident alarmed the Cabinet's Protection Sub-Committee such that it ordered all future escorts between the docks and London to be taken over by the Met, and the Post Office was advised to send mail to London by water for the remainder of the strike. The following afternoon, 12 May, disturbances again racked Tilbury. Just a couple of hours after the news had broken that the strike was called off, a train carrying special constables and volunteer railwaymen back to London was stopped by a five hundred-strong crowd and stoned. It was eventually moved under the guard of a detachment of sailors with fixed bayonets. The stone-throwing stopped but the crowd kept following the train, shouting 'Who won the war, eh?' and 'What about 1914–18?'[23]

The success of the Docklands convoys and the suppression of the Thameshaven riots came at a price. By 8 May the military command was warning the government that due to strike commitments 'the number of naval ships and men available in Home waters is now reduced to a very low figure. The number of troops held in War Office reserve should not be depleted except on very urgent grounds.'[24] Shows of force should be limited to where they were absolutely necessary. By now, troops were committed at fuel depots, power stations, public buildings, and convoys around the country. Further commitments were made when, on 10 May, armoured cars were used to escort three hundred LGOC buses out of the Hendon and Cricklewood bus depots. The following day, in the wake of the train derailment at Cramlington, two armoured trains manned by Royal Engineers were organised to patrol a section of the mainline in the twenty-five miles north of Newcastle. There was clearly a worry that the Army's resources were not inexhaustible. One battalion was brought back to Aldershot from the Channel Islands and another deployed to Glasgow from Belfast, and a further withdrawal of troops from Northern Ireland was considered on 11 May.[25] While military resources were managed well throughout the strike, a longer dispute may have necessitated a mobilisation of the Army Reserve, an idea the generals were far from keen on.

***

Police resources were also being stretched as unrest spread across the country, and the weekend saw more aggressive policing in many areas. Tensions were heightened where the local authorities attempted to restart tram services. In Plymouth, this sparked a riot on the afternoon of the famously amicable football match between strikers and police. Weaker-willed authorities were being encouraged by civil commissioners to get trams and buses back on the roads, and some had sent letters requiring their striking workers to hand in their uniforms – effectively notifying them of termination.

Faced with such escalation, strikers and their supporters held mass meetings all over the country which were, in some cases, even larger than the May Day demonstrations a week earlier. Strikers in Birmingham claimed a turnout of twenty thousand on Sunday.[26] Mary Quaile of the General Council addressed a similar number in Manchester, where a procession was led by the tramwaymen's brass bands.[27] The tone of speeches from the platforms was still notably moderate. Croydon saw the largest labour demonstration in its history 'but only good-humoured comment was made'.[28] Strikers everywhere were urged to stand firm and trust their leaders. The weekly edition of George Lansbury's socialist newspaper urged its readers to go to church and continue to practise 'Christ's doctrine of passive resistance'.[29]

Such pleas for moderation were not enough to rein in the violence that was spreading across the country or deter the police from forcibly dispersing many gatherings over the course of the weekend and ramping up arrests under the emergency regulations. The disturbances that had broken out in Glasgow and the west of Scotland at the end of the previous week continued and spread to Edinburgh. On Saturday Newcastle witnessed significant violence. Ten thousand people gathered in the city centre and the police made several baton charges. They arrested twenty-four people, blaming young hooligans rather than strikers for the disturbances. The chief constable reported that police were finding it difficult to contain the situation and that he had deployed mounted officers and volunteers without notifying the local Watch Committee, as they may have disapproved.[30] The local strikers' newspaper saw the action as deliberate provocation designed to justify the use of the military. 'We will never win this fight standing at street corners,' advised the *Workers Chronicle*. 'Every worker must get into the ranks, into a well organised mass picket, organised by the various unions. Every picket an armlet and controlled by the Council of Action.'[31]

The chief constable at Newcastle pleaded with the Army to help protect vulnerable points in the city, but General Harington of Northern Command was unmoved and urged the use of special constables instead.[32] Down the coast, Middlesbrough also descended into rioting on Saturday night, and a police officer was knocked unconscious with a blunt instrument. To calm the situation, naval ratings were paraded through the town to a church service the following morning, in a show of strength.

In Hull the local TGWU area secretary G. E. Farmery reported police violence on Friday night and all day Saturday. Trouble began on Friday when a crowd gathered at the town hall to dissuade volunteers from signing up. Mounted police charged and hospitalised seven people.[33] The following day numerous baton charges were made against crowds attempting to prevent a skeleton tram service being restored. 'Hull is Hull during strikes,' Farmery noted, referring to the city's tradition of violence during disputes, 'and we are certain the police are responsible for all the friction that has occurred. Hull people will not stand baton charges very long.'[34] As at Middlesbrough, naval ratings were landed from a warship in the dock and marched to the town hall, but the situation remained explosive. The riots continued into Sunday night when a veritable convoy of one hundred cars carrying Cambridge University students to volunteer in the city was attacked. One of those sentenced for assaulting a student was a lance corporal in the Territorial Army (TA), clearly choosing in this instance to put class before country.[35] Many of the students did not stick around; those who did tied their college scarves to the buses and trams they worked, perhaps as a token of class distinction.

A pattern of policing was emerging: a march, demonstration or mass picket was ordered to disperse; people refused; then the police forcibly dispersed the crowd and provoked a response. But there were also more targeted and vicious actions from the police. At Sidcup, eleven were injured on Saturday during raids on the homes of trade unionists. The local committee relayed how one worker saw 'his door forced open, his wife batoned and the police took the husband... We feel it our duty to appeal to you to bring these happenings before the mass of people in this wonderful nation of ours.'[36] At Airdrie in Scotland the local transport committee's rooms were raided, copies of its permits seized, and all present, including those waiting for permits to be issued, warned they could be arrested for sedition.[37]

High-profile arrests included those of Noah Ablett, one of the co-authors of the *Miners' Next Step*, who was now a member of the MFGB's Executive Committee. He was charged after making a speech at Battersea repeating Saklatvala's exhortation on the eve of the strike for soldiers not to obey any orders to shoot strikers.[38]

At Winlaton Mill just outside Newcastle, Will Lawther was one of two men arrested for holding up traffic that was moving without union permits. He was a prominent member of both the Miners' Federation and the Labour Party. Lawther's lodge had been engaged in a local dispute with mineowners in Chopwell since June 1925. Lawther, in the company of Henry Bolton of the local Council of Action, happened to stop off at the same pub as a police convoy escorting a food truck. When the police inspector asked Lawther to help deliver the food, he stated he did not recognise government orders and asked if the police had a permit from the Council of Action.[39] Both men were arrested under the emergency regulations and given a fine of £50 or two months in prison. On sentencing, they were told by the magistrate: 'You may be men of responsible position in your own opinion, but the law of this country takes precedence over any by-laws that any Bolshevik or Socialist or any other organisation thinks it can take upon itself to pass.'[40] Upon being taken to Durham Gaol, a crowd of miners who had turned out to support the two men were baton charged.

These arrests of strike leaders were not without risk, as they could spark a backlash. Many were only brought before the bench after the strike was officially called off, and some magistrates were minded to issue slightly more lenient sentences, fearful of reigniting the conflict. However, others were not so keen to forgive, such as the Newcastle magistrate who, on 20 May, sentenced Edward Wilson for his part in circulating the *Northern Light* strike bulletin:

> If you think that the Council of Action can hold up the inhabitants in a state of tyranny you are very much mistaken. Why you and those associated with you don't go to Russia, I don't know. I am sure the Government, and I personally, would subscribe willingly to get rid of the whole lot of you and let you go and live in that country where everything is so blissful and happy.[41]

Most egregiously, on the night of Monday 10 May every Birmingham Strike Committee member was arrested and charged with publishing a statement likely to cause disaffection among the population. They thought they were simply repeating the news, owing to a miscommunication about a vote on the emergency regulations in Parliament. The numbers of 'Aye' and 'No' votes had been mixed up in a telephone message, and the strike committee therefore, even though some were sceptical, published a bulletin proclaiming that the government had been defeated in the House of Commons. The twenty arrested men included two city councillors, four justices of the peace, and the journalist John Strachey who was Labour candidate for Aston. The aristocratic Labour politician Oswald Mosley, who had come within one hundred votes of toppling Neville Chamberlain at Birmingham Ladywood in the last election, was desperate to be at the centre of the action, but was out of town when the raids occurred. He was said to be 'extremely annoyed when he had presented himself for arrest and had been refused'.[42] Despite the intervention of Ramsay MacDonald, ten of the defendants were given £10 fines or fifty-one days in prison, two were discharged, and the rest bound over.[43]

***

The workload of repression proved too much for the regular police to bear. The government continued apace to enrol volunteer special constables, most of whom, to its disappointment, actually spent their time on humdrum patrols, traffic duty, and other basic tasks to free up the regulars for strike work.

Part of the shift towards harsher methods to break the strike, however, involved the organisation of a new, more militarised volunteer force. At the 7 May meeting, Cabinet approved the creation of the Civil Constabulary Reserve (CCR) based on the force that had been formed during the 1921 miners' lockout.[44] The CCR would essentially be a paramilitary organisation administered by the War Office, but under the operational command of the police. The war secretary was instructed to order the headquarters of all territorial units to form companies of the CCR, 'which will be a paid wholetime force of sworn-in Special Constables organised in unit formation wearing plain clothes but supplied with brassards, steel helmets and truncheons'. For the first few days, its ranks would be open only to Territorial Army personnel and 'known and trusted ex-military men'. After the TA men had been organised, a decision would be made as to whether to open the CCR's ranks to others or to transfer a portion of the home secretary's special constables to the new organisation.[45]

The establishment of the CCR, for which Churchill and Joynson-Hicks were largely responsible, represented a victory for the hardliners in government. As a government spokesman explained to the press: 'If the forces of disorder assumed such dimensions as to be beyond the control of small parties, at the moment the only alternative would be to fall back on the armed forces of the Crown… This would be a condition of affairs all would deplore, as it is felt generally that no shots should be fired nor a bayonet fixed during the present trouble.'[46]

Both the military and the government had resolved that regular troops should be kept away from disturbances where possible and only deployed when there was no alternative. Tear gas had been approved for use in the first instance, in lieu of live ammunition. The CCR was a means by which the government could effectively mobilise the territorials for policing purposes without officially having to call them up. Territorial officers involved were to use the title of 'Administrator' and could not draw rations from the regular Army. Truncheons should be obtained from the police, local manufacturers, or 'suitable substitutions can be extemporized by utilising pick helves, spokes of wheels, etc.'[47]

In actual fact, despite strong official encouragement, many territorials did not join and, rather than risking ordering them to, the Army Council soon threw open recruitment to others. Of the 11,025 recruits that had joined the CCR in London by the end of the strike, only one-third were serving territorials. Most of the remainder were ex-servicemen, probably drawn by the promise of pay – at five shillings a day for a constable and more for officers – or by political motivations.

By the end of the strike the CCR had only just begun to spread to areas outside London, with units formed at Birmingham, Norwich, and elsewhere.[48] A Sea Division of the CCR comprising serving members of the Navy was formed under Admiral Fisher, who could evidently spare the time from his role as director of Naval Intelligence. They were billeted in Admiralty buildings and told to take care not to display any element of their Navy uniforms when called out on CCR duty.[49]

Aside from its role at Thameshaven the CCR was not widely used. Had the strike continued for another few days, however, it is likely the CCR would have grown rapidly and been deployed widely against mass pickets and on convoy duties. There were plans to recruit 1,600 in the county of Buckinghamshire alone.[50] For those with memories of the Irish War of Independence a few years earlier, the CCR seemed uncomfortably close to the paramilitary 'Black and Tans' who had terrorised Irish republicans during the conflict. Deployment of the CCR at scale could have only led to significant violence, spiralling out of either side's control. As the Army noted afterwards, 'the strikers were always unwilling to interfere with regular troops or police but looked on the CCR as a species of "blackleg"…they were quite ready to take on a Harlequin Football team, or a party of medical students'.[51]

***

Hand in hand with repressing the strike by brute force, the government discussed means to challenge its legality. It would hold more weight, however, if the main line of attack in Parliament against the lawfulness of the strike came from outside of its ranks. Whether by luck or design, on 6 May Sir John Simon, the veteran Liberal MP and barrister, rose to speak in the House in a debate on the emergency regulations. The Liberals had been a disunited party since Lloyd George deposed Asquith halfway through the war. Lloyd George had governed after the war with a coalition made up largely of Conservatives, but had now changed tack and was courting the right wing of the Labour Party. During the strike, whereas Asquith and his supporters largely fell in behind the government, Lloyd George attempted to tread a middle road. He had criticised the government's granting of the coal subsidy on Red Friday but now expressed his sympathy with the unions and publicly denounced the government's characterisation of the strike as an attack on the constitution.[52]

Simon, who harboured ambitions to lead a reunited Liberal Party, was a political enemy of Lloyd George and an avid opponent of socialism. He denounced the general strike as illegal in strong and weighty terms. It was not simply a larger version of a normal strike, he argued, because it was directed against the state and not against an employer:

> Every workman who was bound by a contract to give notice. Before he left work, and who, in view of that decision, has either chosen of his own free will or has felt compelled to come out by leaving his employment without proper notice, has broken the law... Every railwayman in that position who is now out in disregard of the contract of his employment is himself personally liable to be sued in the County Court for damages. Let me point out another serious thing. Every trade union leader who has advised and promoted that course of action is liable in damages to the uttermost farthing of his personal possessions.[53]

While Simon denied that his intervention was meant to intimidate, it was printed in full in the *British Gazette* and splashed across the pages of the pro-government press as proof that the strike was an unjustifiable attack on constitutional government. One correspondent pointed out triumphantly: 'Sir John Simon is not a Unionist MP, he is a Radical who has sympathised with and worked for the wage-earners.'[54]

Simon's view was, however, only one interpretation of the law, designed to sow the seeds of doubt in the minds of trade unionists as to the legality and rightness of their cause. It was soon challenged. 'There have been literally hundreds of successful strikes which according to Simon's definition were beyond the law,' mooted the Oxford University Labour Club in a leaflet produced the following day. 'The purely legal definition is of minor importance. It is impossible to bring actions against millions of people. You cannot indict a whole nation.'[55]

Late in the evening of Monday 10 May, as the House was about to adjourn, Sir Henry Slesser, who had served as solicitor general in the 1924 Labour government, rose to speak. He asserted that unless it could be proved that the strike was a seditious conspiracy against the state, a breach of contract could not be considered illegal.[56] The proper place to determine the legality of the strike, Slesser maintained, was not the House of Commons, but a court of law. Unbeknownst to him, events had transpired that would give a judge, John Meir Astbury, the opportunity to do so the very next day.

Havelock Wilson's seafarers' union, the NSFU, had been one of the only unions to oppose the strike at the outset. Wilson had established the NSFU in 1887 as an alternative to parochial unions. He had held it together in the intervening decades, and considered the organisation his prize possession – to be protected at all costs. He had also, unlike most of his peers, never broken with Liberalism and in fact moved rightwards with age.

After the strike vote at the TUC's Conference of Executives, Wilson had informed his officials that the union would be holding a ballot to decide on any action, 'otherwise the consequences may be serious, for if we started to pay out strike money without first taking the opinion of the members, any member could apply to the High Court to obtain an injunction to restrain us'.[57] Wilson probably envisaged the strike would be over before the ballot.

The effect of Wilson's opposition on the unions' united front was disastrous. It meant that commercial cargoes would be able to enter and leave the country if volunteer dock labour could be successfully employed to handle them. Eccleston Square received reports that in some places NSFU members were handling cargo themselves, and smaller sailors' unions were reluctant to take action as Wilson intimated that his union would be ready to provide men to replace them.[58]

Wilson's actions also proved fatal to international solidarity in support of the strike. Many transport unions on the continent were initially keen to 'black' British ships and cargoes, but when they found out that British sailors were still working the ships, the European unions had a hard time persuading their own members to boycott them. From his Amsterdam office, Edo Fimmen of the International Transport Workers' Federation begged the TUC for some clarity on the matter.[59] Citrine explained that the NSFU had gone against the TUC's wishes and implored Fimmen to maintain the boycott, claiming, probably erroneously, that most seamen were on strike despite Wilson's insistence on a ballot. For his part, Wilson simply telegrammed Fimmen: 'When you learn to tell the truth and seek out reliable reports you may expect communications from this office not otherwise.'[60]

Local union officials rebelled in the face of what they saw as Wilson's betrayal of the wider movement. In London and the North-East they worked to bring the men out. At Tower Hill, they held a mass meeting that resolved unanimously to join the strike. The branch officials told Wilson they would take their orders from the TUC, not him. The Merseyside District Committee issued a circular on 3 May:

> The Mersey District Officials…feel it is their duty in order to give all assistance to the TRADE UNION CONGRESS DECISION THAT ALL WORK INCLUDING THE WORK OF SEA TRANSPORT SHALL STOP, therefore, appeal for support in this direction, recognising that this decision by the District Committee WILL NOT ENTITLE MEMBERS TO ANY STRIKE PAY UNTIL THE BALLOT VOTE HAS BEEN TAKEN and that decision must be in favour of supporting the strike otherwise no strike pay will be paid. Your local officials feel that this movement should be supported, and desire to assist in bringing the dispute to a successful and speedy conclusion even without strike pay as we are of the opinion it will be to the very best advantage of the Seamen's movement.[61]

On 8 May, the union suspended twenty-two of its Merseyside officials along with others around the country. The assistant general secretary resigned in support of them. Not content with this, Wilson decided to pursue his own members through the courts to obtain an injunction to prevent them from joining the strike. He chose to make an example out of the Tower Hill branch. Branch secretary George Reed was charged with having led a group of pickets aboard ships to order union members off, although he denied being in London at the time. On 11 May the case came to the High Court before Justice Astbury. Reed complained bitterly to the judge: 'We do not know the law and are unfortunately at the moment unable to employ Counsel, even though Counsel is being employed out of monies that are paid in by ourselves to our Society.'[62]

Although the NSFU's lawyer had stated that 'I am not going to ask your Lordship to interfere in any way with any other union but this; it is this union only that is concerned', Astbury's judgement went far beyond Havelock Wilson's squabble with his troublesome members. Rather, he passed judgement on the general strike as a whole:

> The so-called general strike called by the Trades Union Congress Committee is illegal and contrary to law, and those persons inciting or taking part in it are not protected by the Trades Disputes Act of 1906. No trade dispute has been alleged or shown to exist in any of the Unions affected, except in the miners' case, and no trade dispute does or can exist between the Trades Union Congress on the one hand and the Government and the nation on the other. The orders of the Trades Union Council above referred to are therefore unlawful, and the Defendants are at law acting illegally in obeying them and can be restrained by their own Union from doing so.[63]

Just like Simon's speech, experts questioned the validity of Astbury's decision, one of whom dismissed it as 'an off-hand judgment given in a case where the defendants were not represented by counsel'.[64] Despite this, the Astbury judgement no doubt bolstered the government's case against the strike in the arena of public opinion. 'Illegal strike' and 'TUC's unlawful orders' were splashed across the next day's newspapers. Coverage emphasised the potential consequences of the case: no union member who decided not to strike could be denied their union benefits, and conversely unions would be breaking the law by giving out strike pay to anyone who obeyed an illegal strike order.

There is little evidence that the High Court decision impacted the morale of workers on the ground. For a General Council that by this point was desperately looking for ways to bring the strike to a conclusion, however, it was a different matter. As the chatter in ruling-class circles turned to testing the judgement further in the courts, the union leaders began to fear for their organisations' funds.

Astbury's judicial comment fortified the main pillar of the government's propaganda: the strike was a concerted attack on parliamentary democracy. During the days of the strike itself, the Cabinet and the broader Conservative Party seemed poised to go even further. Just a month before the strike, a Cabinet committee had considered a law for compulsory arbitration – making strikes effectively illegal until a Court of Inquiry had reported on the matters in dispute – but backed away from it on the grounds that 'the introduction of any such legislation would be more likely to precipitate than to prevent a general strike'.[65] Now, with the strike in full swing, some Tory backbenchers urged the government to introduce and rush through a bill that would explicitly ban sympathetic strikes.

Baldwin was not opposed in principle to introducing a new law but typically wanted to ensure it was done in the right way at the right time. On the evening of 8 May the Cabinet discussed a hastily drafted illegal strikes bill that was 'passed round at the outset of the meeting and collected immediately afterwards'. It was proposed that, if passed, it should come into force within twenty-four hours. Its main clause simply read:

> It is hereby declared that it is illegal to commence or continue, or to apply any funds in furtherance or support of, any strike which has any other object than the maintenance or improvement of conditions of labour in the industry or the branch of the industry in which the strikers are engaged, and which is calculated to intimidate or coerce the Government or the community, and that any person instigating or taking part in any such strike is guilty of a misdemeanour.[66]

Tory MPs representing industrial areas and even Sir John Simon cast doubts about such a rushed piece of legislation. Opponents within the civil service, like the mild-mannered Tom Jones, feared that it would push the moderate wing of the union leadership into a closer relationship with the radicals, and dangerously inflame the situation in the country.[67] Jones lobbied the king and sounded out other senior Tories, nervous about being seen to attack trade unionism in toto. The king was also concerned at news that Churchill had laid the groundwork to prepare an addition to the emergency regulations that would give the state the power to prevent transfers of union funds.[68] Ultimately Baldwin's caution won out and he agreed to delay. On 10 May he adjourned the discussion for another two days and, in the meantime, planted a Commons question to which he could answer, disingenuously, that no changes to trade union legislation were being considered.[69]

It has at times been suggested that in the worsening climate of government repression the General Council members came to fear their own arrests. Writing in the 1950s, Julian Symons claimed that, over the weekend of 8–9 May, Alf Purcell came to believe arrest warrants had been issued for him and Bevin.[70] There is no evidence for this, and it is almost certain any such move would have been noted in Cabinet as the arrest of the twelve Communists had been in 1925. There was one story, supposedly from a 'Labour insider', relayed to the *Yorkshire Evening Post* at the end of May, that suggested the TUC leaders had received information about their imminent arrest. At a fraught meeting the night before the strike was called off, in a room in Eccleston Square that used to be Winston Churchill's private library, the General Council supposedly received news through its intelligence operation that 'steps were being taken for their arrest, for the arrest of the committees in charge of the food permits, and for those in whose hands the power rested for stopping the supply of electric light and power'.[71] This unnamed correspondent claimed it was the left-wing members of the General Council who were most worried about this prospect, which could have been a reference to Purcell. No record seems to have survived of the Intelligence Committee passing such a warning to the General Council in writing.

Jimmy Thomas had, of course, predicted the arrest and even execution of the General Council at the strike's outset. He spent much of the strike in histrionics which must have rubbed off on his comrades to some extent. But it's unlikely the General Council had much anxiety about arrest and imprisonment. They did, however, have great cause to worry about their union bank accounts. They had not expected the strike to last more than a few days. It had now lasted a week and showed no sign of abating. Every day at Eccleston Square, they received reports of actions they had neither ordered nor authorised. Both the workers and the government had shown themselves willing to go to great lengths to win the dispute. But the TUC leadership feared such a showdown would rend the trade union movement asunder. And so they looked for a way out.

THE CHAIRMAN OF THE T. U. C. COUNCIL, WHO ANNOUNCED TO THE PREMIER THE TERMINATION OF THE STRIKE : Mr ARTHUR PUGH (IN FRONT) LEAVING DOWNING STREET

TUC leaders leave Downing Street after capitulating to the government.

11

SURRENDER

My executive feels there is something wrong in that certain organisations knew hours before ... that the strike was going to be called off, when we were calling our men out as the last line of attack.

- John Brownlie, Amalgamated Engineering Union (AEU)
January 1927

In general, the situation is one in which we are holding our own. But the Government's organisation is improving, and its policy is becoming more aggressive. Every day the intensity of the struggle will increase.

- TUC Intelligence Committee report, morning of 12 May 1926

The Astbury judgement did not faze the workers out on strike. The 'second line', if they were not already out, responded enthusiastically on 12 May. Others continued to walk out contrary to the orders of the TUC, like the Co-op shop assistants in Newcastle who struck when their shops received goods on blackleg wagons.[1] Across the country, the closure of factories gathered pace as supplies began to run out. Railway passenger and milk train services had slowly improved but were still running less than a quarter of their usual mileage, a figure that was much lower on the LMS and LNER companies that served the industrial north.[2] Other cargo, including that needed for industrial production, was still barely moving on the railways; on 11 May the Great Western shifted only 6.4% of its normal mileage.[3]

There had been remarkably few general moves back to work from any significant workforces. Only isolated grumbling against the strike could be heard from a few union branches, mainly in the printing industry.[4] In some places such as Birmingham, tramwaymen had started to return to work under threat of permanent dismissal from their employers.[5] Nonetheless, on 11 May there were more workers out than on any day since the strike was called.

Despite the continued strength of the strike, the General Council was eager to end it as soon as possible. Yet up to then, it had only made one announcement to that effect, on 6 May in the *British Worker*:

> The General Council is ready, at any moment, to resume negotiations for an honourable settlement. It enforces no conditions for resuming preliminary discussion with the Government on any aspects of the case. It is obvious, however, that at this stage, with no knowledge of the subsequent line of policy that the Government intends to pursue, the General Council cannot comply with the Prime Minister's request for an unconditional withdrawal of the strike notices.[6]

Within a day of this having been printed, however, prominent voices on the General Council like Jimmy Thomas were beginning to talk about calling the strike off. While Thomas represented the extreme end of a spectrum of opinion, he was far from alone. To understand why the union leaders were so keen to get their members back to work, we need to recall their motives for calling the strike in the first place. For them, the strike was fundamentally a response to the issuing of lockout notices by the mineowners, and the subsequent failure to get these withdrawn in the talks held with the government between 30 April and 2 May. Had the lockout notices been withdrawn at any time, they would have immediately called off the strike. The object of the strike was not, as far as they were concerned, to protect the wages and conditions of the miners per se, but to reopen negotiations. From their perspective, they had been forced into using the most radical means possible to pursue a moderate, even meagre, aim.

The bulk of the trade union rank and file, along with the Miners' Federation leaders, saw things differently. For them, the strike was for their oft-stated position of 'not a penny off the pay, not a second on the day' – a slogan that the TUC had never fully embraced but had not publicly repudiated – and to prevent the extension of wage reductions to other industries. The Federation had, however, agreed to turn over the running of the dispute to the TUC as the price of getting any solidarity action at all. This contradiction, ultimately unresolved, explains how the strike was rapidly brought to an end in such a desultory manner. The General Council did not consider themselves to be betraying the strike. If the government opened the door to talks that was, for them, tantamount to victory.

They were not, however, a homogeneous group, and their motives did differ. The most moderate group, represented by Thomas and Charlie Cramp of the NUR, was both ideologically opposed to the strike from the start and convinced on a practical level that it could not win.[7] Thomas thought that the state, if it used all the power at its disposal to crush a general strike, would inevitably be victorious. He spent most of his social time in the company of the ruling class and saw first-hand their determination to beat the unions. He was particularly affronted by Sir John Simon's speech in the House arguing that union leaders could be individually liable for damages arising from the strike, as he had considered Simon a personal friend. As the strike progressed, Thomas increasingly resembled a nervous wreck, fearing for the very future of the trade union movement. By 10 May the NUR leaders were putting it about that the strike could only hold out for another couple of days, exaggerating any sign of returns to work on the railways for their own purposes. Over the course of the strike their relentless pessimism infected other members of the General Council, such as Ben Turner of the textile workers, having an attritional effect on their already shaky resolve.[8]

Bevin was slightly more optimistic. He thought a general strike could last for two to three weeks before it started to cave. This was one reason behind his tactical decision, the cause of so many headaches at Eccleston Square, to bring the workers out in waves. He considered that starting with a full stoppage meant the only way was downhill as soon as any workers started going back. He later reported to his executive that the strike was at full strength on 12 May, the day the 'second line' was brought out, and thereafter would only be able to 'hold out'.[9] For Bevin, therefore, the situation was incredibly time-sensitive, and as early as 6 May he proposed, through the SOC, an approach to the editor of the *Guardian* to act as a go-between for peace talks. Margaret Bondfield of the Shop Assistants' Union had a similar view to Bevin in that, unlike Thomas, she did genuinely want the strike to succeed in achieving its narrow aims. In her role as the General Council's main contact for the south-west of England, she noted that 10 May, when she was visiting Yeovil, was the first day she encountered genuine anxiety among workers to end the strike.[10] This centrist group on the General Council was just as keen to open negotiations as Thomas, but wanted to do so from a position of strength and in a manner that would keep the unity of the trade union movement intact.

The most perplexing group on the General Council was the avowed left-wingers. They were a minority, but included in their number some in important positions. Alf Purcell worked with Bevin on the Strike Organisation Committee, and Alonzo Swales of the engineers was involved in the negotiations with the government. Both men had been built up by the Communists as daring class fighters in the months preceding the strike, as part of the CPGB's Anglo-Russian Committee strategy.[11] In 1924 Purcell had led a TUC delegation to Soviet Russia which also included Herbert Smith and ASLEF leader John Bromley. Purcell described the country as 'a workers' republic…rising, Phoenix like, from the ashes of the most despotic regime of history'.[12] In the months between Red Friday and the outbreak of the general strike, Purcell's speeches and writings were often markedly radical. He claimed 'all the elements for revolution' were coming together and, at a huge Albert Hall rally in March 1926, urged the General Council to use its power to release the jailed Communists from prison.

The left-wing credentials of Purcell, Swales, Hicks, and Bromley were, however, based far more on their desire for friendlier relations between Britain and the Soviet Union than on pursuing a militant industrial policy. During the strike, they never criticised the majority of the General Council, nor proposed any alternative strategies of their own. This was partly out of a sense of collective responsibility and partly from careerism. Kevin Morgan, Purcell's biographer, describes him as 'too wholly committed to the TUC, whether out of loyalty or career interest, to voice his misgivings'.[13] Ultimately, however, the left on the General Council no more saw the general strike as a desirable step towards revolution than did

Bevin or Thomas. For all the government's fearmongering about communist plots, even the union leadership's left-wing could only see as far as a negotiated settlement to end the dispute.

***

The Cabinet, too, contained shades of opinion. The hardline faction around Churchill, including Neville Chamberlain and Lord Birkenhead, wanted more visible and vigorous displays of military force to cow the strikers, and the militarisation of the police operation through the expansion of the CCR. Meanwhile Joynson-Hicks – 'Mussolini Minor' to many of those on strike – behaved in a slightly more reserved and tactful manner during the nine days than his reputation would have suggested.[14] It is likely that Jix's position as chairman of the Supply and Transport Committee both occupied most of his time and let him keep an eye on the emergency machinery without resorting to extreme measures. He resented the fact that Churchill started turning up to committee meetings during the strike, having not previously been involved, and opposed a proposal from the chancellor to install machine-gun posts along the main roads into the London Docklands.[15]

Baldwin has often, at the time and since, been seen as a moderate in hock to these more hardline elements in his Cabinet. Hamilton Fyfe, editor of the *British Worker*, accused him of 'letting them run the show and pushing him into the background'.[16] This perception stems partly from his own claims to be a peacemaker at heart, as expounded in his wireless broadcast to the nation, and from his talent for the underrated political ability to do nothing. A true moderate, it might well be argued, would have found a way to broker an agreement to avoid the strike altogether, but Baldwin was adamantly against too much state intervention in industrial affairs if he could help it. He blamed the war and Lloyd George's governments, from which he had been instrumental in extricating his party, for creating a culture of reliance on the state among employers and workers. In this, he was just as ideologically stubborn as the coalowners or Arthur Cook. For the duration of the strike Baldwin refused to negotiate with a trade union movement that he considered to have gone beyond the realm of constitutional politics.

The more moderate voices in government circles tended to come from civil servants, those who were entrusted to run the machinery of the state smoothly regardless of which party was in power. Tom Jones, the able deputy cabinet secretary, was not unsympathetic to the unions but, like Baldwin, regarded the general strike as an unacceptable attack on the national community. He wanted the government to pursue a strategy of making statements that would embolden the moderate wing of the TUC. When he discussed this idea with Churchill on 7 May the chancellor dismissed it out of hand, saying that the government was 'at war' with the unions and flying into a rage that left Jones feeling 'tossed about like a small boat in an angry sea'.[17] Nevertheless, Jones persisted in his attempts to rein in the wilder elements on both sides, keeping contact with both Churchill's private secretary and with the political scientist Harold Laski, who was close to the labour leaders. Laski also passed on intelligence from Eccleston Square, telling Jones on 8 May: 'I take [Arthur] Pugh home every night. I think I know their minds there. Of the twenty-six known to me not more than three are out and out revolutionaries.' He claimed, erroneously, that Herbert Smith would probably settle for ten-to-fifteen-percent wage reductions.[18] This may have served to convince Jones that there was more room for compromise than actually existed.

While Jones's tireless efforts likely deterred the government from bringing anti-union legislation to the floor of the Commons while the strike was still on, he was otherwise unable to shift the hardliners in government. His exertions were such that he was only able to return to his Belsize Park home to sleep for the first time on 8 May, where evidently he had been having work done. 'The place is still in an awful muddle,' he noted. 'We had supper in one of the bedrooms. The workmen except the foreman have all stopped work.'[19]

There were other informal talks behind the scenes with a view to ending the strike. Over lunch at a West End club on 7 May, the aristocratic writer Osbert Sitwell and his friend Lady Wimborne hatched a plan to obtain peace through the medium of a society luncheon. Lady Wimborne was a popular hostess and the wife of a prominent Liberal. She reached out to the coalowners Lords Londonderry and Gainford, the Liberal peer Lord Reading, and the Labour Party politician Philip Snowden. Inevitably, the one trade unionist who received an invitation to this exclusive lunch was Jimmy Thomas, who was never one to resist passing time in such company.

During four hours of dining Thomas said, entirely without foundation, that the miners were now prepared to accept the Samuel Commission's recommendations, including wage cuts. Thomas was under the impression that Baldwin knew about the Wimborne House talks, which he probably did, and that his wireless broadcast was a coded signal that he was ready to re-establish the coal subsidy, which he certainly was not.[20] For his part, Lord Gainford pledged the coalowners to accept the commission's report, apparently without authority.[21] The Wimborne House group spent a few days trying to make contact with various worthy figures in the world of publishing and journalism to popularise the idea of a negotiated settlement. They achieved little, however, and Lord Reading's approaches to government were received coldly. Baldwin regarded the Liberal Party as a dying beast. He was more than happy to amplify Liberals' public denunciations of the strike but did not want them to involve themselves in its settlement.

***

Other voices of moderation came from the establishment, if not the state itself. The Archbishop of Canterbury, Randall Davidson, had denounced the strike in the House of Lords on 5 May as 'a condition of things so intolerable that every effort is needed, is justifiably called for and ought to be supported, which the Government may make to bring that condition of things as speedily as possible to an end'.[22] Other clergymen, however, showed more sympathy with the workers. An Anglican priest from Warwickshire wrote in support of the miners: 'They simply cannot live on less. They feel – and I fully agree with them – that much of the subsidy was grabbed. They see the wasteful luxury of some owners. Our men are not hotheads like some of the Celts may be but I am convinced they are going to keep up their end desperately.'[23]

Grassroots Christian opinion mobilised in favour of industrial peace. Meetings took place across the country, and a network of Anglican and Nonconformist figures, including the Bishop of London, prevailed on Archbishop Davidson to act. On 7 May he made a joint appeal with the Nonconformist churches for negotiations to resume 'undeterred by obstacles which have been created by the events of the last few days'. The churchmen proposed the simultaneous withdrawal of the strike and lockout notices, and the resumption of the coal subsidy for a 'short, definite period'.[24]

The trade unions and the Labour Party seized on the churchmen's appeal and publicised it as widely as they possibly could; Ramsay MacDonald saw it as the most promising means to end the strike. The government, as we have seen, effectively banned the foremost prelate of the state religion from addressing the nation. This led to complaints from the general public when the appeal was published in the *British Worker* and Saturday's edition of the *Times*.[25]

To make matters worse for the government, on Sunday morning the appeal was read aloud from pulpits across the country. Clergymen praised the strikers' moderation and publicly repudiated the government's line that the strike was an attack on the constitution, while at the same time denouncing the strike as misguided. Free Church minister Dr Norwood probably spoke for many when he said that 'the conviction behind the strike may be mistaken, but it is honest and sincere'.[26] The Free Church Council in Portsmouth urged its congregations to conduct special intercessory prayers for a quick end to the strike. At Bath Abbey the Nonconformists were invited into joint services with their Anglican brethren to pray 'that all party spirit might be set aside and that negotiations might be set on foot which would have a happy fruition'.[27]

As a compromise in the wake of the force of public opinion, Reith broadcast the archbishop's Sunday sermon, a course of action the government could hardly object to. The prelate called for a reasonable and generous settlement. He alluded to the Church appeal but did not advance any more specific proposals. Nevertheless his sermon made enough of a sympathetic impression for Hamilton Fyfe to opine that 'for the first time in its history...the Church of England has put itself on the side of the People against the Privileged Class'.[28] 'Peace among our people', concluded the archbishop, 'is the Will of God.'[29]

J. C. C. Davidson, who had prevented the printing of the Church appeal in the *British Gazette* in case it emboldened 'the unthinking quarters of the population who were for peace at any price', also relented after the matter was raised in Parliament.[30] The Church appeal's impact on the actual course of events was minimal, but it underlined the position of many people in the country of all classes, who were sympathetic to the plight of the miners but regarded the general strike as a step too far. Although some on the labour side held out great hope that it would help them win a moral, if not a material, victory, the appeal was ultimately a naive intervention in the context of the bitter class war that was raging. It was never going to shift the government's position, as is revealed by a letter Baldwin wrote to the Earl of Derby just a couple of days after the strike ended:

> The intellectuals and the clergy have as usual shewn a perfect ignorance of the big questions at issue. They have been in a complete fog as to what was going on, the motive forces, the issues at stake. And they have in consequence talked ROT, and that might have caused serious difficulties if the struggle had been protracted. However thank God we are getting through in spite of 'em.[31]

It's unsurprising that the Church's appeal for peace fell on deaf ears in Whitehall, but it was something of a propaganda victory for the unions. Despite almost universally condemning the strike, the clergy effectively conceded the point that the TUC was not trying to overthrow the government. It was no accident that many trade unionists turned up to Sunday services that weekend wearing their war medals to stress their respectability. Many of their fellow churchgoers would have cause to reassess the strike. Viscount Grey of Fallodon, a veteran Liberal statesman, had been persuaded to write a strong denunciation for the *British Gazette*'s Monday edition. But by Sunday evening he had already partly walked back his position in a BBC broadcast in which he admitted 'if the object of the strike is not revolutionary...then our feeling about the strike would be entirely changed'.[32] These second thoughts did not, however, stop him from toeing the government's line that the strike notices must be withdrawn before any negotiations could take place.

***

The main initiative to end the strike would come not from the clergy but from an aspiring *philosophe*. Sir Herbert Samuel, dismayed that the government had dismissed the recommendations of his Coal Commission, had retreated back to his San Vigilio villa to continue to work, with characteristic modesty, on his book about 'what is wrong with the world'.³³ He phoned Baldwin on the eve of the strike offering to help with negotiations and was politely rebuffed. Undeterred, once it began, he made his way back to England, keen to offer his help in bringing it to an end. In Dover on 6 May, he was met by the celebrity racing driver Henry Segrave, who whisked Samuel up to London in his Sunbeam.³⁴

Samuel's initial plan was to reconvene the erstwhile members of the Coal Commission to present a plan for conciliation, but they were all too burned by their experience to be interested. He resolved to press on alone. Initially he approached the miners and the mineowners, neither of whom were in any mood for compromise. He found a much better reception from the TUC's Negotiating Committee. Naturally, his first phone call was to Jimmy Thomas, and the two arranged a meeting for the afternoon of 7 May. It was to be held at the palatial home of Sir Abe Bailey, a South African diamond tycoon and mutual acquaintance. There, Samuel expressed to the trade unionists his frustration that the wage cuts imposed by the mineowners had gone far beyond what had been proposed by his commission, and they agreed about the desirability of a National Wages Board along the lines of what existed for the railways.

The following day Samuel saw Baldwin and put to him a formula for a potential agreement. This would involve a temporary renewal of the coal subsidy in exchange for the TUC accepting in principle the need for wage cuts for the miners. The prime minister, however, was steadfast that no negotiations could take place until the strike had been called off. The government's position was laid out to Samuel in a letter from Arthur Steel-Maitland, the minister of labour:

> [The government] hold that the General Strike is unconstitutional and illegal. They are bound to take steps to make its repetition impossible. It is therefore plain that they cannot enter upon any negotiations unless the Strike is so unreservedly concluded that there is not even an implication of such a bargain upon their side as to embarrass them in any legislation which they may conceive to be proper in the light of recent events...
>
> While they are bound most carefully and most sympathetically to consider the terms of any arrangement which a public man of your responsibility and experience may propose, it is imperative to make it

plain that any discussion which you think proper to initiate is not clothed in even a vestige of official character.³⁵

This could hardly have been clearer. Samuel was not acting on the government's behalf and it was not prepared to be bound by any promises he made to the TUC in return for calling the strike off.

The following afternoon Samuel and the Negotiating Committee reconvened at Bailey's house, and Samuel informed them of the government's refusal to negotiate. Citrine noted that the hearts of the TUC men began to sink as they realised they would have to abandon the strike to get back in the room with the prime minister:

> I could feel a certain despondency settling on the members who were with us. Here we were, sitting in the house of a South African millionaire, beautifully furnished rooms, with every indication of luxury, cigars on the table, refreshments in plenty, gilt chairs and thick, soft carpets – deliberating on the National Strike. Rather a strange position for men supposed to be aiming at undermining the Constitution.³⁶

It was only after this second meeting with Samuel that the Miners' Federation officials were even made fully aware that talks had been taking place. The exclusion of the miners from the initial discussions caused much rancour, as it had done during the negotiations on the eve of the strike. The TUC negotiators, however, wanted something they could take to the miners as the basis for a settlement before letting them in on the talks.

On the morning of 9 May the MFGB was presented with the 'Samuel memorandum'. It proposed the establishment of a National Wages Board with four representatives of the miners, four of the employers, and four of the government. It advised cutting wages for a 'reorganisation period' of one year, with existing District Boards determining local rates. During this time definitive reforms to the mining industry including the amalgamation of small enterprises 'should be actually carried into effect' under the supervision of the board. It also proposed an extension of the coal subsidy to the end of the month while a new wages agreement was arrived at.³⁷ Crucially, Samuel emphasised that the government and employers should not be expected to reopen negotiations until the principle of wage cuts had been accepted by the trade union side, and that the general strike must be called off before any other measures were taken, including the withdrawal of the lockout notices.[38]

To the miners, this looked like a simple rehash of previous proposals. At a discussion of the MFGB's full executive, Samuel's memorandum was rejected as a basis for negotiations. The following day it was simplified and revised in more discussions between Samuel and the TUC's Negotiating Committee. The only significant shift was that new, reduced wages should only come into effect after a scheme for reorganisation was agreed.

As well as the content of the memorandum, there was the thorny question of whether it was worth the paper on which it was written. Bevin, Turner, and other General Council members pressed the Negotiating Committee for assurances that the termination of the strike would mean the end of the lockout, the Samuel memorandum being made public, and the government accepting it and entering into negotiations. To each of these they answered in the affirmative, despite not having been given any such guarantees by Samuel.[39] It is possible that Thomas and Pugh, for the Negotiating Committee, genuinely thought this would be the case, but it is also certain that by this point they had resolved to end the strike. Bevin, who thought the terms of the memorandum were the best the miners would get, was happy to take them at their word, although he later expressed some regret at having done so.

No one seems to have considered how the coalowners, who had caused the entire dispute, would take the memorandum. They, of course, had already forced down wages through their lockout. In any case, for the MFGB, wage cuts were wage cuts. For the first time during the general strike, the miners' executive met with the General Council on the evening of Monday 10 May. Now the rupture between the MFGB and the TUC became visible. In a heated exchange with Herbert Smith, John Bromley threatened to withdraw ASLEF from the fight. 'I'm not stopping him,' was the miner's curt response.

Citrine recalled the scene: 'Miner after miner got up and, speaking with an intensity of feeling, affirmed that the miners could not go back to work on a reduction in wages. Was all this sacrifice to be in vain?... I glanced round at the hard-set faces of the miners, and I could not see the slightest sign of any compromise of any one of them.' Speaking for the TUC, Arthur Pugh admonished the miners for failing to put forward any counter-proposals. He argued that they were neglecting their responsibility to the wider movement by their obstinacy, and if they had their way, 'We must go on with this struggle until the process of attrition has brought the whole trade union movement to its knees.'[40] To this, Smith simply replied that the miners' executive had their instructions from their members, and could not go back on them. It was a stalemate.

***

The following day, 11 May, Samuel's terms were amended to incorporate a number of changes suggested by the TUC's Negotiating Committee including a freeze on recruitment in the mining industry to prevent overproduction and underemployment. The substantial points, however, remained unchanged. That evening one final attempt was made to persuade the MFGB to sign up to the memorandum, to no avail. Pugh told the leaders there was no more room for manoeuvre; the memorandum would have to be accepted or rejected in its entirety. Following a two-hour discussion, the miners again rejected the terms and walked away from Eccleston Square just before midnight. Bevin suggested giving them one more chance to come round, but by this time the Thomas group on the General Council had had enough. Thomas, and Frank Beard of the Workers' Union, informed their colleagues that they would not keep the strike going without the approval of their executives.[41] This effectively meant reneging on the decision of the pre-strike Council of Executives to put the TUC in charge of the dispute, and breaking the united front of the TUC-affiliated unions.

In the early hours of the morning, Baldwin's secretary rang Eccleston Square from Downing Street. Would the General Council, he asked, like to see the prime minister? It appears Baldwin had been waiting for news of the strike's termination, probably tipped off by Tom Jones who had contacts in the labour camp. It was arranged for TUC representatives to attend Downing Street at noon the following day, with the heavy implication that the purpose of such a meeting would be the unconditional calling-off of the strike.

Upon arriving at the prime minister's residence, the trade union leaders were held outside. Baldwin, they were told, would not see them until they swore to call off the strike. Bevin, who had not been involved in the talks with Samuel but was part of the TUC's delegation, exclaimed: 'For Christ's sake let's call it on again if this is the position.'[42] If so, he was overruled by the others with little fuss. Thomas explained to the government official that they had, indeed, come to announce the strike was over.

Pugh alluded obliquely to the TUC's discussions with Samuel and stated that they had given him hope that the coal dispute could now be settled by negotiations. 'We are here today, sir,' he went on, 'to say that this general strike is to be terminated forthwith in order that negotiations can proceed.'[43] Baldwin replied: 'I thank God for your decision, and I shall lose no time in using every endeavour to get the two contending parties together and do all I can to ensure a just and lasting settlement.'

Few of the other trade unionists were in the mood to talk much. Thomas appealed to Baldwin for help in ensuring that the return to work would be as smooth as possible, 'because the one thing we must not have is guerrilla warfare'. Bevin went further and asked for an assurance against victimisation. He knew that when the decision to end the strike was communicated to people on the ground it would cause chaos and confusion. 'We shall have to send telegrams to Unions whose headquarters are not in London with whom we cannot converse,' he told Baldwin, 'and coupling it with a declaration from yourself would in a way give the lead as to how the thing is to be approached.'

The prime minister was totally non-committal on this point. Closing the door to further discussions with the TUC, and re-establishing the unquestioned authority of the elected government, he refused to guarantee anything: 'I think it may be that whatever decision I come to, the House of Commons may be the best place in which to say it.'[44]

The abject nature of the TUC's surrender stirred some pity in the eyes of their enemies. Lord Birkenhead, no doubt feeling for his friend Jimmy Thomas whose nerves had been fraying more with every passing hour of the strike, wrote of the spectacle at Downing Street that it was 'so humiliating that some instinctive breeding made one unwilling to even look at them. I thought of the Burghers of Calais approaching their interview with Edward III, haltered on the neck.'[45]

When the delegation returned to Eccleston Square, Bevin was exhausted and furious. 'Something has happened and the best way to describe today, if we are not quick, is that we have committed suicide,' he told his colleagues. 'Thousands of members will be victimised as the result of this day's work.'[46] While the evening's edition of the *British Worker* had proclaimed to the faithful that the General Council was 'satisfied that the miners will now get a fair deal', the mood behind the scenes was grim.[47] It was clear as soon as they had seen Baldwin that the unions had achieved no concrete concessions. It would soon become just as clear that there would be no immediate move by the government to resolve the coal dispute at all. Late that night Ben Turner noted: 'G[eneral] C[ouncil] flabbergasted at nothing being settled about Miners' lock-out notices. Retired and felt dismayed... Left at 1.10[a.m.] disappointed and disgusted. Papers out soon about TUC Surrender.'[48]

PART 3

After the Strike

Scenes of chaos and confusion greet the calling off of the strike.

12

THE SECOND GENERAL STRIKE

On the assumption that the lockout notices would be withdrawn and the miners would resume work, we took the view that any victimisation would naturally not be on a large scale at all.
- STRIKE ORGANISATION COMMITTEE REPORT, 16 JUNE 1926

WIGAN: Seven thousand men have been refused reinstatement both by railway and contract firms.
- ONE OF MANY TELEGRAMS TO ECCLESTON SQUARE, 13 MAY 1926

The General Council's announcement of the strike's termination threw the country into chaos. No one knew quite what to believe. Had the government, as the TUC claimed, made real concessions? Had the unions really thrown in the towel when millions of workers were still on strike? It was far from clear what the miners and coalowners thought of the situation or what, if any, negotiations were proposed to solve their dispute. Nor was it clear to the strikers what guarantees they had that they would be able to return to their old jobs.

On the evening of 11 May rumours started to seep out that the strike was about to be called off, compounded by the BBC's wireless broadcasts that obliquely referred to meetings being held with a view to the resumption of negotiations. Telegrams went to Eccleston Square from local committees demanding to know if the rumours were true.

At 1 p.m. on 12 May, the BBC broadcast an official announcement that the strike was over. Many workers naturally took the TUC's claim to have won at face value. The Bradford labour movement's local newspaper claimed that 'after all the stir and excitement, the inconvenience and lying, we are back to where we wish to be, with the miners' cause under negotiation'.[1] Rumours abounded and the details of the discussions with Samuel remained murky. Taking advantage of the general confusion, many union leaders proudly told their members that a huge victory had been won. Both the NUR and RCA claimed that they had achieved the withdrawal of the lockout notices. The NUR leader Charlie Cramp went so far as to tell his branches that the miners would suffer no wage cuts.[2]

In the Commons that afternoon, Baldwin announced the end of the strike in conciliatory terms:

> The peace that I believe has come—the victory that has been won, is a victory of the common sense, not of any one part of the country, but the common sense of the best part of the whole of the United Kingdom, and it is of the utmost importance at a moment like this that the whole British people should not look backwards, but forwards – that we should resume our work in a spirit of cooperation, putting behind us all malice and all vindictiveness.[3]

This raised hopes of a quick return to work without recriminations or victimisation. But just a few hours later came an official announcement of a rather different tone: 'His Majesty's Government have no power to compel employers to take back every man who has been on strike, nor have they entered into any obligation of any kind on this matter.'[4] The day ended with most strikers still unsure of their position and unwilling to return to work. Having previously ordered its constituent unions to abrogate their power to the General Council, the TUC now abandoned its responsibilities. Individual unions were now to make arrangements for their members, intensifying the confusion on the ground.

***

If the gradually leaked gossip, official pronouncements, and telegrams throughout 12 May began to turn the strikers' jubilation into an uneasy sense of dismay, those who reported for work that evening and the following morning were left in no doubt that they had not won a great victory. Across the country, workers found themselves confronted by bosses who were keen to tear up existing agreements with the unions. Others refused to take back the strikers, preferring to retain the services of those who had come forward to take their place.

The situation was uneven. In the main, employers had not had a chance to agree on a common policy; they were as blindsided by the sudden end of the strike as their workers. While relatively few employers imposed immediate wage cuts, many wanted to leave the door open to driving down terms and conditions in the future. To this end they presented returning workers with papers to sign to the effect of acknowledging that they had breached their contracts by walking out. In a handful of places there was even the return of the dreaded 'document', the remnant of the dark days of the nineteenth century when defeated workers had to sign a promise not to join a union as a condition of reinstatement.

Employers' attitudes varied across industries. They all weighed up the threat of provoking further damaging industrial action by pursuing a harsh course. In industries like iron and steel where relations had been relatively harmonious for the past few years, most employers did not want to jeopardise this by attempting to smash the unions. The engineering employers, who had come close to facing a national strike in their industry just two months earlier, were likewise not in the mood to go to war, particularly because those who had come out as part of the 'second line' had only been on strike for a matter of hours before the surrender.

However, there were notable exceptions to this approach of grudging conciliation. In Birmingham, perhaps emboldened by the arrest of the local strike committee and presence of hardline Conservative politicians like Neville Chamberlain, many manufacturing employers forced strikers to sign on at minimum rates and effectively locked out those who refused.[5] The TGWU's victimisation list for Dunlop Rubber in the city, of which Tory politician Eric Geddes was chairman, contains the names of 166 men and 21 women.[6]

Another consideration in the minds of the employers was how replaceable they considered their regular workforce to be. Few of those who volunteered for railway work, for example, aspired to leave their usual careers for a full-time life on the rails. Where volunteers had been drawn from among unemployed workers, however, such as for labouring work, employers were enticed by the prospect of replacing unionists with non-unionists.

If it was hard to attack the unions wholesale, however, many reps and activists fell victim to the bosses' revenge. Jimmy Matthews was the union rep at the Trent Motor Traction company and the last man to report back to work, whereupon he was told that he had been sacked.[7] An Aberdeen blacksmith returned to the company where he had worked for nine years to be told they now considered him an 'incompetent workman'. He happened to also be the union's branch secretary at the firm. He was still unemployed several months later.[8]

Victimisation was naturally worse where union organisation was weaker. For the TGWU, this meant on the trams and in commercial road transport. At the extreme end of the spectrum, W. T. Underwood's Derbyshire bus company simply sacked every worker, including a significant number of women, who had joined the union during the strike.[9] As there was no tradition of organisation there, he got away with it, but the action led to a boycott of his buses and even an attempt by the local labour movement to set up a rival company to employ the sacked workers. Tilling's Buses in London effectively derecognised the TGWU, as did several Conservative-leaning local authorities.[10] By the end of May Bevin estimated that 1,900 of his members on trams and buses had lost their jobs, and around another 1,000 in road haulage where the union's position was weak.[11]

Those outside the core industries who had joined the strike in sympathy were at greater risk of victimisation. The National Union of Vehicle Builders reported 225 cases of victimisation spread across many firms. Isolated strikers with no organisation behind them could be picked off, like Jack Waldon, the only trade unionist at the massive Mazawattee Tea Company processing site in South London, who was sacked after refusing to tear up his membership card upon reporting back to work.[12]

Victimisation extended beyond the workplaces directly involved in the strike, as those who had volunteered for the workers' cause found. In Sunderland a Miss Baker of the paperworkers' union was sacked by her employer of eight years despite being the senior machine minder in her workshop. This was because during the strike she had volunteered in the production of the local edition of the *British Worker*. Thomas Summerbell, the printer of the paper, noted that the male volunteers, who were members of the more powerful printers' unions, had no trouble.[13] Dorothy Clark was dismissed from her teaching job and blacklisted for her role in producing the *Birmingham Worker*, despite a petition from her pupils affirming that they had no knowledge of her political views in the classroom.[14] In a similar case, Communist activist Marjorie Pollitt was dismissed from her teaching job by the London County Council despite the support of prominent Labour politicians.[15] By supporting the unions' outrageous attack on the constitution, these women workers had transgressed the boundaries of respectable behaviour and were punished.

By the day after the strike was called off it became clear that, broadly speaking, employers wanted to force their workers into a humiliating admission of wrongdoing, attack the 'closed shop' – whereby everyone in a workplace was a union member – where it existed by insisting that unionists come back to work alongside non-unionists, and enforce compulsory arbitration before strikes in future. This was unacceptable to a rank-and-file who did not consider that they had been beaten. Plaistow Council of Action summed up the feeling on the ground to the General Council:

> All employers are adopting the same methods which are briefly this:
> They will employ who they like.
> Employment of those who have been blacklegging.
> Treating T.U. Officials with contempt and in some cases ordering them off the premises…
> DANGER! Confusion exists among <u>all workers</u>. It is essential that you send along definite information.
> General feeling <u>no</u> resumption of work <u>until all resume together</u>. No victimisation & unconditionally.
> Please reply quickly. <u>Urgent</u>![16]

Throughout the evening on 12 May and the following morning, protests poured into Eccleston Square from trade unionists around the country. 'Complete dissatisfaction in all grades,' wired the Burnley Central Strike Committee. 'Victimisation and new terms of employment being insisted in all trades. Demand immediate resumption of full general strike at once.'[17] Strike committees in places as varied as Oxford, Stockton-on-Tees, Harrogate, and March pledged themselves to continue the strike.

In Edinburgh, the student and future Labour minister Jennie Lee remembered: 'That evening, while the Central Strike Committee attended to the last funeral rites on the floor above us, we younger ones were huddled together in a corner of our improvised office, stunned and listless, demoralised by the utter fiasco of it all. We ended the day with a cursing competition. I was shocked by the language I suddenly discovered I knew.'[18]

The grassroots posed two separate but closely related demands. Firstly, there was the position that work should not be resumed until victimisation of strikers had been overturned and volunteer replacement workers turned out. This latter feeling was almost universal, far beyond just the areas where the left had a strong influence. It might seem vindictive to modern trade unionists, the vast majority of whom work alongside non-union members every day. But it was not simply motivated by personal hostility towards volunteers. In an era of extreme job insecurity in which sackings and layoffs could happen at any time, the 'closed shop' was a key line of defence. Allowing it to be broken would create a divide-and-rule environment on the shop floor.

Secondly, there was the more radical stance that the strike should be called back on until victory, and even extended to all workers who had not yet been called out. Anger at the General Council's partial approach had been present since the beginning of the strike and now exploded to the surface with demands for the whole movement to be mobilised to defend trade union agreements. At Coventry, where victimisation was reported to be widespread and few had returned to work, the Council of Action pressed the TUC to call out all workers. Hammersmith reported that the situation locally was 'intolerable', with LGOC workers being forced to accept lower wages and longer hours, and urged similar action.[19]

The contradiction that had emerged in the trade union movement in the 1920s – that the more radical wing had pushed for stronger central control – now came to the surface and was well expressed by Tom Garnett of the Sheffield Central Disputes Committee:

We feel that whilst there may have been adequate reason for the decision of the General Council to call off the National Strike, such reason is not contained in the Prime Minister's speech to the House, or in the Press Reports, and whilst we attach little value to the latter normally, the silence of the General Council is ominous when taken in conjunction with these reports. Those of us who had hoped for much from Central Control by the General Council are sadly disappointed at what appears to have been their weakness at a crucial moment, and some of us at any rate are yet hoping that the position can be satisfactorily explained, and the action of the General Council justified.[20]

The radical elements could not extend the strike on their own, and largely confined themselves to appeals to the trade union leaders. There were only some attempts to rally an alternative grassroots leadership. Sheffield circulated a resolution deprecating the calling-off of the strike to other industrial centres and urged them to put pressure on Eccleston Square for a resumption, but stopped short of suggesting that the strike committees themselves should begin to act on their own authority. Charles Flynn of the radical Durham and Northumberland committee wanted the strike to continue until convicted pickets were granted an amnesty – a demand that was unlikely to be taken up by the TUC or fulfilled by the government in any short amount of time – but even he asked for the General Council's permission for the strike committee to remain in existence to coordinate this.[21]

This call for a huge extension of the strike to defend the status quo ante was unsuccessful, but the pressure did have some impact. The unions held most of their members out and, in an ill-tempered exchange with Bevin in Downing Street in the evening, the War Secretary Worthington-Evans accused the TUC of effectively having called the strike back on. Bevin did not deny this but drew a distinction between 'the strike against the constitution, as you put it' and 'a constitutional strike to defend our wages and agreements'.[22] The following afternoon of 13 May the General Council issued a 'manifesto' which, while stopping far short of acceding to the demands of the grassroots, acknowledged the situation on the ground:

Peace depends upon employers abstaining from attempts at victimisation. It depends upon their declining to follow the example some are setting of using this position to attack the position of trade unionism... The Government, if it means what the Prime Minister said, must stop this attack on trade unionism. It must demand that the employers abstain from victimisation. Unless this obligation is fulfilled the trade unions will have no alternative but to resist to the uttermost.[23]

***

By the evening of 13 May there were more workers on strike that day than any previous. Some had returned to work to find themselves working with blacklegs and walked out again. Others in the 'second line' had only just come out that day. The leadership of ASLEF had met and declared an all-out national strike, and Bevin had wired all TGWU area secretaries instructing them to take an 'all in or all out' position.[24] The instructions from the centre, combined with the determination of the grassroots, were decisive. Effectively, a second general strike had begun.

Both the government and the TUC teetered on a precipice. The former had proclaimed victory but now faced an even more organised and militant working-class movement that saw itself as engaged in a battle for the very survival of trade unionism. The latter could feel its control of the movement, hitherto almost unquestioned, suddenly beginning to slip away.

For the revolutionary left, it was the opportunity they had been waiting for. Despite the forces of the Communists being numerically minuscule and the number of targeted arrests that had been carried out against them in the past days, conditions were in some ways favourable for them. Their activists were playing leading roles in many important strike committees. They were a coherent and organised group and capable of disseminating their propaganda in challenging circumstances, and they had a significant following in the major coalfields. Most importantly, workers who were facing returns to work under humiliating conditions were in no mood to take this lying down, giving the Communist Party a much bigger potential audience for its ideas among moderate trade unionists.

Realising belatedly that the left-wing members of the General Council had fallen in behind the moderates, the Communists finally proposed the creation of an alternative leadership through a delegate conference of strike committees. Nothing like this had ever been posed before; no groundwork had been laid for this demand. The logistics of pulling off such an event while under state harassment, with trade unionists busy fighting local defensive battles, would have been difficult to say the least. The party was not in a particularly healthy state at the end of the strike. Some of the leaders arrested in October were still in prison and many hundreds of members had been arrested under the emergency regulations since 3 May, mainly for producing and distributing material 'likely to cause disaffection'. Tom Mann, the face of the Minority Movement, missed the strike altogether, as he was in Russia meeting with fellow communist trade unionists.

Some local party branches were able to produce and circulate material, such as this from the Sheffield District Committee on 13 May:

> The responsibility for this debacle rests on the shoulders of a 'Right wing' General Council and the timid Parliamentary leaders of the Labour Party, who anxious for peace on any terms, were conducting their defeatist propaganda behind the scenes.
>
> So-called 'left' wingers cannot escape their responsibility. Not a single protest has been heard against the negotiations that were being carried on during the dispute. Not a single condemnation has been voiced by these phase-mongers [sic] against the treacherous decision calling off the General Strike without any terms and relying on a Tory Government to be merciful...
>
> Treachery will come home to roost. Those responsible must be impeached. At every meeting of organised workers the demand must be raised for an immediate Special Trades Union Congress and a thorough spring cleaning of the whole of the Labour machinery.[25]

Ultimately, though, the CPGB could only add its voice to the chorus of outrage. The second general strike was primarily driven not by Communists but by a much broader layer of trade union militants. In Manchester a huge demonstration of railwaymen marched through the city demanding unconditional reinstatement. On the Great Western Railway it was reported that 'the position is no better than yesterday – and the change if any is for the worse'.[26] Southampton dockers reported being 'more solid than a week ago' as workers who had returned came back out.[27] In town after town, mass meetings were held at which workers resolved, almost unanimously, to remain on strike. Resumptions of work only occurred where employers unequivocally guaranteed reinstatement on old terms.

In the industrial areas on 13–14 May, the mood was sullen and ominous. In the highly charged atmosphere crowds once again mobilised and there were outbreaks of violence. Thousands gathered in Swindon to attack the first trams back on the roads and successfully stopped the service. Railwaymen in the town resolved to stay out not just for full reinstatement of strikers, but for the release of everyone who had been arrested under the emergency regulations.[28] In Gloucester seven dockers were arrested after police broke up a crowd blocking a canal bridge. Subsequently supporters gathered outside the local police station and were again dispersed by force.[29] East London, where hardly anyone had yet returned to work, was patrolled by police and armoured cars. Perhaps flush with their victory or perhaps nervous about the explosive possibilities of the situation, Poplar police violently broke up a rally outside the town hall before raiding the local NUR office. The mayor, who was a railwayman himself, and a local vicar were among forty who suffered wounds from the police batons.[30] The situation in the North-West, where the numbers of pickets were actually growing, alarmed the police, who urged the government to hold off on disbanding the CCR, and the chief constable of Cardiff enrolled another 150 special constables as he expected the situation to deteriorate 'if employers insist on unconditional surrender'.[31]

The adjournment debate in the House of Commons on the evening of 13 May was therefore held in a tenor of utmost seriousness. Ramsay MacDonald reiterated that both the king and the prime minister had called for the country to come together the previous day, and contrasted this with the triumphalist tone of the *British Gazette* and the attitude of the employers:

> We have had industrial disputes before; we have had people threatening to crush out trade unionism… But common sense came over them, the common sense of both parties, so that when peace came, and the fight was over, the first thing that the combatants on both sides did was to shake hands. That has not happened now. That has not happened in the newspapers, it has not happened in the streets, it has not happened in some wild

and heady demonstrations, it has not happened regarding the conditions imposed upon the men who have presented themselves for work... Threats are the last thing I should think of, but let there be no mistake about this. If there is any attempt to smash up trade unionism, if any section of the country, or any foolish person in the country, thinks that after the events of last week and yesterday he can scrape the faces of trade unionists in the dust, he is very much mistaken. We want a settlement. We want no guerrilla warfare to begin, and to go on and on and on. We want no resentment left behind. But if that is going to be avoided, it has got to be avoided by treating men as independent, self-respecting working men, who are not going to crawl back, and have not got to be treated as human beings with the yoke of absolute subordination riveted on to their necks.[32]

In response, Baldwin defended his actions and dismissed as 'propaganda' the idea that there was a general offensive to drive down wages, but felt compelled in the face of the situation to make a remarkably unequivocal concession: 'I will not countenance any attack on the part of any employers to use this present occasion for trying in any way to get reductions in wages below those in force before the strike commenced or any increase of hours.'[33]

The prime minister's intervention went a long way to calming the immediate situation but did not commit the government to support the immediate reinstatement of all strikers, as this would have meant going back on the guarantees they had made to the volunteers during the strike. It did, however, give impetus to efforts to find settlements in the major industries where workers were still out.

***

It was the settlement on the railways that broke the logjam and allowed for a general return to work. The 'big four' railway companies, who essentially saw themselves as the victims of an unauthorised wildcat strike, initially took a fairly belligerent attitude. Great Western had issued a circular to managers on 9 May stating that returning strikers should be informed that they are only rehired 'on the understanding that you are not relieved of the consequences of having broken your contract of service with the Company'. Some in the management of the 'big four' wanted to go further and re-employ strikers only on base-rate terms and conditions regardless of their length of service.[34]

On 13 May Cramp told the companies he could not prevail on his members to return under these conditions. The employers realised that to impose these terms would extend the national rail strike. Many of the few railwaymen who had returned that morning walked out again the following day, and with the febrile situation in the country, other workers would probably follow.

There were twenty-four hours of negotiations between the three main rail unions (NUR, ASLEF, and RCA) and the 'big four' companies. The railway settlement that was reached on 14 May represented a significant climb down from the employers' initial offensive but was still a bitter pill for the unions to swallow. Strikers, except those guilty of violence or intimidation, would be taken back on their old terms in order of seniority. The attempt to drive down the wages and conditions of the railwaymen had been defeated, but with several major caveats. Firstly, the companies reserved 'their legal rights to claim damages arising out of the strike from strikers and others responsible'. The unions had to acknowledge that they had committed a wrongful act by calling the strike, and would not strike in future without negotiating with the companies. Crucially, the unions also agreed 'to give no support of any kind to their members who take any unauthorised action'.[35] Railwaymen, except those who had not struck, also lost their guaranteed weekly working hours, with the situation to be reviewed as the coal lockout continued.

Special punishment was meted out to those in supervisory white-collar roles who had joined the strike, many of whom were demoted as a result. In the eyes of the companies, these salaried men should have known better than to throw their lot in with the unions. A stationmaster recalled he and his striking colleagues being 'banished to the far ends of the system, put to humiliation, lectured and reproached by the top bosses'.[36] Most damaging for the railwaymen was the lack of any commitment to a timescale for re-employment. The companies maintained that, as traffic would take a long time to get back to normal levels, they would not be able to reinstate everyone. As the coal lockout continued this was put to devastating effect for many. Towards the end of the year, Thomas reported to the Labour Party conference that 200,000 railwaymen were working part-time, and a further 45,000 had not been taken back at all since the end of the general strike.[37]

It was not immediately clear that the men would accept these terms and as late as the afternoon of 15 May the Supply and Transport Committee was informed that on the LNER 'there will be no services tomorrow and the Company are hoping that the men will thus have time to think matters over, and that the Unions will bring their influence to bear'. Railway pickets were still out at Darlington as late as 16 May.[38] Ultimately, though, with their leaders ordering a return to work, there was no rank-and-file organisation among railway workers that was strong enough to stem the tide. By the end of the weekend railwaymen were reporting for duty across the country, their unions intact but, in many cases, their own futures uncertain. The union leaders thanked the companies for showing enough magnanimity to stop short of attempting to smash them, and Thomas went so far as to recommend in a wireless broadcast that other employers should follow the example of the settlement they had reached.

It would prove harder to come to an agreement on the docks, where workers were more accustomed to longer strikes than the railwaymen. Liverpool was the only major port to see a quick return to work, as a result of the Docks and Harbour Board discharging their volunteers on 13 May. The Merseyside Council of Action pressed other employers to follow their example, but this fell on deaf ears in an industry that was addicted to casualised and semi-casualised labour. As soon as the strike had been called off, TGWU London area secretary Tom Scoulding had posted an unequivocal notice at the entrances to the London Docks:

> To all members of Docks, Waterways, and Clerical Groups
> Dear Sirs and Brothers
> <u>National Strike</u>
>   Under the terms of the settlement reached by the TUC today it was decided that members resume work at a time to be arranged by employers and Union Officials.
>   As we have not yet met Port Employers regarding time of starting work, a complete reinstatement of all members and the immediate dismissal of free labour, there will be no resumption of work until an agreement upon these three main essentials is reached.

All maintenance, docks, clerical, waterways and other grades of workers attached to the docks, wharves, and river are therefore instructed to remain out on strike until definite instructions to the contrary are received from the undersigned.

Yours fraternally

J. T. Scoulding, Area Secretary

F. Thompson, Docks Group Secretary

T.W. Condon, Clerical Group Secretary[39]

The London dockers did not fully resume work until 17 May. In a similar humiliation to that endured by the railway union, the TGWU had to admit it had broken its agreement with the company and commit not to call any strike in future without first exhausting the conciliation process. This was somewhat ameliorated, however, by the fact that all permanent men would be taken back at their old rates. This agreement was the model by which work was resumed in the ports. Bristol dockers, who stayed out until 21 May, also won, after a personal intervention from Bevin in his home port, a no-victimisation pledge and a cap on the number of volunteers that would be employed.[40] Dockers on Teesside were among the last to go back, as the employers initially stated they could only offer day-to-day work due to the coal trade having ground to a halt. This the union refused to accept, and work only resumed, on pre-existing terms, on 25 May.[41]

The two big settlements on the railways and the docks became an example for other industries. In the flour-milling industry, workers secured a return to work on their old terms on 20 May, but they would only be taken on as and when required, and the companies reserved the right to keep on those who had been employed during the strike.

Union power was perhaps worst-hit in the printing trades where in some parts of the country support for the strike had been less than solid. Workers were reinstated on an as-and-when basis and hours were to be cut in order to facilitate more men being taken back. Many printers abandoned their practice of only working in fully unionised shops or tore up their union membership altogether. The *Guardian* created its own company union with a non-strike agreement.[42] At other employers, union meetings were banned during work time, and, in revenge for the *Daily*

Mail incident, it was stressed that any union 'interference' with the press would not be countenanced.[43]

Although the return to work was broadly settled by such national agreements, in some areas, solidarity action against victimisation held strong for a few more days. This was particularly the case where local authorities had attempted to dismiss striking tramwaymen who tended to be less heavily unionised than their fellows on the docks and railways. Merseyside, which had been remarkably quiet during the strike, saw local railway union branches along with other workers stay out for several days in an effort to secure the reinstatement of tramwaymen in Birkenhead.[44]

In Hull, where the strike had been marked by police violence and bitter feeling more than most other towns, hundreds of tramway men had been dismissed by the Corporation. TGWU organiser G. E. Farmery complained of having to deal with 'the most stupid and tricky set of employers that could possibly exist'.[45] In spite of their national settlement, local railwaymen resolved to stay out until everyone was reinstated.

Hundreds of volunteers had been hired on the trams and promised that their jobs would be made permanent if they wished. A similar situation existed in the city's power station. 'We are not going to allow the unions to dictate who we should take back,' one councillor put it bluntly.[46] The majority on the council's Tramways Committee even voted to expel the two Labour members who had aligned themselves with the unions. On 16 May an agreement was reached that was largely a defeat for the union; the only concession they had wrung was that previous employees would be considered for future vacancies before new people. The committee, however, shorn of its Labour members, retained the right to refuse employment and effectively achieved its goal of turning the tramway into an 'open shop'.[47]

As late as 22 May Farmery claimed that 350 tram workers had not been reinstated. As well as fighting this rearguard action, he still kept his eyes on helping the miners, now the general strike had been abandoned. He informed Bevin that imported coal was due to be landed at the port next week, but it would be impossible to persuade members not to handle it unless the railwaymen did the same.[48] The united front was broken.

Eastbourne Council took a similar 'volunteers first' approach regarding reinstatement at their municipal bus company. This sparked a decision among the town's three thousand striking workers to stand by the busmen. Here too, though, the workers failed to get the volunteers discharged and had to reconcile themselves to working alongside them. By 22 May they had, in the words of the local paper, 'resumed work with an alacrity and a desire to regain their tarnished character that does them every credit'.[49]

Unions did their best to fight for reinstatement, but in depot after depot and factory after factory the closed shop was prised open. In the conditions of mass unemployment that prevailed across much of the country, there were plenty of people happy to take jobs as non-unionists. It would take many months and years after the strike for the shop-floor strength of the unions to be built back up.

***

While the trade union movement struggled to retain its cohesion and licked its wounds, the other side basked in its triumphs. 'The Nation Wins' was the verdict of the *Daily Mirror*, still appearing in a truncated four-page format.[50] The feted volunteers now reaped their reward in the thanks of a grateful nation. This, at least, was the intended story. Dinners and banquets were held in their honour by employers, Rotarians, and private members' clubs. Certificates of thanks and even medals were bestowed on the veterans of the strikebreaking effort. The Great Western Railway handed out over one thousand solid silver ashtrays.[51]

Never since 1926 has such a large section of the population been mobilised to undermine a social struggle being waged by their fellow citizens. The praise for their service, good humour, and cheerful countenance was effusive. 'Bless them!' wrote one woman to the *Yorkshire Evening Post*. 'They have saved England from panic.'[52] There was relief at the reassertion of normality, that the nation's innate moderation had triumphed again. The defeated trade unionists, now no longer a sinister revolutionary threat, were spoken of magnanimously and praised, in the main, for their good behaviour. They were a proud army led into a futile battle by generals who should have known better.

It was the volunteers and not the strikers who, in this rapidly crystallising interpretation of events, represented the best of Britain. Those unemployed workers who had stepped up should of course be kept on, as they had now proved their worth as against the idle trade unionist.[53]

'By your efforts and sacrifice you are proving your loyalty to King and Country,' wrote the Chairman of the LGOC to his volunteers, 'and carrying for yourselves the gratitude and admiration of every loyal citizen of the Empire'. At his Chiswick depot, where buses had to be taken out under armed escort during the strike, a morale-boosting newsletter had been produced by white-collar staff for the volunteers. It signed off in a hopeful tone, optimistic that nothing like the nine days in May would ever happen again:

> For our own part, in bidding you God's Speed we thank you for all you have done for our Company. We lose you with regret, but that regret loses its sharp edge in welcoming back our old men. Neither they nor us have been crushed by the small minority. Neither they nor us will recriminate. This generation will see no recurrence of a General Strike expedient. We will relegate it to the limbo of forgotten things turning our faces hopefully to the future.[54]

THE LEVER BREAKS.

The Liberal *Chronicle* satirises the failed revolution.

13

THE EXPERIENCE OF DEFEAT

In any prolonged struggle between labour and capital, where both sides were fully organised, labour would have to give way, as the capitalist was more likely to hold out in a struggle in which starvation was the ultimate factor.

- Sir Adam Nimmo, *Colliery Guardian*, 1913

Mundus the Wolf said to the shepherds: 'Why should there not be peace between you and us, seeing that both depend on the sheep for a living so our interests are the same?' And with this most of the shepherds agreed, for they thought: 'Why should we have the danger and trouble of fighting the wolves who speak so pleasantly?'

- Preface to *Mond's Manacles* by Arthur Cook, 1928

When the TUC capitulated, the miners were left with the stark choice of whether to fight on alone.

The strength of the General Council's faith in the Samuel memorandum – in the integrity of the 'British gentleman who had been Governor of Palestine' – meant that they could hardly conceive of a situation where the MFGB would not accept it. In reality, they were never really given the choice. Several members of the Cabinet including the minister of labour and minister for mines urged Baldwin to disown the memorandum as soon as the strike was called off. For them, adopting proposals so wholeheartedly endorsed by the TUC seemed to hand over victory to the unions.

Upon receiving Cook and Smith at Downing Street on the evening of 13 May, Baldwin stressed that the government was not at all bound by Samuel and would, in fact, be presenting its own proposals. The following day the minister of labour published these. There would be immediate wage cuts and a National Wages Board that would fix rates on a district-by-district basis. Nationalisation, either of the pits or of royalties, was ruled out, but the government committed to legislate for some reorganisation of the industry.[1] Of course these proposals were unacceptable to the miners. The owners, having ridden out the storm of the general strike, saw no reason to give any ground on the question of reorganisation. All the government had achieved was a way forward that re-established the gridlock existing before the general strike.

Ultimately the TUC had never really shared the miners' position of absolute opposition to wage cuts. The miners, for their part, may have begrudgingly accepted the General Council's leadership over the general strike but they reserved the right to make their own final decision on any terms. Not unreasonably, as the representative body of the workers concerned, and having been shut out of talks, the MFGB needed time to discuss any proposed settlements. On 19 May a delegate conference of the MFGB met and rejected the government's proposals. For their part, the mineowners were even more stubborn, refusing to accept any National Wages Board. Underscoring their long-held opposition to any compromise, the owners went further. 'It is time to state plainly', they informed the government, 'that a number of the conclusions in the report of the Samuel commission...would spell ruin to British industry.'[2] Just as the last sections of strikers were returning to work, it became clear to everyone that the lockout in the coalfield would continue. At the end of May, the government reactivated the emergency regulations.

Bitter recriminations ensued. There was no prospect of the TUC calling the strike on again and, while the heart of the rank and file remained with the miners' cause, no unofficial strike movement developed. Workers who had just experienced the crushing realisation of defeat were hardly likely to walk off the job again. This was compounded by the fact that such action would be unofficial and likely unlawful. On top of this, many had been taken back under agreements by which the unions had acknowledged that the general strike was a 'wrongful act' and employers explicitly reserved their rights to punish any worker for breaking contract. With this hanging over their heads, it is hardly surprising that the semi-official action that had immediately followed the strike did not organically develop into widespread unofficial action.

The union leaders did, however, feel pressure from their members, angry at what was considered by many to be a major act of betrayal and breach of the principle of solidarity. Criticism of the conduct of the dispute came from far beyond the miners' ranks. The Independent Labour Party's *New Leader* alleged 'faulty preparation, weak leadership, and an end unworthy of this great effort of loyalty'. The ETU made public its criticism of the partial nature of the strike call that had caused its members such trouble. One Dewsbury Trades Council delegate summed up the General Council's actions with a typically economical Yorkshire sentiment: 'Simply daft.'[3] Even Jimmy Thomas faced a raft of criticism at the NUR's July conference but, after a two-hour speech lambasting a supposed communist plot in the union, received an overwhelming vote of confidence from the delegates.[4]

In response to grassroots dissatisfaction in the TGWU Bevin wrote to his members to disassociate himself from the fiasco:

> With regard to the calling off of the strike you can take it from me that we, who were not on the Negotiating Committee, were assured that the Samuel Document would be accepted, that the Lockout notices would be withdrawn, and that methods of resumption would be discussed forthwith; and, when these assurances had been given us, we naturally felt we had accomplished the purpose for which the strike was called.[5]

A few weeks later, surer of himself, Bevin had changed his tune somewhat, telling a TGWU branch secretary that the whole trade union movement would have been 'smashed to atoms' if the strike had continued another two or three days.[6] In an article for the union's journal, he accused the miners of failing to appreciate the sacrifices the TGWU had made for them. He defended both the calling of the strike and its abandonment as necessary and inevitable. In view of the positions of the coalowners and the government, Bevin argued, there would have been widespread unofficial action 'which would have produced anarchy in the Movement' if the TUC had not grasped the nettle. But he rather contradicted himself by also describing the strike as a spontaneous and emotional response to the lockout, for which preparations could not have been made.[7]

From within the TUC itself, criticism was more muted but it did exist. Margaret Bondfield blamed the confusion over permits on a lack of prior consultation with trades councils.[8] Others expressed dissatisfaction with specific elements of how the dispute had been run. The most common criticism was of the decision to call out printworkers. It came to be regarded in hindsight as a damaging own goal that alienated public opinion and left much of the country at the mercy of government propaganda.

Short of a strike, what could the movement now do to help the miners? Millions of tonnes of imported coal were pouring into the country, and each shipful unloaded in British ports weakened the miners' position. The prospect of a coal embargo, which had been mooted in the run-up to Red Friday, was raised again by the MFGB in mid-July. When the rail unions rejected this, the MFGB did not take up the matter with the General Council, acknowledging that such a discussion would be futile.[9]

In the end, the wider movement's backing for the miners was strictly moral and financial. In the straitened climate, the financial backing was significant. Many unions had suffered serious hits during the short strike, particularly those that paid strike pay and out-of-work benefits – over £2.6 million in all. ASLEF, the NUR, and the RCA had all spent over half of their funds by the end of May, made worse by the fact that so many railworkers were now working short-time. The TGWU's funds had totally run dry and the union had gone into debt in order to keep up full strike pay and victimisation payments.[10] 'We could have kept our money,' wrote Bevin, 'but we would have lost our soul.'[11]

The MFGB's proposal for a compulsory levy on all union members was rejected, but some unions whose own finances had taken a battering during the general strike still dug deep for the miners. The TGWU and NUR had spent £1 million each in strike pay, and total union reserve funds declined by a third.[12] By August, the TUC itself had donated £46,000, although this was dwarfed by £250,000 from the Soviet trade unions which, unlike the General Council, the MFGB had no qualms about accepting.[13] This predictably outraged the Tory right, who raised hue and cry about 'Russian gold'. Moves to prevent these donations aroused opposition from an unlikely source. The king's private secretary wrote to Joynson-Hicks:

> His Majesty is sure you and the Government will differentiate between money sent in the aid of the General Strike (to which we could unquestionably take exception) and that contributed on behalf of those suffering from the Coal Strike [sic]. It would be disastrous if the Government's action could in any way justify a cry from the Socialist party that the former were attempting to stop financial aid from Russia or from any other country to save the miners' women and children from starvation.[14]

With the threat of revolution nipped in the bud, the miners had reverted from nefarious agents of anarchy and chaos to honest poor working men to be pitied.

***

Seeing the miners struggling on their own had a profound effect on other workers, dismayed that standing in solidarity with them had come to naught. The union leaders could not ignore these feelings and, as accusations of betrayal began to take hold, looked to justify their actions. A special conference of union executives was proposed by the General Council for 25 June, at which the TUC's official report of the strike would be discussed. Citrine hoped this process would reveal widespread support for the manner in which the General Council had conducted the strike. Surprisingly, the miners urged the postponement of this conference. When it became clear that the lockout was going to be a long one, and would still require the support of fellow trade unionists if it was to be broken, they wanted to maintain a veneer of unity. The miners were, at this stage, holding on to the slim hope of persuading the TUC to back a coal embargo and thought that a public airing of the movement's internal fissures would be counterproductive.

The exception was Cook, who initially pulled no punches in his criticism of the General Council. He told a rally on 23 May on his home turf in South Wales:

> We have been fighting not just against the Government and the owners but against a number of Labour leaders... I have had experience of being bullied in colliery offices; I have had experience in 1920 and 1921 of meeting various Prime Ministers, but never have we been bullied by the employers or the Government to the extent that we were bullied by certain trade union leaders to accept a reduction in wages.[15]

In a polemical pamphlet, *The Nine Days*, Cook expanded on his argument. He claimed that the change of personnel on TUC committees in 1925, when Thomas returned to the General Council and Pugh became chairman of the Industrial Committee, hampered efforts to prepare for the general strike. Most damningly Cook argued that by conceding on the principle of wage cuts even before the strike had been declared, the General Council had gone against the agreed position of the whole trade union movement. He blamed Thomas and the Negotiating Committee for immediately looking for a pretext to call the strike off, which they readily found in the noncommittal discussions with Herbert Samuel. 'They had been prepared to force *us* to retreat in order that *they* might carry out the retreat they longed for. When the truculence of the Tory Cabinet thrust them willy nilly into the General Strike they had not ceased in their endeavour to "smooth it over".'[16]

The TUC agreed to postpone the conference until after the lockout, on the provision that Cook's pamphlet was withdrawn from sale and the MFGB ceased public attacks on the General Council. The left, therefore, lost both the urgency of their criticisms and, in Cook, their loudest voice.

Despite this uneasy truce, as the lockout dragged on it did not take long for bad feelings to resurface. ASLEF general secretary John Bromley had been considered a left-winger on the General Council before the strike, but during the nine days he fell in behind Thomas in regarding it as a futile endeavour. In the July issue of his union's journal, Bromley laid out a view of events highly critical of the miners' leaders for sticking to their position without regard to the sacrifices made by the rest of the movement. The miners considered Bromley to have broken the truce of silence they had agreed and never forgave him. Cook was soon publicly criticising the TUC again and, speaking at an ILP summer school in August, squarely blamed them for selling out the miners.

At the TUC's annual congress in Bournemouth in September temperatures boiled over. The press reported Bromley as saying the miners were paying a lavish £1 a day to each of their sixty delegates. This infuriated Cook, who attacked Bromley in the press and sent him a private letter calling him a 'dirty swine not for to be in the Labour Movement. Surely you have done enough against the miners, their wives and children without adding insult to injury. Remember we shall not forget.'

When Bromley stood to speak in favour of the appeal for the miners' relief fund there was almost a fistfight on the conference floor. The MFGB delegates got up and walked out, singing the 'Red Flag'. Bromley denied making his remarks but in his response insinuated that Cook was in receipt of personal funds from Soviet Russia. His letter reveals the strength of feeling and extent of the division between the two leaders by this point:

> You assure me the miners will not forget, but I am afraid that they have forgotten, or at least their leaders have, many things which my Union and I have in the past done to help them. They have forgotten our generous contributions of the past to the sufferers of mining disasters. They have forgotten that although our Union was not part of the Triple Alliance in 1921, it readily responded and joined with that Federation in support of the miners... They have forgotten that in August 1925, my Executive and I took the lead in declaring that our members should not move any coal under any circumstances should the miners be locked out, which action with that of the other railways and transport unions secured to the miners a Royal Commission and £23,000,000 subsidy... They have forgotten that our 62,000 members, with the exception of some 200 in all Great Britain, struck for a fortnight in support of the miners, and had no need to be anxious for the calling off of that strike, because they were as solid on the last day as they were on the first, and they assisted to win a magnificent victory, but that the crass stupidity of some of you threw it into the wind... let me tell you that I frankly think your management of the affairs of your Federation has been a disaster, and your noisy and untruthful attacks on members of the General Council, and on the members of the Unions

which have sacrificed so much in support of the miners, is beneath contempt, and your latest statements as to the paucity of the financial assistance given to the miners by other Unions is the measure of your lack of appreciation and gratitude to men who have sacrificed themselves on the altar of your infernal egotism.[17]

Cook withdrew his remarks. There was to be no reckoning at the Bournemouth congress, for Cook used his considerable influence to prevent the MFGB delegates voting for a Communist motion that would have forced a debate on the strike. Although his own denunciations of the TUC leaders had been fierce, Cook was not prepared for the movement to have the argument out in the open while the lockout was still on. He still, against all odds, hoped to rally the movement behind a proposal for a compulsory levy for the miners' hardship fund.[18] By this point, though, even that was a step too far for the TUC.

***

The lockout dragged through summer, the miners and their families sustained by donations from home and abroad, fundraising, and social activities in their communities. With impressive self-organisation, communities staged soup kitchens, carnivals, and processions as a spirit of solidarity spread across the coalfields. Local Labour Parties, co-operatives, and chapels came to the fore. Many thousands were fed every day in South Wales in canteens with fresh tablecloths and freshly cut flowers. There were concerts, sermons, and wedding celebrations in these improvised working-class institutions.[19] Miners' wives, who unlike their husbands were eligible for poor relief, suffered the indignity of going before the poor law guardians for the dreaded means test. By the summer 2.5 million people were claiming relief across England and Wales, including over eighty percent of families in some mining areas.[20]

The conditions that had prevailed across the country during the strike continued in the coalfields: heavy-handed policing, baton charges, tough sentences for pickets. One West Midlands picket reported:

Every colliery is protected by the police. We cannot get to the colliery. We cannot speak to anyone. We have no means of approaching them… We have prosecutions going on galore, every week, every day nearly, even women and children who are walking alongside these people [working miners] actually with a toy drum are taken before the magistrates and are convicted very readily.[21]

In Nottinghamshire the novelist D. H. Lawrence noted, somewhat disapprovingly, the role of women in confrontations with police and blacklegs: 'In the past they would have died of shame at having to go to court. But now, not at all. They had a little gang of women with them in the marketplace waving red flags and laughing loudly and using bad language... Good luck, old girl! Let 'em have it! Give it the bluebottles [police] in the neck!'[22]

Edith Cartwright was arrested for throwing a stone at a working miner outside Hatfield Main colliery, even though it was too dark for any real proof of the assailant's identity to be gathered. Her case became a *cause célèbre* for the movement as she was jailed along with her newborn baby who soon took ill.[23] Fortunately, both Edith and her baby survived. Upon her release in November after serving her month-long sentence she was received at a large rally at the Albert Hall, alongside Harry Pollitt, a Communist who had himself been recently released after twelve months in prison.[24]

Seeing the suffering around him, Arthur Cook refused his general secretary's salary, living on the same lock-out pay as other miners. He constantly toured the coalfield areas to keep up the miners' morale in a hectic schedule that took a serious toll on his physical health. As the weeks went on his voice, literally, began to crack and fade. Now convinced that there was no way the rest of the labour movement was going to come back to the field of battle, he began to look for a settlement.

In mid-July the clergy again proposed peace terms along the lines that they had sketched out during the general strike. Cook and the majority of his executive proposed their acceptance to an MFGB that was increasingly divided between militant and moderate elements. 'Is it leadership to sit still and drift to disaster?' he asked his delegates. 'I say if this conference believes we can fight another six weeks I will do my best, but as long as I am Secretary I ask you as I ask myself to face facts, to come out of the struggle not demoralised, but to retain confidence in each other and not to tell everyone that labour is dead.'²⁵ The miners rejected the bishops' terms by a slim majority in a secret ballot. By that point the government had already repudiated them, with Baldwin telling the clergy in confidence that he considered the miners and owners to be 'equally stupid and equally bigoted'.²⁶

Churchill, despite his bellicosity during the general strike, had become more amenable to the miners' case after its defeat. Having seen off the threat to the constitution, he was now keen on pursuing a settlement. As chancellor, he was concerned about the effect of a prolonged lockout on the public purse. The number of people claiming poor relief rose by a staggering 337% throughout the summer, mostly the dependants of locked-out miners.²⁷ The Empire lost £400 million in trade over the course of the year; £42 million was spent on imported coal. Along with others in the Cabinet, Churchill began to settle on the idea of lengthening the working day as a solution to the industry's impasse. '[The miner] is not going to get a lot of sympathy if he is obliged to work as long as the railwayman,' noted Neville Chamberlain.²⁸ This was politically appealing as it seemed more palatable than just reducing wages, but it would potentially cost the state even more from resulting unemployment.

Baldwin, content with his victory in May, retreated to his default *laissez faire* approach to industrial relations and was uninterested in expending much energy on finding a compromise. He was reluctantly won round to introduce the necessary legislation to lengthen the working day in the mines back to eight hours before going on his summer holiday and leaving Churchill in charge of the situation. 'May I say this in perfect frankness,' Baldwin wrote, exasperated, 'the frightfully difficult task I have to do is to wean this great industry from the breasts of the State, where it has been for ten years, and until that industry is on its own feet, we shall have this recurring over and over again.'²⁹

The passage of the coal mines bill lengthening the working day to eight hours severely damaged the miners' already weak position. Aware of the prime minister's attitude, the mineowners were obstinate as ever. They saw the possibility of breaking up their nemesis MFGB as a national organisation. So disgusted was Churchill at the owners' attitude that he purportedly remarked to a colleague: 'I am all on [the miners'] side now.'³⁰ The Fabian academic R. H. Tawney warned the civil servant Tom Jones that the owners' determination for a complete and humiliating victory could turn the coalfields into an 'internal Ireland' and thousands more miners into revolutionaries.[31]

In September the miners' resolve began to falter in places. George Spencer, general secretary of the Nottinghamshire Miners' Association and MP for Broxtowe, opened negotiations with local coalowners for a return to work in his district, a move for which he was expelled from both the MFGB and the Labour Party. The 'Spencer Union' attracted little support in other areas but gave impetus to miners who wanted to go back. In some places the bosses began setting up their own 'company unions'. For a dangerous moment it looked like the survival of the MFGB itself was at stake. Seeing the writing on the wall, Cook successfully worked to win the MFGB delegates round to the acceptance of a national agreement that would include wage cuts. Only the South Wales and Lancashire federations opposed this.

Cook, so often portrayed as an intransigent and uncompromising firebrand, ended up laying the groundwork for the miners to return to work in good order with some pride intact. He explained his thinking in military terms: 'I shall tell [the members] that we must have our Mons; a well-led army must retreat before a stronger army; we shall win like the British Army did – perhaps four years hence.'[32]

A government proposal that would have retained the principle of a national agreement in exchange for wage cuts was overwhelmingly rejected by miners in another national ballot, but the minority were feeling the strain and emboldened to start returning to the pits. Despite this, by mid-October over 200,000 miners were back at work. A last-ditch attempt by the MFGB to escalate the dispute by ordering the withdrawal of safety men, proposed by Nye Bevan, failed. This nuclear option was opposed by the safety men's own specialist unions and by a sizeable minority of the MFGB's own members.[33]

In November another proposal, which would see the dispute settled on the basis of district-by-district negotiations, was rejected by MFGB members but by a much smaller margin of 460,806 to 313,200. While this was quite a remarkable result given the months of hardship the miners had faced, it was enough to persuade the MFGB's conference that national unity had been broken, and they instructed the district federations to make terms. Across the coalfields men went back on varied conditions, almost all working eight hours a day for less pay. The minimum rates were pushed down to the levels of 1921. Scotland and Durham suffered particularly harsh cuts. The exceptions were the members of the Spencer Union in Nottinghamshire who, for their role in breaking the miners' national unity, were given raises of four shillings a week.[34] There was absolutely no commitment to industry reorganisation from the owners. They were once again the undisputed masters of their fiefdoms.

With the miners back at work, the way was clear for the long-awaited TUC special conference to be held. It would deal specifically with the question of whether to accept or reject the General Council's report of the strike. In the General Council's defiant words: 'The Council have no excuses to offer and no apologies to make for the conduct of the strike or for its termination.'[35] It had convinced itself that it had done everything it could for the miners and received only ingratitude. There could not have been better preparation for the struggle, it declared, because to prepare would have been to show its hand to the government. It could not have done better in negotiations because no side had accepted the Samuel report in good faith. And it could not have organised the strike better because it was an event with no precedent.

Not everyone agreed that the General Council had nothing to apologise for. Just before the conference, the Communist paper *Sunday Worker* published an interview with Arthur Cook. He quoted extracts of the TUC's draft report, and accused the General Council of keeping it a secret from the rank and file for too long. Citrine didn't take kindly to such reproaches:

> The *Sunday Worker* has kept up a barrage of glaring headlines asserting with every variety of emphasis that it was trying to obtain for the rank and file information which the General Council was trying to keep 'secret'. All the time you were aware that the Report, so far from being in any sense 'secret' was to be made public as soon as the responsible Executives of the Unions from whom the General Council had received its mandate for the National Strike had had an opportunity to consider it. The facts are so plain that no evasion on your part can extenuate your action.[36]

Citrine was supported by Robert Williams, the general manager of the *Daily Herald* and former Communist fellow-traveller, who told him somewhat hyperbolically: 'These people have no morals and no principles and appear to believe the most foul and unspeakable means justify their ends.'[37] Communists had previously been accepted as a radical, if troublesome, wing of a respectable labour movement. Now mainstream trade union leaders hardened their attitudes towards them, suspicious of what they saw as hysterical criticism and wrecking behaviour.

After many wars of words printed in the labour movement's press, the conference met on 20 January 1927. George Hicks, in the chair, appealed to the assembled trade unionists to look to the future and act as judge and jury over the past. Nevertheless, there were still strong criticisms to be made. After Hicks somewhat laboriously read the whole report verbatim to the hall, the questions poured in. Bevin was asked why workers were being called out at the same time preparations were being made to end the strike. He claimed a lack of communication between his SOC and the Negotiating Committee. An ASLEF member asked who had given assurances to the government at the outset of the strike that there would be no interference with food supplies, something the rail unions had vociferously opposed. H. H. Morton of the ETU asked if the General Council had overstepped its authority by calling the strike putting union executives in a position of having to call their members out without notice in contravention of their own rulebooks. This echoed the NSFU leader Havelock Wilson's legal case against his own members in the Astbury judgement. It was perhaps the relatively high level of victimisation experienced by ETU members that caused this resentment.

However, the General Council's loyalists soon grew exasperated with the barrage of questions from every direction. 'If this is going to be an inquest,' grumbled veteran dockers' leader James Sexton, 'how many corpses are we going to deal with?'[38]

The case against the General Council charged it with failing to prepare for the strike, exceeding its authority in the manner it called it off, and failing to sufficiently protect workers against victimisation. For its part, the General Council argued that it had been imbued with absolute authority to run the dispute by all unions, including the miners, at the outset. Simultaneously, however, it argued it was the unions' individual responsibility to prevent victimisation. To the charge of a lack of preparation Bevin pleaded that they were operating in an unprecedented situation, and had no such authority to make any preparations until the union executives met on the eve of the strike.

The miners also made the charge that the Samuel memorandum contained no worthwhile guarantees and should not have been used as a pretext to call off the strike. To this, the General Council simply restated its view that, had the miners accepted the memorandum, the government would have been painted into a corner and forced to use it as a basis for negotiations. Arthur Pugh, in acknowledging that the General Council was aware that Samuel was not acting upon the government's authority, gave a telling response:

> Sir Herbert Samuel indicated in his statement that he was not acting for the Government or anyone else. That was accepted, but those who understand how these things work will not, I think, be disposed to doubt that the thing was not entirely unknown to the government. Anybody who appreciates the position of a Government that has got the control of the whole nation and not a part, and that is responsible to the whole nation, must appreciate...no Government could bring in someone to intervene between itself and a section of the people to whom it was responsible.[39]

Put simply, Pugh had completely accepted the government's logic that no negotiations could take place while the strike was ongoing. This response must have left many in the room wondering why, if that were the case, they had embarked on the strike at all.

In a long speech stating the MFGB's case, Herbert Smith stressed that at all times the miners' leaders had consulted their union before making decisions. It was not the stubbornness of Smith or Cook or any other individual that led to the MFGB rejecting terms, but the decision of the majority of miners in the country through their delegates. Cook, also eminently reasonably, pointed to the statements made by the General Council before the strike that it was entirely behind the miners' position against wage cuts and longer hours:

> Did we come to the General Council to get a reduction in wages? We could have got a reduction without going there...let our report go out, and let the rank and file decide who was right in this great struggle. First they

committed us to a wages reduction, then to district agreements, and then to hours. Therefore it is clear and true on the three questions that they said they would stand by us on, they committed us, and the miners are suffering. But we will rebuild and reorganise and the movement will get stronger, but it will get new leaders who will have the courage to lead.[40]

Others on the left attacked the General Council's timidity throughout the strike. A delegate of the furnishings trade union, Alex Gossip, criticised the *British Worker* for its unenthusiastic tone. In his view, the General Council should not have assumed the good faith of those with whom they had to negotiate. 'You want to treat the employing class as what they are,' he argued, 'our bitter and vindictive enemies, and fight them with all the power at your disposal in the same way as they fight us.'[41]

Thomas and Citrine, despite their differences, both attacked the miners for neglecting their responsibility to the wider movement. Citrine admitted that the movement was not prepared for a strike. However, he pointed out that if they had been openly laying the groundwork for one they would have opened themselves up to legal challenges from inside the unions about the lack of a ballot. In Citrine's view, the MFGB's refusal to accept the Samuel memorandum was the fatal event that had broken the united front of the unions. Citrine asked the assembled trade unionists to put aside personal bitterness: 'Neither the Miners' Federation nor the General Council can be held entirely blameless for what happened. I ask you to try to dismiss personalities as far as you can, and to look at this thing objectively and to say to yourselves, what was wrong? Could, in the circumstances, any other set of men have acted differently?'[42]

Bevin had been genuinely annoyed that the strike had ended so suddenly with no guarantees for his members. He could have used the conference as an opportunity to air this criticism. Instead, he lined up behind the majority on the General Council. Like Citrine he criticised the miners for having little regard for the position of other unions. 'If the General Council came to my aid and the aid of my union, and if they said "Bevin you must go out and face a hostile membership, but this is the best we can do," I would face the hostility of my members.'[43] For him, the integrity and cohesion of trade union organisation as a whole was more important than the views of the rank and file.

When the vote came to endorse the General Council's report, only the Woodworkers and a few other small unions joined the miners in opposing it. The report was accepted by 2,840,000 votes to 1,095,000.

***

The General Council had won a somewhat pyrrhic victory in securing the retrospective approval of the movement for its version of events. The vote did nothing to lessen the grim effects of the defeat.

The victimisation of workers dragged on through the months and years after the general strike. To support those who were sacked and blacklisted, the TUC set up a special fund which granted £2 to each victimised worker upon their name being submitted by their trade union. In October the Widnes branch of the Building Trade Workers applied to its general secretary to support an application for a grant for a brother Duggan, dismissed from the United Alkali Company after fifty-four years. He had been a member of the union since 1889.[44] The winter of 1926–7 was a particularly harsh one for the many thousands of workers who remained unemployed after the strike. The wife of one TGWU member captured the pain, frustration, and wounded pride these families felt in a letter asking the union for assistance: 'Each week he goes for the dole and I expect him to come home and say it is stopped, what is going to happen to us, I am worried to death. Xmas, what Xmas for me and mine, through no fault of our own, laughed at by people who know you for a real unionist. You can and must do something for us.'[45]

The problem reached much farther than the out-and-out blacklisting of trade unionists. The dislocation caused by the strike and coal lockout gave employers an excuse to restructure. Where workers had walked out of factories, or the industry had been put on short-time, employers took the opportunity to reduce their headcounts. Cammell Laird's ordnance factory in Nottingham shed twenty percent of its workforce.[46] Some 160 members of one glassworkers union lost their jobs when their employer used the coal shortage to shut a factory in Castleford, which it had been trying to offload for three years.[47] Heavy metal manufacturing was particularly badly affected; the Iron and Steel Trades Confederation reported after the strike that the majority of its eighty thousand members would remain unemployed until the coal lockout was finished. The knock-on effect went far beyond the factories, though, with the Shop Assistants' Union reporting in June that 'claims are now coming in and owing to the continued stoppage in the mining industry the volume of suspension cases is growing very rapidly'.[48]

Every instance placed a demand on union funds as the unemployed members started to draw their benefits. Some unions were paying out thousands of pounds every week even several months after the strike. This would of course affect their ability to fight their own defensive battles as well as drive more of their members to the poor law guardians for relief.

This consequent unemployment contributed to an immediate drop in trade union membership after the strike. Trade union membership declined from 5.5 million in 1926 to 4.8 million in 1928.[49] Not all of this came down to workers being out of jobs. After the general strike's collapse, workers' faith in the power of unions faltered. The TGWU alone shed tens of thousands of members. Unions whose financial position was more precarious suffered the most, such as the paper workers, who could only afford to pay out one-third of the amount members were entitled to in benefits.[50] An exodus from the union naturally followed. However, the unions proved themselves to be remarkably resilient, especially when compared to past defeats. Whereas the general unions had almost fallen apart under the employers' offensive in the 1890s, their organisation, and the bulk of their membership, remained intact in the late 1920s. Trade unionism had not been smashed; it was here to stay as a major social force.

Prepared to rub salt in the trade unions' wounds, the government revived proposals for curbing union power by legislation. Baldwin still had his solid parliamentary majority, and the unions lacked the confidence to oppose such a sweeping move after their bruising defeat. It was necessary to make sure a general strike could never happen again. In existing law, the Astbury judgement was shaky at best.

Grassroots Tory opinion chimed with that of the National Confederation of Employers' Organisations, which wanted the legal immunity granted to strikers for breaking contract removed and picketing rules to be tightened up again.[51] They also wanted to damage the Labour Party by requiring union members to 'opt in' to political levies as had been proposed in Macquisten's bill the year before the strike.

The trade disputes and trade unions bill introduced in March 1927 addressed the Tories' favourite union bugbears. It banned any form of sympathy strike or any strike 'designed or calculated to coerce the Government either directly or by inflicting hardship upon the community'. Anyone taking part in a general strike – not just its leaders – could be jailed for two years. Picketing rules were tightened up. The 'opt in' provision was passed. Civil servants' unions were banned from affiliation to the TUC or pursuing political goals. Against the recommendations of some of the more aggressive employers' organisations, however, the Tories left the Trade Disputes Act 1906 on the books, so that unions could not be held liable for damages incurred. It was pressure from Conservative trade unionists on the ground, who did not want the Act to go too far, that ensured this.[52]

The labour movement's campaign against the bill was broad but shallow. The National Trade Union Defence Committee held more than 1,100 public meetings around the country. But there was no question of using industrial action to stop the law and the TUC advised its constituent unions to comply with it once passed.[53] Constitutionalism once again won the day.

The Conservatives found other ways to drive home their victory. Many had been critical of Labour-run local poor law guardians, who, they said, were being too generous to the families of strikers. Certainly the amount spent in these areas had increased, but this was due to the unemployment consequent of the dispute rather than a deliberate political campaign to keep the strike and lockout going by surreptitiously funding strikers through the disbursement of poor relief. Nonetheless it provided the excuse for Neville Chamberlain, the minister of health, to push through a Board of Guardians (Default) Act. This staggering act of vindictiveness enabled the government to disband local boards that were being too 'generous' in their grants to miners' families.[54] The class war did not stop at the factory gate but pervaded the home of every worker.

However, although the government was out for blood, not everyone sought retribution. There were those on the employers' side who, seeing how close the country had come to catastrophe in 1926, wanted to pursue a more moderate course. In doing so, they reasoned, they could reach out to the now unquestionably dominant elements of the trade union leadership who preferred partnership to conflict. Initial moves were made by Sir Arthur Steel-Maitland, the minister of labour, who tried to open talks between Bevin and prominent industrialists. This process was wrecked by Baldwin's determination to proceed with the anti-union law, which temporarily pushed the two sides further apart.[55]

On the employers' side, the process was largely driven by bosses representing the expanding new industries – electronics, chemicals, vehicle manufacturing – that relied more on technological innovation and were less burdened with the baggage of troubled industrial relations. They were primarily concerned that British industry needed to be made more competitive through rationalisation, and that both workers and employers had a shared interest in this. The interests of 'industry' in the abstract were to override class or sectional interests. This was not in fact too far from the position the unions had taken towards the coal industry itself in the early 1920s.

This group of employers coalesced around Sir Alfred Mond. Mond was a relatively progressive-minded coalowner who in 1926 became the first chairman of the massive Imperial Chemical Industries conglomerate. Within Imperial Chemical Industries, Mond was pioneering a new industrial relations structure whereby workers would be given a measure of profit sharing to tie them to the interests of the company, and a system of works councils would be put in place to try to resolve disputes without strikes.

In January 1928 the first meeting between this group and the TUC took place. In Mond's words, the discussions had 'the twin objects of the restoration of industrial prosperity and the corresponding improvement in the standard of living of the population'.[56] In the reports that came from the resulting 'Mond-Turner' talks – Ben Turner was serving as president of the TUC that year – the employers' side conceded that union recognition was the best way to achieve harmonious industrial relations, and that workers victimised after the general strike should be reinstated. Rationalisation of industry was to be carried out with the cooperation of the unions.

The prospect of union recognition and expansion in these new industries made the TUC keen on the talks. Opposition from within union ranks was fairly muted, except from Arthur Cook who strongly denounced 'Mond's manacles' as the death of independent trade unionism. For this he was attacked not only by the General Council but also from within the

Miners' Federation by his old ally Herbert Smith.[57] Cook's isolation was a sign of how far the mood in the movement had shifted since the Conference of Executives met at Memorial Hall in April 1926.

The Mond-Turner talks struggled to get past the hurdle of the major employers' associations, who rejected the reports. The more traditional employers, having just beaten the unions in a major national strike, were not inclined to look past wage cuts as their panacea for solving industrial problems.

***

While the unions turned to partnership, the revolutionaries enjoyed a brief boon from the widespread disgust at the TUC's surrender. The CPGB doubled its membership over the course of 1926. Many of the new joiners were miners impressed by the party's steadfast support for their cause. After the trade union movement closed ranks behind the General Council in January 1927, however, the Communists were increasingly marginalised. In February 1927 the General Council disavowed local trades councils that could not be entreated to disaffiliate from the Minority Movement. The large National Union of General and Municipal Workers (NUGMW) withdrew its delegates from many trades councils that refused to disassociate from the Communist-influenced group.[58]

Citrine authored several articles attacking the revolutionaries and launched a national inquest into Communist 'infiltration'. In his memoirs, he explained how throughout the 1920s his attitude to the Communists changed, as did that of many of his fellow moderates. Initially, he had sympathy with the Russian revolution and regarded Communists as just slightly more enthusiastic union militants. After the general strike he came to see them as a malign and disruptive influence that needed to be removed. In *Democracy or Disruption?* he explained:

> After two years of careful thought, observation, and mature deliberation, I am convinced that it is the duty of all who have a sincere concern for the welfare of the trade union and Labour movement to abandon a negative attitude towards this problem of Communist propaganda, and to make up their minds positively on the question of whether the cancer of Communist influence is allowed to grow.[59]

A growing view took hold in trade union officialdom that the general strike had always been doomed to fail and those who had supposedly egged the unions on in such a folly – the Communists – had gambled with the movement's very existence. With the weight of opinion and the bureaucratic machinery of the movement turning against it the Communist Party struggled to consolidate its growth and remained a relatively small force in the labour movement.

A further blow to the Communists came on 12 May 1927, exactly one year after the general strike was called off, when the London offices of the All-Russian Co-operative Society (ARCOS) were raided by the police and security services. ARCOS ostensibly existed to promote economic ties between Britain and the USSR but doubled as a front for Russian intelligence. The government had decided to break off diplomatic relations with the Soviets and hoped to use incriminating evidence seized from the raid as a pretext to do so. Unfortunately, no such evidence was found.[60] Baldwin pressed ahead with the plan, justifying it with some intercepted telegrams. More opprobrium was heaped on the CPGB as agents of a foreign power, and the Anglo-Russian Trade Union Committee, which had just about staggered on despite the political rows following the general strike, was finally put in its grave. By the end of 1927 the standing of the Communists in the wider labour movement had never been lower.

The union leaders of 1926, denounced for leading an attempted overthrow of constitutional government, almost all became pillars of the establishment within a remarkably short period of time. For Walter Citrine, the strike marked the beginning of a twenty-year career as general secretary of the TUC. During this time, the unions' influence in the Labour Party and national politics grew, culminating in the party's landslide election victory of 1945. This government, Labour's first with a majority in the Commons, elevated Citrine to the Upper House as the 1st Baron of Wembley.

Ernest Bevin remained general secretary of the TGWU until that same election. He emerged from the general strike with his standing enhanced both within and outside the trade union movement. Many trade unionists appreciated the tireless work and organisational strengths he showed during the strike, even if they disagreed with his tactic of calling the workers out in waves. Outside the movement he was unfairly portrayed as the strike's Napoleon, single-handedly calling the shots. This of course was a disservice to the many thousands of trade unionists who contributed to the strike's organisation, but it created a grudging respect for Bevin even among his political opponents. During the 1930s he showed his strident opposition to appeasement of Fascism and the pacifists in the labour movement and came to be regarded as one who had all the trappings of a statesman. He entered Parliament in 1940 to serve as minister of labour in the wartime national government of his old adversary Winston Churchill. After Labour's 1945 victory he was made foreign secretary by Clement Attlee.

Part of the party's election platform was the repeal of the hated Trade Disputes and Trade Unions Act 1927. Speaking for this in Parliament, Bevin attempted to lay his ghosts from 1926 to rest:

> I propose this afternoon to deal with the historical side of the general strike. I have been waiting 20 years to do this... They cast the trade unions for the role of enemies of the State, and while as an individual I have been a trade union leader for 20 years, I never have been an enemy of the State. I have been as big a constitutionalist as any Member on the other side of the House, and I am fighting to remove the stigma which the Tory Party in 1927 put upon me, as the leader of a trade union... The Tory Party would use all the forces of the State to prepare to fight Labour at the end. I say that that is quite wrong. We are subjects of the King as much as anybody else. We are part of the State.[61]

Many union leaders had already taken such warm words about the state to heart, not least Jimmy Thomas. He returned to government in 1929 when Ramsay MacDonald formed his second minority administration. Two years later, when MacDonald created a national government coalition with the Tories in response to the Wall Street Crash, both men were expelled from the Labour Party and Thomas was kicked out of his beloved NUR. He ended up in the Cabinet of MacDonald's successor, one Stanley Baldwin, until being forced to resign in disgrace in 1936 when details of some of his unsavoury financial dealings became public.

Arthur Cook's trajectory was somewhat different. He never achieved, nor did he seek, the approval of the British establishment. He remained the MFGB's popular and militant general secretary, but in the economic conditions prevailing after the strike became more convinced of the need for a Labour government to save the coal industry. He broke fully with the Communist Party during its ultra-left turn in the late 1920s, when it attempted to set up a separate revolutionary miners' trade union in Scotland. When, in the 1929 election, the Communist Harry Pollitt challenged Ramsay MacDonald in the mining constituency of Seaham, Cook spoke for the Labour leader.[62] MacDonald polled 35,615 votes to Pollitt's 1,451 and formed his second minority government. Like many trade unionists Cook was bitterly disappointed with the orthodox austerity economics of the second Labour government. This briefly aligned him with Oswald Mosley and John Strachey, latterly of the Birmingham Strike Committee, and others who unsuccessfully pushed the government to take a more interventionist line on unemployment.

By the time MacDonald was thrown out of the Labour Party for forming his national government with the Tories in 1931, Cook was very ill. During one of his many speaking engagements in 1926 an adversary had kicked him, aggravating his old mining injury. Rather than seeing a doctor, he simply carried on with his duties. In 1931 his leg was amputated. He withstood the operation well but was found shortly afterwards to have cancer, and his condition rapidly deteriorated. On his hospital bed he was visited by Walter Citrine and relayed to him a message to the voters of Seaham to vote Labour against MacDonald in the forthcoming election.[63] It would be the last time the two saw each other; Cook died in the early morning of 2 November 1931, just shy of his forty-seventh birthday.

The labour movement's great and good gathered at Cook's funeral to pay tribute to the man who had so often been a thorn in their side. John Bromley, who had clashed so fiercely with Cook in the aftermath of the general strike, represented the General Council, and Cramp, who in 1926 had found Cook's radicalism so intolerable, was there for the railwaymen. William Lee even attended for the coalowners. 'The British labour movement has lost a devoted friend,' MFGB president Ebby Edwards intoned, 'the miners have lost a giant for their cause.'[64] One tribute described Cook as 'the St Paul of the English Labour movement – probably the greatest agitator this country has had since Jack Cade – the most hated Labour leader in the country but the most loved, too.'[65]

The subsequent careers of those on the government side are of course more familiar. Joynson-Hicks continued as Baldwin's home secretary and became better known for his censorship of D. H. Lawrence's *Lady Chatterley's Lover* and attempts to clamp down on London's nightclubs than for his role in the general strike. He retired from the House in 1929 and was elevated to the Lords.

Churchill's subsequent political resume scarcely needs repeating. As Britain's wartime prime minister during 1940–5 he has become the closest the country has to a secular deity. Yet in his lifetime he was never loved by the industrial working class. This is reflected in the heavy defeat he suffered in 1945. As late as 1950, his role in the tumultuous period of 1910–26 haunted him on the campaign trail, as historian Dai Smith has noted: 'On the cinema screens of South Wales whenever Churchill appeared on the Movietone newsreels his image was booed, and his very name met with the hiss of collective hostility.'[66]

Feted in the immediate aftermath of the strike, Stanley Baldwin's grip over the warring factions in his government soon began to decline, and he failed to retain a majority at the 1929 election. In 1931 he led his party into MacDonald's national coalition and together the two men presided over the misery of that austere decade. The Great Depression saw 3.5 million workers unemployed at its height. As usual, it was the industrial areas and coalfields that were hit the hardest. MacDonald tried to balance the nation's books on the backs of the poor, cutting public sector wages and unemployment benefits by ten percent. Baldwin replaced the ailing MacDonald in 1935, serving as prime minister for two more years until his own retirement.

MacDonald and Baldwin. Bevin and Churchill. Such partnerships would have seemed unlikely during the year of post-war Britain's greatest conflagration. But they were perhaps presaged by a chance meeting that summer. In August 1926 Baldwin was holidaying in Aix-les-Bains near the Alps, attempting to recover from his heavy workload with some fresh mountain air. Back home, the miners were still out, collections for their relief fund being taken in every town. Thousands of railwaymen had not been reinstated since the strike. Whole factories were idle, steelworkers on short-time or laid off. Hundreds still languished in prison under the emergency regulations.

A world away, in the Hôtel Bernascon, a grand palace hotel from the Belle Époque, the prime minister chanced upon a few members of the TUC's General Council. 'Your Majesty will be amused to hear', he wrote to the king, 'that I crossed yesterday with a number of members of the Council of the TUC. We had a most friendly conversation and parted with mutual protestations of affection, and on their side, I hope, respect as well.'[67] Sadly, the exact identities of these trade union luminaries are lost to history.

Postal workers rally in London during the 2022–3 strike wave.

14

THE LEGACY OF 1926

Do you remember 1926? The great dream and the swift disaster,
The fanatic and the traitor, and more than all,
The bravery of the simple, faithful folk?
'Ay, ay, we remember 1926,' said Dai and Shinkin,
As they stood on the kerb in Charing Cross Road,
'And we shall remember 1926 until our blood is dry.'

— IDRIS DAVIES, THE ANGRY SUMMER

The general strike was not, in any real sense, general.

— THE TUC'S OFFICIAL CENTENARY HISTORY, 1968

Every single day of the strike, the government and those on strike sensed that at any moment, the situation could spiral out of control. For Baldwin on 6 May, it was the 'road to anarchy and ruin'. On the same day, Leon Trotsky, watching from afar, wrote: 'The real victory of the General Strike lies only in the winning of power by the proletariat.'[1] Naturally, he had no faith that the British trade union leadership desired such a victory. When *Lansbury's Labour Weekly* performed a post-mortem a few weeks later, it presented the government and the unions as being on the brink of civil war had the strike not been called off.[2] The Army hierarchy was adamant that 'the general strike was the best training for war young officers had obtained since the War'.[3]

Could the general strike have won? And how close was Britain really to revolution?

The strike was more solid than any of its supporters could ever have dared hope. Despite fears of a break, and a handful of instances of significant numbers of workers, particularly on the trams, returning on 10–11 May, there were more out at the time the strike was called off than there had been on its first day. The chief civil commissioner noted in his post-strike report that factories were closing apace due to the inability to transport coal. The government's emergency operation had successfully staved off most major food shortages but was not hauling anything like the normal levels of commercial and industrial traffic. 'It seems probable', Mitchell-Thomson wrote, 'that if the strike had lasted longer it would have soon become necessary to render assistance on a much wider scale than had hitherto been contemplated.'[4]

Generally the opinion of historians has been that the government would have been able to ramp up its operation to deal with this. There was a glut of volunteers and vehicles available in most localities across the country, more than there were jobs for. The large available pool of unemployed workers made it much easier to undermine a general strike in 1926 than it would have been if one had occurred in 1919.

The main problem for the government, had the strike dragged on, would have been the country's continued reliance on coal. There was no prospect of volunteers being introduced to work the mines. While there were coal stocks available these, as well as any imports, were useless unless they could be moved. A longer strike would have tested the government's ability to do this, and the workers' ability to stop it, much more sharply. By 11 May many factory workers who had not yet been brought out were not only refusing to handle coal but considering stopping any work that required 'black juice'. Widespread civil disorder would have likely resulted in the following days as the situation grew acute.

Just as large numbers of workers coming out on strike do not guarantee victory, large-scale civil unrest does not necessarily lead to revolution. The serious and potentially revolutionary implications of the strike have been written out of our national story. But they were keenly felt by those who actually lived through it.

Fears of a revolution certainly weighed on the minds of the government, police, and state officials in the run-up to and during the strike. The combative South Wales Police chief Lionel Lindsay, who had asked for military intervention at Tonypandy in 1910, expressed to the Home Office in December 1925 the extent to which he saw the forthcoming struggle as a kind of social war in which an anti-union majority needed to be mobilised to smash the labour movement: 'I am sure that the vast majority of the population are sick of Labour tyranny, and are ready to put it down the moment they can feel confident that their Government is going to lead them, but they must have proof that the Government will lead them before they show their hands.'[5]

On the union side, the leaders certainly feared losing control to more radical elements. This was admitted by Charles Dukes of the NUGMW when, at the 1927 Council of Executives called to discuss the strike's conduct, he declared:

> Every day the strike proceeded, the control and authority of that dispute was passing out of the hands of responsible Executives into the hands of men who had no authority, no control, no responsibility, and was wrecking the movement from one end to the other... I deplore this attitude of presuming that we had the movement thoroughly organised, thoroughly disciplined; that we could move our sections and our battalions almost upon military plans.[6]

Those on the Marxist left have married the two questions by arguing that the strike was not successful *because* it was not revolutionary. The quantity of a mass strike did not tip over into the quality of a direct challenge to state power.

For the Communist Party and its fellow travellers, no revolution was possible in 1926. And therefore Communists bear no responsibility for not pulling one off. James Klugmann, writing in 1969, argued the party's main task during the strike was to raise class consciousness and provide trade unionists with a fuller political understanding; given its weaknesses it could not be expected to do much more.[7] This accepts the party line first posed by J. T. Murphy, the Communist official imprisoned for seditious libel in 1925, on the eve of the general strike: 'Our party does not hold the leading positions in the trade unions. It is not conducting the negotiations with the employers and the Government. It can only advise and place its press and its forces at the service of the workers – led by others.'[8]

If Communists see 1926 as a virtuous defeat, their estranged Trotskyist siblings see it as a cautionary tale: that of a crisis of leadership. As the general strike unfolded in Britain, the ideological struggle for leadership of the Soviet Union between supporters and opponents of Joseph Stalin was reaching its sad conclusion. The tactic of the Anglo-Russian Trade Union Committee was a ripe target for Leon Trotsky. He considered it a doomed attempt by Zinoviev to short-cut the creation of a mass revolutionary party in Britain by cosying up to left-leaning trade union leaders. This unavoidably blunted the revolutionary zeal and agitation of the Communist Party. After the general strike was called off Trotsky went further, seeing in the determination of the Soviet leadership to persevere with the committee despite the General Council's behaviour, the abandonment of the Bolshevik policy of international working-class revolution:

> Can the trade unions be utilized at one time in the interests of international class policy, and at another time for any sort of alleged diplomatic aims? Can such a situation be established where the same representatives of [Stalin's faction] say at one moment that the General Council is a traitor and strike-breaker, and at another time that it is a friend with whom we are in hearty accord? Is it sufficient to whisper secretly that the former must be understood in the revolutionary class sense and the latter in a diplomatic sense? Can such a policy be spoken of seriously?[9]

To this day, Trotskyist groups lament the selling-out of the strike by the timidity and conservatism of those tasked with leading it.[10]

It is certainly the case that the prospects for a successful revolution in 1920s Britain suffered due to a paucity of revolutionary leadership. Both communist and Trotskyist interpretations created a narrative of betrayal that is true, but is also a truism; it almost goes without saying that the men leading the British labour movement in 1926 were not revolutionaries. Jimmy Thomas was never going to storm Buckingham Palace in his bowtie and dinner jacket. Trade union leaders, after all, will behave like trade union leaders. But there is more to be learned from the incredible feats of working-class self-organisation and the kernel of alternative leadership that was beginning to develop during the strike.

The mainstream Labour Party, which feared revolution like sin, chose to forget that this kernel might take root and, finding fertile ground, flourish. For the Fabian Beatrice Webb, whose rather caustic and ungenerous remarks have been over-relied on by historians, the general strike was 'the death gasp of that pernicious doctrine of "workers' control" of public affairs through the trade unions, and by the method of direct action'.[11] For Webb and other Labourites, the strike's defeat meant the labour movement could shake off its childish attachment to direct action and class struggle, and concentrate on the electoral road to socialism.

The Mond-Turner talks, for all their lack of practical value, seemed to reinforce this. Labour historians have tended to see this as part of a trend towards social partnership that was already happening in the trade union movement, but the failure of the general strike certainly emboldened those who wanted to pursue that road. This, coupled with the bleak conditions of the 1930s when mass unemployment made prosecuting national strikes in industry very difficult, swung the pendulum of working-class activity back into the political sphere. The Labour Party roared back from its wilderness years under MacDonald's and Baldwin's national governments, helped in no small part by the Second World War, to win its convincing victory in 1945. The strategy of the reformers had appeared to pay off.

We know no revolution took place in 1926. But on 11 May, millions of workers were prepared to strike until victory and momentum appeared to be building for an 'all out' policy. The government had mobilised a paramilitary force to smash pickets. Violence was spreading across the country. It was an open question how far things would go. The answer was provided by the TUC on 12 May; indeed, the seriousness of the situation was one of the motivating factors behind its keenness to capitulate.

***

But when we think of the general strike, if we think of it at all, it hardly figures as the revolutionary convulsion its participants feared – or hoped – it was. We picture happy well-heeled volunteers peeling potatoes in Hyde Park, in a noble attempt to keep Britain fed. The contemporary

British press was only too happy to publish such cheerful images. In the decades that followed, these smiling students penned memoirs and novels, all solidifying the image of the general strike as a grand old time. Novelist Christopher Isherwood, who volunteered for the TUC during the strike, recalled that 'the Poshocracy had won, as it always did win, in a thoroughly gentlemanly manner...so now it was quite prepared magnanimously to pretend that nothing more serious had taken place than, so to speak, a jolly sham fight with pats of butter'.[12]

The strike came to emblematise a peculiar Englishness, where one could take pride in the nation's level-headedness, moderation, and common sense. After all, it was often repeated, no one was killed. This was untrue, but facts have rarely disturbed our national memory too much. The general strike was a triumph of the British spirit, especially when compared to the wilder and bloodier social struggles of its European neighbours, in which communists were fighting fascists in the streets. John Galsworthy, whose *Modern Comedy* trilogy (1928) concluded in 1926, certainly saw the strike in these terms: 'We [the English] are still a people that cannot be rushed, distrustful of extremes, saved by the grace of our defensive humour, well-tempered, resentful of interference, improvident and wasteful, but endowed with a certain genius for recovery.'[13] It was likewise a rite of passage for those too young to have fought in the Great War. 'We'll show the dead chaps we can fight too,' as Mulcaster says to Charles in Evelyn Waugh's *Brideshead Revisited* (1945) when the two discuss volunteering.

It is hardly surprising, given the dominance of Oxbridge graduates in shaping Britain's twentieth-century cultural output, that this attitude of the intelligentsia percolated into the public history of the strike in the post-war years. The strike was an aberration – 'the Nine Days' Wonder' – never to be repeated. The real underdogs were not the downtrodden workers but the plucky young volunteers facing down the mob. Strikers themselves, even when sympathised with, were seen to be undertaking a folly that was basically doomed from the start.[14]

Nowadays, with the strike having slid out of living memory, it has vanished from the national story we tell ourselves. At most it was nine days of collective madness that had no real impact. Millions of Britons tuned in to watch the travails of an appealing aristocratic family in

Downton Abbey as they navigated the interwar world. Strikingly, the TV series comes to an abrupt end on New Year's Day 1926. The much-anticipated film sequels start in 1927. The fourth series of *Peaky Blinders* (2017) takes place against a heavily fictionalised lead-up to the strike. The revolutionaries, and by extension the organised working class, are just another criminal gang causing chaos on the streets of Birmingham. The role of Jessie Eden – a real shop steward who helped bring out women at Lucas Electronics during the strike – is reduced to a seductress, luring the protagonist, Tommy Shelby, to the cause of socialism.

There is of course an alternative story told by those on the left, where the strike represents the unfulfilled promise of working-class power. Working-class writers picked up their pens to capture the real possibilities of a world turned upside down. In *The Angry Summer* (1943) poet and former miner Idris Davies gives voice to the citizens of a small Welsh community: the locked-out miners; their suffering wives; the sullen and resentful local grocer. In 1929 Ellen Wilkinson, the left-wing Labour MP who had spent the nine days touring the country addressing strikers' meetings, wrote her first novel, *Clash*, partly based on her experiences. Sympathetic to the view of the labour movement's left wing, it situated the strike in the context of a general period of militancy and social progress going back to 1910.[15] Also critical of the General Council was *The Striker Stricken, or the Thirty Sleepers of Eccleston Square* (1926), a satirical operetta penned by Wilkinson's fellow socialist G. D. H. Cole reflecting the views of the majority of trade unionists in the wake of the strike's failure. In it, a rather cartoonish character representing the rank and file admonishes Walter Citrine: 'Call this a General Strike? Know what I calls it? I calls it a blooming Church Parade. Fakers, the 'ole bleeding lot of yer!'[16]

For the TUC itself, the strike has been an embarrassment, something to forget. Memoirs of the union leaders are replete with protestations that they never wanted it, never thought it would work, and never want to see anything like it happen again.[17] On the strike's fiftieth anniversary the TUC merely arranged a small, barely advertised exhibition in its head office and said no more about it.[18]

In the coalfields, by contrast, the strike and lockout were long remembered. A common refrain among men and women who lived through the strain of 1926 was that the general strike lasted nine months, not nine days. Recollections were varied. Some remembered hardship and humiliation, others communal meals, dances, and solidarity. Eventually in the post-war years the stories and memories of 1926 would give rise to 'a second and third generation of union militants intent on avenging the deep wounds inflicted on their forebears'.[19]

***

The strike's defeat left its indelible mark on the labour movement, and yet industrial militancy has persisted. There has been no general strike in Britain since 1926, but the country has come closer than many people think. In July 1972 five shop stewards were arrested for breaching a court injunction preventing picketing at a warehouse on the London Docks. This led to a series of unofficial stoppages and mass demonstrations outside Pentonville Prison where they were being held. Such was the groundswell of support for the Pentonville Five that the TUC was compelled to call a 'national day of action' – as in 1926, they could not bring themselves to use the term 'general strike' – for their release. By the direct intervention of the government, the five were set free two days before Britain's second general strike was due to take place.

That same year, the miners also took their revenge for 1926. Under the Attlee government, the mines were at long last nationalised, a worthy prize for decades of struggle. In 1945 a single National Union of Mineworkers (NUM) replaced the MFGB, albeit with the districts still holding a lot of autonomy. This union was to remain in the vanguard of the working-class movement for the next four decades.

In 1972, when miners once more faced a decline in their living standards, they undertook their first official national strike since 1926. 'Flying pickets' of miners visited railway yards, power stations, and coking plants to spread solidarity action among other workers. The miners had made their point: the country could not function without their labour. Two years later they scored another victory and in the process brought down Edward Heath's Tory government.

Cultural depictions of the general strike during the wave of industrial militancy in the 1970s therefore took on a different tone. One episode of the 1970s historical soap *Upstairs, Downstairs* (1975) is set during the strike and distils many of the popular images of 1926. For example, an aristocratic volunteer driving a bus nips into his Belgravia townhouse for a tea break and has a damp confrontation with a group of surly but essentially good-natured Cockney pickets. The episode ends with two miners, who have stopped by the house to visit a relative 'downstairs', learning of the TUC's betrayal. As they leave, rolling their eyes at a carload of Union Jack-waving toffs, the 1975 audience seems invited to consider whether it may be the miners who have had the last laugh.

Jim Allen's four-part *Days of Hope* (1975) follows a working-class family through the First World War, the 1921 lockout, and the general strike. The protagonists of the epic didactic drama, directed by Ken Loach, are two brothers. One begins as a working-class patriot and becomes a communist, and the other is jailed during the war as a conscientious objector and subsequently elected in 1924 as a moderate Labour MP. They end up on opposite wings of the labour movement during the strike in the series' final episode. Broadcast in prime time in a period of revived union militancy, the series put the betrayal narrative back in the popular consciousness.[20] For Allen and Loach the strike, and the period preceding it, are stepping stones in the forward march of labour, a struggle that, while often brutal and uneven, appeared to many in the 1970s to be finally on the verge of victory.

∴

The days of hope would not last long. In the 1980s the Conservative government launched a deliberate and ultimately lethal attack on the mining industry and the miners' union. A year-long strike raised the memories of 1926 once again as the forces of the state were mobilised against coalfield communities. The levels of occupation and surveillance, and police violence at places like Orgreave in June 1984, if anything surpassed what had been seen half a century earlier. The miners' leader, Arthur Scargill, was both named for his predecessor Arthur Cook and a great admirer of his. Prime Minister Margaret Thatcher had, like Baldwin, promised to bring peace and harmony upon her election to office. The country once again teetered on the brink of civil conflict. Sympathy with the miners was immense but, despite some heroic unofficial action from workers on the ground, there was to be no national strike in their support this time. The TUC and the Labour Party washed their hands of the affair, and the miners were beaten.

Following the defeat of the NUM in 1985, strike action fell to historically low levels. But stage-managed mass strikes, tightly controlled by the trade union leadership, remain an occasional feature of British life, such as the public sector pensions strike of November 2011. Here, unions across health, education, and the civil service coordinated a single day of action that was billed as the biggest strike in the country since 1926, with perhaps as many as two million workers coming out. The following year, the TUC congress debated and passed a motion to 'consider the practicalities of a general strike' against the government's austerity measures. Nothing came of the vote.

Despite a century of almost complete indifference from the TUC towards coordinating industrial action, even when called for by its constituent unions, the far left has continued to place the demand on the General Council. The faith in a general strike called and controlled from above – the example of 1926 – surprisingly persists even though it was criticised as a strategy by revolutionaries at the time. The revolutionary Rosa Luxemburg, who witnessed the 1905 strike wave in the Russian Empire, drew a distinction between a tightly controlled general strike, which in Europe was usually undertaken as a show of force in support of passing some specific legislation, and a mass strike with genuinely revolutionary potential. The latter would emerge as the escalation and convergence of multiple ongoing struggles. If the TUC shrinks at the suggestion of the former, it is vanishingly unlikely that they will ever involve themselves in the 'many small channels of partial economic struggles and little "accidental" occurrences [flowing] rapidly to a raging sea' that Luxemburg argued constitutes the latter.[21] Of course, as in 1926, the inability and unwillingness of trade union leaders to call a strike exculpates self-professed revolutionaries from critically examining their own lack of influence in the broader movement.

Trade union leaders themselves have long since stopped ascribing any industrial role to the TUC General Council. The idea of a general strike periodically raises its head in the rhetoric of the more left-leaning general secretaries with little substance or strategy behind it. Even elementary material solidarity between different unions has been difficult to achieve. When industrial militancy returned to the agenda in Britain in 2022–3, during an acute cost of living crisis, rail workers, postal workers, and NHS nurses all engaged in long-running sustained strike action. But there was little coordination, even among unions in the same industry. NHS nurses struck on different days from their doctor colleagues, as did the ASLEF and RMT unions on the railways. Unite-CMA members at Royal Mail cheerfully drove delivery vans while their postie colleagues were on strike. There are very few organised rank-and-file networks to push union leaders into more radical action as the National Minority Movement was able to do in the 1920s, still fewer who could develop an alternative leadership.

Without the re-emergence of such grassroots trade unionism it is difficult to envisage what a general strike would look like in the 2020s. It would certainly face more legal obstacles than its antecedent. In 1926, it was possible to debate the legality of the general strike. In twenty-first-century Britain, it would be straightforwardly illegal. The industrial unrest of the 1970s prompted a tightening of anti-trade union legislation inspired by Baldwin's 1927 Act. Thatcher's governments explicitly banned sympathy action, destroyed the closed shop, and put ever-tighter restrictions on picketing. Britain now has the most restrictive trade union laws in Western Europe. Injunctions are frequently used to invalidate lawful strike action on flimsy technical pretexts. During the 2025 Birmingham bin dispute, where agency workers were unlawfully employed to replace striking workers, it was the strikers, not the employer, who faced a court order, to prevent their effective peaceful picketing.

The criminalisation of effective trade unionism has gone hand in hand with the criminalisation of broader forms of protest. While in 1926 thousands fell foul of the emergency regulations, and with the caveat that hard labour still formed part of many prison sentences at that time, most jail terms were relatively short. The magistrates who doled out three-to-six-month sentences for breaking a bus window or inciting the overturning of a tram would baulk at the draconian four-year sentences handed to Just Stop Oil protesters for non-violent direct action on the M25 in 2024. It has become far more mainstream to quash protest with the blunt instrument of the law.

Of course the landscape of the British economy is very different today. Fewer than eight percent of workers are employed in manufacturing.

Docklands that once employed tens of thousands have been replaced by highly mechanised ports with smaller, more skilled workforces. The million-strong army of coalminers has reduced in number to fewer than three hundred. Nevertheless, certain fundamentals are the same. We still rely on the world of physical things ultimately produced by human labour. In a globally interconnected economy logistics and transport workers occupy a crucial strategic position, perhaps more so than ever. The trade union movement's centre of power in Britain has shifted with the economy. Its strengths now tend to be among white-collar public-sector employees. A 2020s general strike would likely see workers coming out who would not have dreamed of joining the movement in 1926 – teachers, nurses, doctors, civil servants – but who are also able in their own way to paralyse the social life of the country.

Co-ordinated industrial action is still eminently possible, even within the bounds of the law, but the 2022–3 strike wave demonstrated that the will to unity that characterised the actions of even moderate leaders of the 1920s, like Bevin and Citrine, has not yet concretely re-emerged, and rank-and-file organisation across the movement is weak at best.

More than anything, the general strike of 1926 was an act of both extreme selflessness and extreme self-interest. Millions of workers supported the miners at the risk of their own jobs and livelihoods, because they knew that the fight was a crucial one for them and their whole class. The result was a demonstration of working-class power the like of which Britain has not seen since. In the face of a government acting openly in the interests of the bosses, they were prepared to hold firm. As the Birmingham socialist J. Stuart Barr noted after the strike: 'A lot has been said in the past of the need for the workers having faith in their leaders; I would humbly suggest that if the strike taught us nothing else, it certainly taught us that it is just as important for the leaders to have faith in the workers.'[22]

Regardless of the strength of the law and state power, it is this attitude, and the confidence and organisation to put it into practice, that need to be rediscovered. If it is, the 1926 general strike will no longer stand alone in British history.

Acknowledgements

My foremost thanks go to my partner Rebecca, without whose love, support, insight, and patience this book would not have been possible. I love you.

Thanks to my editor Rida Vaquas, whose suggestions were uniformly helpful, to Paul Nash and Laura McFarlane, Julian Ball and Francesca Dawes, Margot Weale, and the rest of the Oneworld team. Many thanks also to my copy-editor Sam Wells.

I am grateful to Holly Smith for her help with sources and feedback on parts of the draft.

My thanks also go to the staff at the Modern Records Centre, the Labour History Archive and Study Centre, and my old colleagues and union comrades at the National Archives.

Finally to all friends and comrades – particularly Jo, Mark, and Ed – who have put up with me constantly holding forth about the general strike in recent months and helped to clarify my arguments.

Any errors in the book are of course mine alone.

Bibliography

Archival collections
Churchill Archives Centre, Cambridge (CAC)
Labour History Archive and Study Centre, Manchester (LHASC)
Modern Records Centre, Warwick (MRC)
The National Archives, Kew (TNA)

Newspapers and periodicals
Bath Chronicle and Herald
Blyth News
British Gazette
British Worker
Buckingham Advertiser and Free Press
Chelmsford Chronicle
Daily Express
Daily Herald
Daily Mail
Daily Mirror
Diss Express
Dundee Evening Telegraph
Eastbourne Chronicle
Evening News
Exeter and Plymouth Gazette
Gloucestershire Echo
Hansard
Hartlepool Northern Daily Mail
Hull Daily Mail
Illustrated Sunday Herald
International Socialist Review
Leicester Evening Mail
Luton News and Bedfordshire Chronicle
Merthyr Express
Northern Whig
Plebs

Portsmouth Evening News
Sheffield Daily Telegraph
Sheffield Independent
Southwark and Bermondsey Recorder
Sunderland Daily Echo
Tatler
Thanet Advertiser
The Record
Times
Western Morning News
Workers' Weekly
Yorkshire Evening Post

General histories

Andrew, Christopher, *The Defence of the Realm: The Authorized History of MI5* (London: Penguin, 2010)

Bailey, Catherine, *Black Diamonds: The Rise and Fall of an English Dynasty* (London: Penguin, 2008)

Bash, Graham & Fisher, Andrew, *100 Years of Labour* (Labour Representation Committee, 2006)

Benbow, William, *Grand National Holiday and Congress of the Productive Classes* (London: Journeyman Press, 1977)

Benson, John, *British Coalminers in the Nineteenth Century: A Social History* (New York: Holmes & Meier, 1980)

Benyon, Huw & Hudson, Ray, *The Shadow of the Mine: Coal and the End of Industrial Britain* (London: Verso, 2021)

Blythe, Ronald, *The Age of Illusion: England in the Twenties and Thirties 1919–1940* (London: Hamilton, 1963)

Bor, Michael & Bor, Jethro, *Come Together: Trades Councils 1920–50* (Market Harborough: The Book Guild, 2024)

Bowley, Arthur L, *Wages in the United Kingdom in the Nineteenth Century* (Cambridge: Cambridge University Press, 1900)

Brandon, David, *The General Strike 1926: A New History* (Barnsley: Pen and Sword Transport, 2023)

Broadberry, Stephen & Burhop, Carsten, 'Real Wages and Labor Productivity in Britain and Germany 1871–1938' in *The Journal of Economic History* 70(2) (2010)

Brown, Oliver, *British Right-wing Antisemitism 1918–1930* (University of Gloucestershire, MA thesis, 2021)

Bullock, Ian, *Under Siege: The Independent Labour Party in Interwar Britain* (Edmonton: AU Press, 2017)

Burns, Emile, *The General Strike May 1926: Trades Councils in Action* (London: Labour Research Department, 1926)

Butler, William, '"The British Soldier is no Bolshevik": The British Army, Discipline, and the Demobilisation Strikes of 1919' in *Twentieth Century British History* 30(3) (2019)

Campbell, Alan, 'Reflections on the 1926 Mining Lockout' in *Historical Studies in Industrial Relations* 21 (2006)

Charlton, John, *It Just Went Like Tinder: The Mass Movement and New Unionism in Britain 1889* (London: Redwords, 1999)

Clegg, Hugh Armstrong, *A History of British Trade Unions since 1889*, vol. 2 (Oxford: Clarendon Press, 1985)

Cliff, Tony & Gluckstein, Donny, *Marxism and Trade Union Struggle: The General Strike of 1926* (London: Bookmarks, 1986)

Clinton, Alan, *The Trade Union Rank and File: Trades Councils in Britain 1900–40* (Manchester: Manchester University Press, 1977)

Coal Industry Commission, *Reports and Minutes of Evidence on the Second Stage of the Inquiry* (1919)

Coates, Ken & Topham, Tony, *The Making of the Labour Movement: The Formation of the Transport & General Workers' Union 1870–1922* (Nottingham: Spokesman, 1994)

Coates, Ken (ed.), *British Labour and the Russian Revolution: The Leeds Convention, a Report from the* Daily Herald (Nottingham: Spokesman, n.d.)

Cook, Arthur James, *The Nine Days: The Story of the General Strike told by the Miners' Secretary* (London: Co-operative Printing Society, 1927)

Copsey, Nigel & Renton, David (eds.), *British Fascism, the Labour Movement and the State* (London: Palgrave Macmillan, 2005)

Crook, Wilfrid Harris, *The General Strike: A Study of Labor's Tragic Weapon in Theory and Practice* (Chapel Hill: University of North Carolina Press, 1931)

Dangerfield, George, *The Strange Death of Liberal England* (London: Constable & Co, 1936)

Darlington, Ralph, *Labour Revolt in Britain 1910–14* (London: Pluto Press, 2023)

Davis, Mary, *Comrade or Brother? The History of the British Labour Movement 1789–1951* (London: Pluto Press, 1993)

Desmarais, Ralph H., 'The British Government's Strikebreaking Operation and Black Friday' in *Journal of Contemporary History* 6(2) (1971)

Desmarais, Ralph H., 'Strikebreaking and the Labour Government of 1924' in *Journal of Contemporary History* 8 (1973)

Desmarais, Ralph H., 'Lloyd George and the Development of the British Government's Strikebreaking Organisation' in *International Review of Social History* 20(1) (1975)

Farman, Christopher, *The General Strike, May 1926* (London: Rupert Hart-Davis, 1972)

Florey, R.A., *The General Strike of 1926* (London: John Calder, 1980)

Foot, Paul, *The Vote: How It Was Won and How It Was Undermined* (London: Penguin, 2006)

Galsworthy, John, *A Modern Comedy*, (London: William Heinemann, 1929)

Glasgow, George, *General Strikes and Road Transport* (London: Geoffrey Bles, 1927)

Glynn, Sean, & Oxborrow, John *Interwar Britain: A Social and Economic History* (London: Allen & Unwin, 1976)

Goodhart, Arthur L., 'The Legality of the General Strike in England' in *Yale Law Journal* 36 (1927)

Graves, Robert & Hodge, Alan, *The Long Week-end: A Social History of Great Britain 1918–1939* (London: Penguin, 1971)

Harmon, Mark D., 'A War of Words: The *British Gazette* and the *British Worker* During the 1926 General Strike' in *Labor History* 60(3) (2019)

Hobsbawm, Eric, *The Age of Extremes* (London: Abacus, 1995)

Jeffery, Keith and Hennessy, Peter, *States of Emergency: British Governments and Strikebreaking Since 1919* (London: Routledge & Kegan Paul, 1983)

Jenkins, Mick, *The General Strike of 1842* (London: Lawrence & Wishart, 1980)

Keynes, John Maynard, *The Collected Writings of John Maynard Keynes*, vol. 9 (Cambridge: Cambridge University Press, 2012)

Kirby, Maurice W., *The British Coalmining Industry 1870–1946: A Political and Economic History* (London: Archon Books, 1977)

Klugmann, James, *History of the Communist Party of Great Britain*, vol. 2 (London: Lawrence & Wishart, 1969)

Kushner, Tony & Lunn, Kenneth (eds.), *Traditions of Intolerance: Historical Perspectives on Fascism and Race Discourse in Britain* (Manchester: Manchester University Press, 1989)

Lamb, Dave, *Mutinies: 1917–1920* (Solidarity, n.d.)

Lansbury, George, *The Secret History of the Great Strike and the Blackleg State* (London: Lansbury's Labour Weekly, 1926)

Lawrence, Jon, 'Forging a Peaceable Kingdom: War, Violence, and Fear of Brutalization in Post-First World War Britain' in *The Journal of Modern History* 75(3) (2003)

Laybourn, Keith, *The General Strike of 1926* (Manchester: Manchester University Press, 1993)

Laybourn, Keith, *A History of British Trade Unionism* (Stroud: Sutton Publishing, 1997)

Laybourn, Keith, *The General Strike Day by Day* (Stroud: Sutton Publishing, 1999)

Leon, Clare Katherine, *Special Constables: An Historical and Contemporary Survey* (University of Bath, PhD thesis, 1991)

Luxemburg, Rosa, *The Mass Strike, the Political Party and the Trade Unions* (London: Bookmarks, 2023)

Lyddon, Dave, 'Walter Milne-Bailey, the TUC Research Department, and the 1926 General Strike' in *Historical Studies in Industrial Relations* 29/30 (2010)

MacDonald, G.W. & Gospel, Howard F., 'The Mond-Turner Talks, 1927–1933: A Study in Industrial Co-operation' in *The Historical Journal* 16(4) (1973)

Macfarlane, L.J., 'Hands Off Russia: British Labour and the Russo-Polish War, 1920' in *Past and Present* 38 (1967)

Mason, Anthony, 'The Government and the General Strike, 1926' in *International Review of Social History* 16(1) (1969)

McIlroy, John, Campbell, Alan & Gildart, Keith (eds.), *Industrial Politics and the 1926 Mining Lockout: The Struggle for Dignity* (Cardiff: University of Wales Press, 2009)

McIlroy, John, 'Memory, Commemoration and History – 1926 in 2006' in *Historical Studies in Industrial Relations* 21 (2006)

McKillop, Norman, *The Lighted Flame: A History of the Associated Society of Locomotive Engineers and Firemen* (London: Thomas Nelson, 1950)

McLynn, Frank, *The Road Not Taken: How Britain Narrowly Missed a Revolution, 1381–1926.* (London: Vintage Books, 2013)

Moore, Nathan, '"The courtrooms of the working class are the streets": Demonstrations During the "Great Communist Trial of 1925"' in *Twentieth Century Communism* 30 (2026)

Morgan, Jane, *Conflict and Order: The Police and Labour Disputes in England and Wales 1900–1939* (Oxford: Clarendon Press, 1987)

Morris, Margaret, *The General Strike* (London: The Journeyman Press, 1980)

Murphy, John Thomas, *The Political Meaning of the Great Strike* (London: CPGB, 1926)

Outram, Quentin, 'The Stupidest Men in England? The Industrial Relations Strategy of the Coalowners between the Lockouts, 1923–1924' in *Historical Studies in Industrial Relations* 4 (1997)

Page Arnot, Robin, *The General Strike, May 1926* (Wakefield: EP Publishing, 1975)

Page Arnot, Robin, *The Miners: A History of the Miners' Federation of Great Britain 1889–1910* (London: Allen & Unwin, 1949)

Paxman, Jeremy, *Black Gold: A History of How Coal Made Britain* (London: William Collins, 2021)

Pearce, Brian & Woodhouse, Michael, *A History of Communism in Britain* (London: Bookmarks, 1995)

Pearson, Lynn, *England's Co-operative Movement: An Architectural History* (Liverpool: Liverpool University Press, 2020)

Pelling, Henry, *A History of British Trade Unionism* (5th ed., London: Penguin, 1992)

Perkins, Anne, *A Very British Strike: 3 May–12 May 1926* (London: Pan Books, 2007)

Phillips, G.A., *The General Strike: The Politics of Industrial Conflict* (London: Weidenfeld & Nicolson, 1976)

Postgate, Raymond, Wilkinson, Ellen & Horrabin, Frank, *A Workers' History of the Great Strike* (London: Plebs' League, 1927)

Pugh, Martin, *'Hurrah for the Blackshirts!': Fascists and Fascism in Britain Between the Wars* (London: Pimlico, 2006)

Raw, Louise, *Striking a Light: The Bryant and May Matchwomen and Their Place in History* (London: Continuum, 2011)

Raynes, J.R., *Coal and its Conflicts: A Brief Record of the Disputes Between Labour and Capital in the Coal Mining Industry of Great Britain* (London: Ernest Benn, 1928)

Redmayne, Sir Richard Augustine Studdert, *The British Coal-Mining Industry During the War* (Oxford: Clarendon Press, 1923)

Reid, Anna, *A Nasty Little War: The West's Fight to Reverse the Russian Revolution* (London: John Murray, 2023)

Renshaw, Patrick, *The General Strike* (London: Eyre Methuen, 1975)

Richards, Huw, *The Bloody Circus: The* Daily Herald *and the Left* (London: Pluto Press, 1997)

Rosenberg, Chanie, *Britain on the Brink of Revolution: 1919* (London: Bookmarks, 1987)

Ryan, Liam, 'Citizen Strike Breakers: Volunteers, Strikes, and the State in Britain, 1911–1926' in *Labour History Review* 87(2) (2022)

Saltzman, Rachelle Hope, *A Lark for the Sake of Their Country: The 1926 General Strike Volunteers in Folklore and Memory* (Manchester: Manchester University Press, 2014)

Skelley, Jeffrey (ed.), *The General Strike, 1926* (London: Lawrence & Wishart, 1976)

Symons, Julian, *The General Strike* (London: House of Stratus, 2001)

Taaffe, Peter, *1926 General Strike: Workers Taste Power* (London: Socialist Books, 2006)

Taylor, Robert, 'Citrine's Unexpurgated Diaries, 1925–26: The Mining Crisis and the National Strike' in *Historical Studies in Industrial Relations* 20 (2005)

Thomas, Ian, *Confronting the Challenge of Socialism: The British Empire Union and the National Citizens' Union 1917–1927* (University of Wolverhampton, MPhil thesis, 2010)

Torrance, David, *The Wild Men: The Remarkable Story of Britain's First Labour Government* (London: Bloomsbury, 2024)

Unofficial Reform Committee, *The Miners' Next Step* (1912)

Ward, Jack Grimley, 'Bolshevik Bogies: Red Scares in Britain, 1919–24' in *Contemporary British History* 38(1) (2024)

White, Stephen, 'Soviets in Britain: The Leeds Convention of 1917' in *International Review of Social History* 19(2) (1974)

Wrigley, Chris, 'The General Strike, 1926 in Local History Part I: The Government's Volunteers' in *The Local Historian* 16(1) (1984)

Wrigley, Chris, 'The Lloyd George Coalition Government: Labour and Industrial Relations' in *Journal of Liberal History* 119 (2023)

Local histories

Ainsworth, Jim, *Accrington 1926: A Comprehensive History of the General Strike as It Affected Accrington and District* (Hyndburn TUC, 1994)

Barnsley, Tony, *Breaking Their Chains: Mary MacArthur and the Chainmakers' Strike of 1910* (London: Bookmarks, 2011)

Bruley, Sue, *The Women and Men of 1926: A Gender and Social History of the General Strike and Miners' Lockout in South Wales* (Cardiff: University of Wales Press, 2010)

Burke, Barry, *Rebels With a Cause: The History of Hackney Trades Council 1900–1975* (Hackney Trades Council, 1975)

Craig, Maggie, *When the Clyde Ran Red* (Edinburgh: Mainstream Publishing, 2011)

Griffiths, Robert, *Killing No Murder: South Wales and the Great Railway Strike of 1911* (London: Manifesto Press, 2009)

Hills, R.I., *The General Strike in York, 1926* (York: University of York, 1980)

Hutcherson, Margaret, *Let No Wheels Turn: The Wrecking of the Flying Scotsman, 1926* (Washington: TUPS Books, 2006)

Johnson, Barry, *Nine Days that Shook Mansfield: The General Strike in the Mansfield Area* (Chesterfield: The Ragged Historians, 2005)

Large, Margaret, *The Nine Days in Birmingham: The General Strike 4–12 May 1926* (Birmingham: Birmingham Public Libraries, 1976)

Newitt, Ned, *The General Strike in Leicester – 1926* [https://www.nednewitt.com/?page_id=1378]

Porter, J.H., 'Devon and the General Strike' in *International Review of Social History* 23(3) (1978)

Potts, Christopher R., *The GWR and the General Strike* (Oxford: The Oakwood Press, 1996)

Sephton, Robert S., *Oxford and the General Strike 1926* (Oxford: Robert Sephton, 1993)

Smith, Dai, 'The Tonypandy Riots, 1910 – Winston Churchill's Nemesis' in *Finest Hour* 193 (2021)

Southwark Trades Council, *Nine Days in May: The 1926 General Strike in Southwark* [https://libcom.org/article/nine-days-may-1926-general-strike-southwark]

Taylor, David, *The 1926 General Strike in Wolverhampton and the Black Country: A Revolution or a Dispute?* (Oxford: Youcaxton, 2017)

Towers, Brian, *Waterfront Blues: The Rise and Fall of Liverpool's Dockland* (Lancaster: Carnegie, 2011)

Trory, Ernie, *Brighton and the General Strike* (East Sussex: Crabtree Press, 1975)

Wright, Ian, 'Pity the Poor Buttyman: The Butty System in the Forest of Dean 1921–1938' (Bristol Radical History Group, 2020)

Wyncoll, Peter, *The Nottingham Labour Movement 1880–1939* (London: Lawrence & Wishart, 1985)

Memoirs and biographies

Bevan, Aneurin, *In Place of Fear* (London: William Heinemann, 1952)

Blaxland, Gregory, *A Life for Unity* (London: Frederick Muller, 1964)

Bondfield, Margaret, *A Life's Work* (Tiptree: The Anchor Press, 1948)

Bullock, Alan, *The Life and Times of Ernest Bevin*, vol. 1 (London: William Heinemann, 1969)

Callwell, Major-General Sir Charles Edward, *Field Marshal Sir Henry Wilson, His Life and Diaries*, vol. 2 (London: Cassell & Co, 1927)

Campbell, John, *F.E. Smith: First Earl of Birkenhead* (London: Jonathan Cape, 1983)

Cannadine, David (ed.), *Oxford Dictionary of National Biography* (Oxford: Oxford University Press)

Childs, Sir Wyndham, *Episodes and Reflections* (London: Cassell & Co, 1930)

Citrine, Lord Walter, *Men and Work* (London: Hutchinson & Co, 1964)

Cole, Margaret (ed.), *Beatrice Webb's Diaries 1924–32* (London: Longmans, Green & Co, 1956)

Darlington, Ralph, *The Political Trajectory of J.T. Murphy* (Liverpool: Liverpool University Press, 1998)

Davies, Paul, *A.J. Cook* (Manchester: Manchester University Press, 1987)

Dorril, Stephen, *Blackshirt: Sir Oswald Mosley and British Fascism* (London: Viking, 2006)

Fyfe, Hamilton, *Behind the Scenes of the Great Strike* (London: The Labour Publishing Company, 1926)

Hyde, Harford Montgomery, *Baldwin, the Unexpected Prime Minister* (London: Hart-Davis MacGibbon, 1973)

Hyndman, Henry Mayers, *Further Reminiscences* (London: Macmillan & Co, 1912)

Jones, Thomas, *Whitehall Diary*, vol. 2 (London: Oxford University Press, 1969)

Lawson, Jack, *The Man in the Cap: The Life of Herbert Smith* (London: Methuen & Co, 1941)

Lee, William Alexander, *30 Years in Coal* (The Mining Association of Great Britain, 1954)

Mann, Tom, *Memoirs* (London: MacGibbon & Kee, 1967)

Moher, Jim, *Walter Citrine: Forgotten Statesman of the Trades Union Congress* (JGM Books, 2021)

Morgan, Kevin, *Bolshevism, Syndicalism and the General Strike: The Lost International World of A.A. Purcell* (London: Lawrence & Wishart, 2013)

Radice, Giles & Radice, Lisanne, *Will Thorne: Constructive Militant* (London: George Allen & Unwin, 1974)

Rhodes James, Robert, *Memoirs of a Conservative: J.C.C. Davidson's Memoirs and Papers, 1910–37* (London: Weidenfeld & Nicolson, 1969)

Rhodes James, Robert, *Churchill: A Study in Failure 1900–1939* (London: Weidenfeld & Niolson, 1970)

Samuel, Herbert, *Memoirs* (London: Cresset Press, 1945)

Sitwell, Osbert, *Laughter in the Next Room* (London: Macmillan & Co, 1949)

Thomson, Basil, *Odd People: Hunting Spies in the First World War* (London: Biteback, 2015)

Turner, Ben, *About Myself 1863–1930* (London: Humphrey Toulmin, 1930)

Williams, Thomas, *Digging for Britain* (London: Hutchinson, 1965)

Williamson, Philip, *Stanley Baldwin: Conservative Leadership and National Values* (Cambridge: Cambridge University Press, 1999)

Williamson, Philip & Baldwin, Edward (eds.), *Baldwin Papers: A Conservative Statesman 1908–1947* (Cambridge: Cambridge University Press, 2004)

Young, George Malcolm, *Stanley Baldwin* (London: Rupert Hart-Davis, 1952)

The strike in fiction

Cole, G.D.H., *The Striker Stricken* reproduced in *Historical Studies in Industrial Relations* 22 (2006)

Davies, Idris, *The Angry Summer: A Poem of 1926* (Cardiff: University of Wales Press, 1993)

Ferrall, Charles & McNeill, Dougal, *Writing the 1926 General Strike: Literature, Culture, Politics* (Cambridge: Cambridge University Press, 2015)

Haywood, Ian, ' "Never Again?": Ellen Wilkinson's *Clash* and the Feminization of the General Strike' in *Literature & History* 8(2) (1999)

Wilkinson, Ellen, *Clash* (London: Greenprint, 2018)

Notes

Introduction
1. C. Farman, *The General Strike, May 1926*, p. 29.
2. The theory is expressed in William Benbow's pamphlet *Grand National Holiday and Congress of the Productive Classes*.
3. See M. Jenkins, *The General Strike of 1842* for a comprehensive account of the strike in that year.
4. I. Davies, *The Angry Summer: A Poem of 1926*, p. 3.

1 THE FIRST REQUISITE OF EMPIRE
1. J. Paxman, *Black Gold: The History of How Coal Made Britain*, pp. 115–16.
2. R. Page Arnot, *The Miners: A History of the Miners' Federation of Great Britain 1889–1910*, vol. 1, pp. 22–4.
3. H. Benyon & R. Hudson, *In the Shadow of the Mine: Coal and the End of Industrial Britain*, p. 8.
4. P. Renshaw, *The General Strike*, p. 78.
5. H. Benyon & R. Hudson, *In the Shadow of the Mine*, p. 19.
6. J. Benson, *British Coalminers in the Nineteenth Century: A Social History*, p. 127.
7. J. Benson, *British Coalminers in the Nineteenth Century*, pp. 93–103.
8. As contemporaries did, I use the words coalowner and mineowner interchangeably throughout this book.
9. W.A. Lee, *30 Years in Coal*, p. 11.
10. See C. Bailey, *Black Diamonds*, ch. 1.
11. J. Paxman, *Black Gold*, pp. 71–80.
12. See Q. Outram, 'Nimmo, Sir Adam (1866–1939)' in D. Cannadine (ed.), *Oxford Dictionary of National Biography*.
13. M.W. Kirby, *The British Coalmining Industry 1870–1946: A Political and Economic History*, p. 10.
14. On another occasion he ranked them the other way around, stating that 'if Mr Herbert Smith and Mr Cook had not existed, I should have had to admit plainly that I thought the mine owners were the stupidest people in the world'. See Q. Outram, 'The Stupidest Men in England? The Industrial

Relations Strategy of the Coalowners between the Lockouts, 1923–1924' in *Historical Studies in Industrial Relations* 4, p. 66.
15 J. Benson, *British Coalminers in the Nineteenth Century*, p. 31.
16 P. Davies, *A.J. Cook*, p. 4; J. Lawson, *The Man in the Cap: The Life of Herbert Smith*, p. 32.
17 J. Benson, *British Coalminers in the Nineteenth Century*, p. 180.
18 T. Williams, *Digging for Britain*, p. 16.
19 A.L. Bowley, *Wages in the United Kingdom in the Nineteenth Century*, pp. 96–110; S. Broadberry & C. Burhop, 'Real Wages and Labor Productivity in Britain and Germany 1871–1938' in *The Journal of Economic History* 70(2), p. 420.
20 J. Benson, *British Coalminers in the Nineteenth Century*, p. 79.
21 See G.A. Phillips, *The General Strike: The Politics of Industrial Conflict*, pp. 297–300.
22 See for example I. Wright, 'Pity the Poor Buttyman: The Butty System in the Forest of Dean 1921–1938', *Bristol Radical History Group*.
23 J. Benson, *British Coalminers in the Nineteenth Century*, p. 91.
24 R. Page Arnot, *The Miners*, p. 37.
25 J. Benson, *British Coalminers in the Nineteenth Century*, pp. 191–4.
26 R. Page Arnot, *The Miners*, p. 50.
27 P. Renshaw, *The General Strike*, p. 38.
28 The terms 'strike' and 'lockout' have both been used to describe the 1893 dispute and many subsequent miners' disputes including that of 1926. Generally, they began as lockouts when the owners attempted to unilaterally impose new conditions, and developed into strikes when the union instructed its members not to accept the new terms.
29 R. Page Arnot, *The Miners*, pp. 368–9.
30 J. Paxman, *Black Gold*, pp. 164–6.
31 P. Davies, *A.J. Cook*, pp. 8–12.
32 Unofficial Reform Committee, *The Miners' Next Step*, p. 17.
33 J.R. Raynes, *Coal and its Conflicts*, pp. 120–1.
34 R.A.S. Redmayne, *The British Coal-Mining Industry During the War*, p. 146.
35 H.A. Clegg, *A History of British Trade Unions since 1889*, vol. 2, pp. 127–30.
36 See P. Davies, *A.J. Cook*, pp. 24–5.
37 M.W. Kirby, *The British Coalmining Industry 1870–1946*, pp. 29–31.
38 R.A.S. Redmayne, *The British Coal-Mining Industry During the War*, pp. 216–17.
39 P. Renshaw, *The General Strike*, p. 60.
40 J.R. Raynes, *Coal and its Conflicts*, pp. 167–70.
41 J.R. Raynes, *Coal and its Conflicts*, p. 181.
42 P. Davies, *A.J. Cook*, pp. 44–6.
43 W.A. Lee, *30 Years in Coal*, pp. 16–17.

44 K. Coates & T. Topham, *The Making of the Labour Movement: The Formation of the Transport & General Workers' Union 1870–1922*, pp. 774–6.
45 P. Davies, *A.J. Cook*, pp. 53–8.
46 J. Lawson, *The Man in the Cap*, pp. 150–1.
47 G.A. Phillips, *The General Strike*, pp. 24–5.
48 Q. Outram, 'The Stupidest Men in England?', pp. 75–6.
49 M. Morris, *The General Strike*, pp. 111–12.
50 J.M. Keynes, 'The Economic Consequences of Mr Churchill' in *The Collected Writings of John Maynard Keynes*, vol. 9, p. 211.
51 Frank Hodges, whose reputation never recovered from the 1921 debacle, jumped before he was pushed and focused on his other role of secretary of the Miners' International Federation.
52 *Daily Herald*, 31 July 1925.
53 R. Page Arnot, *The General Strike, May 1926*, pp. 29–31.
54 P. Renshaw, *The General Strike*, pp.121–2.
55 R. Page Arnot, *The General Strike, May 1926*, p. 35.
56 R. Page Arnot, *The General Strike, May 1926*, p. 36.
57 M. Morris, *The General Strike*, p. 146.
58 C. Farman, *The General Strike, May 1926*, p. 51.
59 G.A. Phillips, *The General Strike*, pp. 74–5.
60 C. Farman, *The General Strike, May 1926*, pp. 53–4.
61 C. Farman, *The General Strike, May 1926*, p. 54.

2 'A POWER STRONGER THAN THE STATE ITSELF'?

1 R. Griffiths, *Killing No Murder: South Wales and the Great Railway Strike of 1911*, p. 10.
2 S. Glynn & J. Oxborrow, *Interwar Britain: A Social and Economic History*, p. 92.
3 See T. Barnsley, *Breaking Their Chains: Mary MacArthur and the Chainmakers' Strike of 1910*.
4 S. Glynn & J. Oxborrow, *Interwar Britain*, p. 221.
5 S. Glynn & J. Oxborrow, *Interwar Britain*, p. 145.
6 R. Graves & A. Hodge, *The Long Week-end: A Social History of Great Britain 1918–1939*, p. 65.
7 See L. Raw, *Striking a Light: The Bryant and May Matchwomen and their Place in History*, ch. 6.
8 K. Coates & T. Topham, *The Making of the Labour Movement*, pp. 56–8.
9 K. Coates & T. Topham, *The Making of the Labour Movement*, pp. 88–9.
10 L. Raw, *Striking a Light*, pp. 155–6.
11 H. Pelling, *A History of British Trade Unionism*, pp. 92–100.
12 H.M. Hyndman, *Further Reminiscences*, ch. 19.

13 J. Charlton, *It Just Went Like Tinder: The Mass Movement and New Unionism in Britain 1889*, pp. 69–70.
14 T. Mann, *Memoirs*, pp. 26–7.
15 E.A. Radice & G.H. Radice, *Will Thorne: Constructive Militant*, p. 12.
16 G. Bash & A. Fisher, *100 Years of Labour*, p. 13.
17 R. Darlington, *Labour Revolt in Britain 1910–14*, pp. 77–80.
18 R. Darlington, *Labour Revolt in Britain 1910–14*, pp. 97–105.
19 R. Griffiths, *Killing No Murder*, pp. 31–2.
20 C. Bailey, *Black Diamonds*, pp. 118–20.
21 R. Darlington, *Labour Revolt in Britain 1910–14*, p. 96.
22 Quoted in R. Darlington, *Labour Revolt in Britain 1910–14*, p. 175.
23 *International Socialist Review*, May 1911.
24 G. Dangerfield, *The Strange Death of Liberal England*, pp. 380–5.
25 H. Pelling, *A History of British Trade Unionism*, p. 155.
26 *British Labour and the Russian Revolution: The Leeds Convention*, a report from the *Daily Herald*, pp. 29–30.
27 See S. White, 'Soviets in Britain: The Leeds Convention of 1917' in *International Review of Social History* 19(2).
28 C. Wrigley, 'The Lloyd George Coalition Government: Labour and Industrial Relations' in *Journal of Liberal History*, 119, pp. 58–60.
29 H.A. Clegg, *A History of British Trade Unions since 1889*, vol. 2, pp. 204–7.
30 M. Craig, *When the Clyde Ran Red*, ch. 18.
31 C. Rosenberg, *Britain on the Brink of Revolution: 1919*, pp. 58–9.
32 A. Bevan, *In Place of Fear*, pp. 20–1.
33 K. Laybourn, *A History of British Trade Unionism*, p. 141.
34 See K. Coates & T. Topham, *The Making of the Labour Movement*, pp. 790–797.
35 H. Pelling, *A History of British Trade Unionism*, pp. 166–7.
36 Prior to joining the CPGB Cook was in fact a member of a group close to Sylvia Pankhurst, the Communist Party of South Wales and the West of England, considered too left-wing even by the CPGB for its outright rejection of parliamentary politics and extreme hostility to the Labour Party.
37 B. Pearce & M. Woodhouse, *A History of Communism in Britain*, p. 169.
38 M. Bor & J. Bor, *Come Together: Trades Councils 1920–50*, pp. 12–17.
39 W. Churchill, 'Bolshevism and Imperial Sedition, 1920'. See https://www.nationalchurchillmuseum.org/bolshevism-and-imperial-sedition.html.
40 H.A. Clegg, *A History of British Trade Unions since 1889*, vol. 2, pp. 394–5.
41 MRC, *MSS.292/PUB/4/1/25*.

3 THE CORRIDORS OF POWER
1 E. Hobsbawm, *The Age of Extremes*, p. 67.

2   TNA, *HO 45/10743/263275.*
3   See MRC, *15X/2/63/12.*
4   J.G. Ward, 'Bolshevik Bogies: Red Scares in Britain, 1919–24' in *Contemporary British History* 38(1), pp. 5–6.
5   *Leicester Evening Mail,* 21 February 1922.
6   B. Pearce & R. Woodhouse, *A History of Communism in Britain,* p. 100.
7   R.H. Desmarais, 'The British Government's Strikebreaking Operation and Black Friday' in *Journal of Contemporary History* 6(2), p. 125.
8   See C.E. Callwell, *Field Marshal Sir Henry Wilson, His life and Diaries,* vol. 2, pp. 148–70.
9   See A. Reid, *A Nasty Little War: The West's Fight to Reverse the Russian Revolution,* pp. 194–5.
10 *Illustrated Sunday Herald,* 8 February 1920.
11 MRC, *292/947/1/29.*
12 L.J. Macfarlane, 'Hands Off Russia: British Labour and the Russo-Polish War, 1920' in *Past and Present* 38, p. 147.
13 MRC, *36/R30/23.*
14 W. Butler, '"The British Soldier is no Bolshevik": The British Army, Discipline, and the Demobilisation Strikes of 1919' in *Twentieth Century British History* 30(3), pp. 9–22.
15 D. Lamb, *Mutinies: 1917–1920,* pp. 19–20.
16 W. Childs, *Episodes and Reflections,* p. 162.
17 C. Andrew, *The Defence of the Realm: The Authorized History of MI5,* pp. 122–3.
18 W. Childs, *Episodes and Reflections,* pp. 216–17.
19 B. Thomson, *Odd People: Hunting Spies in the First World War,* p. 285.
20 TNA, *HO 144/6682.*
21 R.H. Desmarais, 'Lloyd George and the Development of the British Government's Strikebreaking Organisation' in *International Review of Social History* 20(1), pp. 3–4.
22 L. Ryan, 'Citizen Strike Breakers: Volunteers, Strikes, and the State in Britain, 1911–1926' in *Labour History Review* 87(2), pp. 125–9.
23 R.H. Desmarais, 'The British Government's Strikebreaking Operation and Black Friday', pp. 115–20.
24 R.H. Desmarais, 'Strikebreaking and the Labour Government of 1924' in *Journal of Contemporary History* 8, p. 167.
25 R. Rhodes James, *Memoirs of a Conservative: J.C.C. Davidson's Memoirs and Papers, 1910–37,* p. 178.
26 R. Rhodes James, *Memoirs of a Conservative,* pp. 179–80. Smillie and Hodges were both prominent MFGB leaders in this period.
27 A. Mason, 'The Government and the General Strike, 1926' in *International Review of Social History* 16(1), p. 4.

28 R.H. Desmarais, 'Strikebreaking and the Labour Government of 1924', p. 173.
29 R. Rhodes James, *Memoirs of a Conservative*, p. 180.
30 R.H. Desmarais, 'Strikebreaking and the Labour Government of 1924', pp. 173–4.
31 *Workers' Weekly*, 25 July 1924.
32 For a full account of the collapse of the 1924 Labour government see D. Torrance, *The Wild Men: The Remarkable Story of Britain's First Labour Government*, ch. 13.
33 *Daily Mail*, 25 October 1924.
34 C. Andrew, *The Defence of the Realm*, pp. 148–51.
35 P. Williamson, *Stanley Baldwin: Conservative Leadership and National Values*, pp. 123–5, 193–4.
36 P. Williamson, *Stanley Baldwin*, p. 3.
37 P. Williamson, *Stanley Baldwin*, pp. 181–2.
38 D. Cesarani, 'Joynson-Hicks and the Radical Right in England after the First World War', in T. Kushner & K. Lunn (eds.), *Traditions of Intolerance: Historical Perspectives on Fascism and Race Discourse in Britain*, pp. 118–40.
39 R. Blythe, *The Age of Illusion: England in the Twenties and Thirties 1919–1940*, pp. 24–5.
40 P. Williamson & E. Baldwin (eds.), *Baldwin Papers: A Conservative Statesman 1908–1947*, p. 166.
41 J. Campbell, *F.E. Smith: First Earl of Birkenhead*, p. 768.
42 K. Jeffery & P. Hennessy, *States of Emergency: British Governments and Strikebreaking since 1919*, pp. 93–4.
43 R. Rhodes James, *Memoirs of a Conservative*, pp. 227–8.
44 TNA, *CAB 23/50/23*.
45 TNA, *CAB 23/50/25*.
46 TNA, *HO 144/6682*.
47 TNA, *CAB 23/51/2*.
48 *Daily Herald*, 21 November 1925.
49 *Daily Express*, 26 November 1925.
50 N. Moore, '"The courtrooms of the working class are the streets": Demonstrations During the "Great Communist Trial of 1925"' in *Twentieth Century Communism* 30, pp. 11–12.
51 J. Klugmann, 'Marxism, Reformism, and the General Strike,' in J. Skelley (ed.), *The General Strike, 1926*, pp. 66–7.
52 TNA, *MEPO 38/20*.
53 P. Williamson, *Stanley Baldwin*, pp. 79–80.
54 M. Pugh, *'Hurrah for the Blackshirts!': Fascists and Fascism in Britain Between the Wars*, p. 96.

55 R.C. Maguire, ' "The Fascists…are…to be depended upon." The British Government, Fascists and Strike-breaking during 1925 and 1926' in N. Copsey & D. Renton (eds.), *British Fascism, the Labour Movement and the State*, p. 16.
56 TNA, *CAB 24/174*.
57 TNA, *CAB 24/174*.
58 TNA, *CAB 23/50/22*.
59 TNA, *CAB 24/175*.
60 TNA, *CAB 24/174*.
61 TNA, *CAB 23/51/1*.
62 R.C. Maguire, ' "The Fascists…are…to be depended upon." The British Government, Fascists and Strike-breaking during 1925 and 1926', p. 8.
63 *Times*, 25 September 1925.
64 TNA, *CAB 24/174*.
65 *Times*, 1 October 1925.
66 M. Pugh, *'Hurrah for the Blackshirts!'*, pp. 58–9.
67 *Evening News*, 17 September 1925. One of the Fascists was also injured in the fight.
68 *Evening News*, 10 November 1925.

4 BREAKDOWN

1 P. Renshaw, *The General Strike*, pp. 143–4.
2 TNA, *CAB 24/179*.
3 G.A. Phillips, *The General Strike*, pp. 100–1.
4 G. Blaxland, *A Life for Unity*, p. 184.
5 See for example *Western Morning News*, 25 March 1926.
6 J. Klugmann, *History of the Communist Party of Great Britain*, vol. 2, pp. 101–2.
7 LHASC, *CP/CENT/IND/11/01*.
8 TNA, *HO 144/6682*.
9 T. Jones, *Whitehall Diary*, vol. 2, pp. 10–16.
10 MRC, *MSS.292/252.61/29/3*.
11 MRC, *MSS.292/252.61/29/3*.
12 MRC, *MSS.292/252.61/29/4*.
13 MRC, *MSS.292/252.61/29/5*.
14 G.A. Phillips, *The General Strike*, pp. 109–11.
15 MRC, *MSS.292/252.61/29/6*.
16 A. Perkins, *A Very British Strike*, p.94.
17 MRC, *MSS.292/252.61/29/7*.
18 G.A. Phillips, *The General Strike*, pp. 153–4.
19 Quoted in K. Laybourn, *The General Strike Day by Day*, p. 38.

20 MRC, *MSS.292/252.61/29/9*.
21 MRC, *MSS.292/252.61/29/10*.
22 W. Citrine, *Men and Work*, p. 157.
23 K. Morgan, *Bolshevism, Syndicalism and the General Strike: The Lost Internationalist World of A.A. Purcell*, pp. 240–2.
24 K. Morgan, *Bolshevism, Syndicalism and the General Strike* pp. 252–4.
25 Quoted in K. Laybourn, *The General Strike Day by Day*, p. 43.
26 MRC, *MSS.292/252.62/5/13*.
27 P. Wyncoll, 'The East Midlands' in J. Skelley (ed.), *The General Strike, 1926*, p. 177.
28 G. Barnsby, 'The Black Country' in J. Skelley (ed.), *The General Strike, 1926*, p. 204.
29 J. Jacobs, 'From Hackney' in J. Skelley (ed.), *The General Strike, 1926*, p. 360.
30 The text of these telegrams can be found in TNA, *HO 144/6116*.
31 W. Citrine, *Men and Work*, pp. 164–5.
32 Quoted in K. Laybourn, *The General Strike Day by Day*, p. 49.
33 Quoted in K. Laybourn, *The General Strike Day by Day*, p. 53.
34 M. Morris, *The General Strike*, p. 228.
35 H.M. Hyde, *Baldwin, the Unexpected Prime Minister*, p. 268.
36 Dave Lyddon believes this was written by Milne-Bailey. See D. Lyddon 'Walter Milne-Bailey, the TUC Research Department, and the 1926 General Strike' in *Historical Studies in Industrial Relations* 29/30.
37 MRC, *MSS.292/252.62/13/17*.
38 *Hansard*, 3 May 1926.
39 W. Citrine, *Men and Work*, pp. 175–6. As home secretary in January 1911, Churchill had overseen an operation against a small revolutionary gang in Sidney Street, East London, which involved the mobilisation of hundreds of police, troops, and artillery, for which he had been widely criticised.
40 Quoted in R. Page Arnot, *The General Strike, May 1926*, pp. 167–9.
41 *Western Morning News*, 4 May 1926.
42 *Exeter and Plymouth Gazette*, 4 May 1926.

5 THE FIRST DAY

1 I. MacDougall, 'Edinburgh' in J. Skelley (ed.), *The General Strike, 1926*, p. 146.
2 MRC, *MSS.292/252.62/16/14*.
3 P. Renshaw, *The General Strike*, p. 176.
4 MRC, *MSS.292/252.62/21/2*.
5 P. Renshaw, *The General Strike*, p. 178.
6 R. Page Arnot, *The General Strike, May 1926*, p. 173.
7 *Belfast Newsletter*, 5 May 1926.

8 M. Morris, *The General Strike*, p. 27.
9 *Belfast Newsletter*, 5 May 1926.
10 M. Morris, *The General Strike*, pp. 24–5.
11 *An account of the proceedings of the Northumberland and Durham General Council Joint Strike Committee, May 1926*, p. 4.
12 D.A. Wilson, 'From Bradford' in J. Skelley (ed.), *The General Strike, 1926*, p. 354.
13 P. Wyncoll, 'The East Midlands', pp. 178–9.
14 A. Perkins, *A Very British Strike*, pp. 114–15.
15 D. Brandon, *The General Strike 1926: A New History*, pp. 147–8.
16 I. MacDougall, 'Edinburgh', p. 147.
17 P. Renshaw, *The General Strike*, p. 179.
18 A. Tuckett, 'Swindon' in J. Skelley (ed.), *The General Strike, 1926*, p. 289.
19 *An account of the proceedings of the Northumberland and Durham General Council Joint Strike Committee, May 1926*, p. 3.
20 MRC, *MSS.292/252.62/21/3*.
21 P. Renshaw, *The General Strike*, p. 181.
22 R.P. Hastings, 'Birmingham' in J. Skelley (ed.), *The General Strike, 1926*, pp. 213–14.
23 *Hartlepool Northern Daily Mail*, 5 May 1926.
24 *Hartlepool Northern Daily Mail*, 5 May 1926.
25 E & R. Frow, 'Manchester Diary' in J. Skelley (ed.), *The General Strike, 1926*, pp. 161–3.
26 M. Morris, *The General Strike*, p. 33.
27 MRC, *MSS.292/252.62/5/52*.
28 M. Morris, *The General Strike*, pp. 35–8.
29 MRC, *MSS.292/252.62/20/5*.
30 *Sheffield Daily Telegraph*, 4 May 1926.
31 MRC, *MSS.292/252/62/5/52*.
32 M. Morris, *The General Strike*, p. 32.
33 *Sunderland Daily Echo*, 4 May 1926.
34 B. Davies, 'From St Helens' in J. Skelley (ed.), *The General Strike, 1926*, p. 332.
35 J. Symons, *The General Strike*, pp. 57–8.
36 *Sheffield Independent*, 5 May 1926.
37 *Yorkshire Evening Post*, 4 May 1926.
38 D. Brandon, *The General Strike 1926*, p. 147.
39 MRC, *MSS.292/252.62/16/14*.
40 R. Page Arnot, *The General Strike, May 1926*, pp. 174–5.
41 MRC, *MSS.292/252.62/20/6*.
42 MRC, *MSS.292/252.62/13/25*.

6 VOLUNTEERS

1. TNA, *CAB 23/52/21*.
2. P. Wyncoll, 'The East Midlands', p. 174.
3. R.H. Saltzman, *A Lark for the Sake of their Country: The 1926 General Strike Volunteers in Folklore and Memory*, pp. 66–7.
4. See O. Brown, 'British Rightwing Anti-Semitism, 1918–1930', MA thesis, University of Gloucestershire.
5. Quoted in I. Thomas, *Confronting the Challenge of Socialism: The British Empire Union and the National Citizens' Union 1917–1927*, MPhil thesis, University of Wolverhampton, p. 96.
6. R.H. Saltzman, *A Lark for the Sake of their Country*, p. 72.
7. L. Ryan, 'Citizen Strike Breakers', pp. 132–3.
8. See J. Symons, *The General Strike*, ch. 4.
9. MRC, *MSS 126/TG/11/5/3*.
10. P. Carter, 'The West of Scotland' in J. Skelley (ed.), *The General Strike, 1926*, pp. 134–5.
11. *Northern Whig*, 15 May 1926.
12. *Tatler*, 12 May 1926.
13. C.R. Potts, *The GWR and the General Strike*, pp. 61–6.
14. MRC, *MSS.126/TG/11/1/10*.
15. See G.A. Phillips, *The General Strike*, pp. 152–3.
16. For a geographical breakdown of the OMS lists see C. Wrigley, 'The General Strike, 1926 in Local History Part I: The Government's Volunteers' in *The Local Historian* 16(1), pp. 42–8.
17. A. Mason, 'The Government and the General Strike 1926', pp 18–19; P. Renshaw, *The General Strike*, pp. 186–7.
18. P. Renshaw, *The General Strike*, pp. 185–6.
19. TNA, *HO 144/6116*.
20. A. Mason, 'The Government and the General Strike 1926', p. 20.
21. Only around five thousand students received degrees in 1920, rising to just over ten thousand in 1920. See P. Bolton, *Education: Historical Statistics* (House of Common Library, 2012).
22. G.A. Phillips, *The General Strike*, p. 154.
23. I. MacDougall, 'Edinburgh', pp. 143–4.
24. J. Symons, *The General Strike*, p. 68.
25. R.H. Saltzman, *A Lark for the Sake of Their Country*, p. 76.
26. MRC, *MSS.21/3285/13*.
27. R.H. Saltzman, *A Lark for the Sake of Their Country*, pp. 141–5.
28. R.H. Saltzman, *A Lark for the Sake of Their Country*, p. 103.
29. J. Symons, *The General Strike*, p. 95.
30. D. Brandon, *The General Strike 1926*, pp. 168–9.

31 *Diss Express*, 14 May 1926.
32 *Southwark and Bermondsey Recorder*, 21 May 1926.
33 G.A. Phillips, *The General Strike*, p. 163.
34 G. Glasgow, *General Strikes and Road Transport*, pp. 10–13.
35 L. Ryan, 'Citizen Strike Breakers', p. 122.
36 TNA, *HO 144/6902*.
37 G. Glasgow, *General Strikes and Road Transport*, p. 53.
38 *Tatler*, 12 May 1926.
39 TNA, *HO 144/6751*.
40 TNA, *HO 144/6751*.
41 G.A. Phillips, *The General Strike*, pp. 155–7.
42 *Hansard*, 6 May 1926.
43 TNA, *CAB 23/52/19*.
44 See *An Account of the Proceedings of the Durham and Northumberland General Council Joint Strike Committee, May 1926*, pp. 8–10 for the strikers' version of events.
45 TNA, *CAB 27/331-2*.
46 *Sunderland Daily Echo and Shipping Gazette*, 8 May 1926.
47 A. Mason, *The General Strike in the North East*, pp. 59–60.
48 TNA, *HO 144/6116*.

7 THE STATE RESPONDS

1 M.D. Harmon, 'A War of Words: The *British Gazette* and the *British Worker* During the 1926 General Strike' in *Labor History* 60(3), p. 197.
2 TNA, *CAB 23/52/24*.
3 R. Rhodes James, *Memoirs of a Conservative*, pp. 235–8.
4 T. Jones, *Whitehall Diary*, vol. 2, p. 38.
5 TNA, *CAB 23/52/29*.
6 R. Rhodes James, *Memoirs of a Conservative*, pp. 238–42. Davidson claimed that he kept the original copy of these articles but they were destroyed by fire during the Second World War.
7 For a quantitative analysis of the terms used in the *Gazette* see M.D. Harmon, 'A War of Words: The *British Gazette* and the *British Worker* During the 1926 General Strike', pp. 198–200.
8 *British Gazette*, 7 May 1926.
9 R. Rhodes James, *Memoirs of a Conservative*, pp. 244–5.
10 G.M. Young, *Stanley Baldwin*, p. 116.
11 I. Bullock, *Under Siege: The Independent Labour Party in Interwar Britain*, p. 119.
12 H. Fyfe, *Behind the Scenes of the Great Strike*, pp. 26–7.
13 *British Worker*, 5 May 1926.

14 See H. Richards, *The Bloody Circus: The Daily Herald and the Left*, ch. 4.
15 MRC, *MSS 292/252.62/125*.
16 P. Renshaw, *The General Strike*, p. 190.
17 TNA, *KV 4/246*.
18 P. Renshaw, *The General Strike*, pp. 200–1.
19 R. Rhodes James, *Memoirs of a Conservative*, pp. 246–7.
20 R. Rhodes James, *Memoirs of a Conservative*, p. 248.
21 F. McLynn, *The Road Not Taken: How Britain Narrowly Missed a Revolution, 1381–1926*, pp. 455–6.
22 TNA, *CAB 23/52/29*.
23 TNA, *CAB 23/52/27*.
24 MRC, *MSS.292/252.62/21/24*.
25 TNA, *KV 4/282, Luton News and Bedfordshire Chronicle*, 7 May 1926.
26 C. Farman, *The General Strike, May 1926*, pp. 183–4.
27 L. Ryan, 'Citizen Strike Breakers', pp. 116–19.
28 See C.K. Leon, *Special Constables: An Historical and Contemporary Survey*, pp. 370–1.
29 TNA, *HO 144/6902*.
30 TNA, *HO 144/6902*.
31 MRC, *MSS.292/252.62/146*.
32 TNA, *HO 144/6902*.
33 C.K. Leon, *Special Constables* pp. 386–8.
34 MRC, *MSS 292/52.62/105*.
35 TNA, *HO 45/24860*.
36 *Daily Herald*, 6 October 1925, *Birmingham Daily Gazette*, 8 October 1925.
37 TNA, *HO 45/24860*.
38 TNA, *KV 4/282*.
39 MRC, *MSS 292/52.62/113*.
40 TNA, *CAB 27/331*.
41 TNA, *HO 144/6898*. The Watch Committee was the body of the local authority that oversaw the police.
42 TNA, *HO 144/6116*.
43 TNA, *HO 144/6751*.
44 TNA, *WO 30/143*.
45 TNA, *WO 32/3455*.
46 P. Kerrigan, 'From Glasgow' in J. Skelley (ed.), *The General Strike, 1926*, pp. 322–3.
47 TNA, *WO 30/143*.
48 TNA, *ADM 1/8705/184*.
49 TNA, *HO 144/22372*.
50 TNA, *KV 4/246*.

51 TNA, *KV 4/246*.
52 TNA, *WO 30/143*.
53 TNA, *KV 4/246*.
54 TNA, *WO 30/143*.
55 TNA, *HO 144/6894*.
56 TNA, *WO 32/3455*.
57 TNA, *KV 4/246*.
58 TNA, *KV 4/246*.
59 TNA, *KV 4/246*.

8 WHO RUNS THE STRIKE?

1 M. Morris, *The General Strike*, pp. 48–9.
2 G.A. Phillips, *The General Strike*, p. 137.
3 MRC, *MSS.292/252.62/28*.
4 J. Symons, *The General Strike*, p. 136.
5 J. Symons, *The General Strike*, pp. 146–7. Casson later served as President of the British Actors' Equity Association, a forerunner of today's Equity union.
6 M. Bondfield, *A Life's Work*, pp. 266–8.
7 M. Morris, *The General Strike*, pp. 79–80. The TUC had asked all members of the parliamentary Labour Party who could do so to return to their constituencies to assist with organisation and public speaking.
8 MRC, *MSS.292/252.62/62*.
9 MRC, *MSS.292/252.62/28*.
10 In R. Page Arnot, *The General Strike, May 1926*, p. 170.
11 MRC, *MSS.292/252.62/28*.
12 MRC, *MSS.292/252.62/113*.
13 C. Farman, *The General Strike, May 1926*, p. 160.
14 MRC, *MSS.292/252.62/102*.
15 MRC, *MSS.21/4385/2*.
16 MRC, *MSS.126/TG/11/1/10*.
17 MRC, *MSS.126/TG/11/1/10*.
18 MRC, *MSS.126/TG/11/1/51/8*.
19 C. Farman, *The General Strike, May 1926*, pp. 158–9.
20 M. Morris, *The General Strike*, pp. 44–5.
21 G.A. Phillips, *The General Strike*, pp. 136–7.
22 A. Clinton, *The Trade Union Rank and File: Trades Councils in Britain 1900–40*, pp. 34–43.
23 A. Clinton, *The Trade Union Rank and File: Trades Councils in Britain 1900–40*, pp. 109–13.
24 M. Bor & J. Bor, *Come Together*, pp. 38–9.
25 E. Burns, *The General Strike May 1926: Trades Councils in Action*, p. 13.

26 R.S. Sephton, *Oxford and the General Strike 1926*, pp. 9–10.
27 P. Kerrigan, 'From Glasgow', p. 324.
28 C. Farman, *The General Strike, May 1926*, pp. 153–4.
29 See for example J. Skelley (ed.), *The General Strike, 1926*, pp. 148–9, 163, 176.
30 A. Mason, *The General Strike in the North East*, pp. 15–19.
31 *An account of the proceedings of the Durham and Northumberland General Council Joint Strike Committee, May 1926*, p. 20.
32 *Merthyr Tydfil Central Strike Committee Souvenir Report*, p. 7.
33 L. Pearson, *England's Co-operative Movement: An Architectural History*, p. 109.
34 R.W. Postgate, E. Wilkinson & J.F. Horrabin, *A Workers' History of the Great Strike*, p. 35.
35 C. Farman, *The General Strike, May 1926*, p. 163.
36 MRC, *MSS.126/TG/11/1/10*.
37 TNA, *HO 144/6894*.
38 S. Benton, 'Sheffield' in M. Morris, *The General Strike*, pp. 434–5. MRC, *MSS 292/252.62/100*.
39 G.A. Phillips, *The General Strike*, pp. 137–8.
40 MRC, *MSS 292/252.62/76*.
41 MRC, *MSS 292/252.62/146*.
42 A. Mason, *The General Strike in the Northeast*, p. 22.
43 MRC, *MSS 292/252.62/100*.
44 *Nine days in May: The 1926 General Strike in Southwark* [https://libcom.org/article/nine-days-may-1926-general-strike-southwark]
45 R.P. Hastings, 'Birmingham', p. 216.
46 MRC, *MSS.292/252.62/146*.

9 ALL OUT?

1 C. Farman, *The General Strike, May 1926*, p. 157.
2 R. Mace, 'Battersea, London' in M. Morris, *The General Strike*, p. 390; J. Jacobs, 'From Hackney', p. 363.
3 S. Benton, 'Sheffield', p. 433.
4 TNA, *HO 144/6894*.
5 D. Taylor, *The 1926 General Strike in Wolverhampton and the Black Country*, pp. 44–5.
6 P. Carter, 'The West of Scotland', p. 133.
7 A. Mason, *The General Strike in the North East*, p. 70.
8 A. Tuckett, 'Swindon', pp. 294–5.
9 TNA, *KV 4/282*.
10 N. Newitt, *The General Strike in Leicester – 1926* [https://www.nednewitt.com/?page_id=1378].

11 J. Attfield & J. Lee, 'Deptford and Lewisham' in J. Skelley (ed.), *The General Strike, 1926*, pp. 270–1.
12 J. Jacobs, 'From Hackney', pp. 363–4.
13 MRC, *MSS.292/252.62/146*.
14 K. Laybourn, *The General Strike, Day by Day*, pp. 75–6.
15 R. Mace, 'Battersea, London', p. 387.
16 C. Farman, *The General Strike, May 1926*, p. 186.
17 TNA, *KV 4/282*, TNA, *MEPO 2/3133*.
18 P. Carter, 'The West of Scotland', pp. 120–1.
19 TNA, *KV 4/282*.
20 TNA, *ADM 1/8697/70*.
21 For a full account of the Cramlington incident and subsequent trial see M. Hutcherson, *Let No Wheels Turn: The Wrecking of the Flying Scotsman, 1926*.
22 M. Hutcherson, *Let No Wheels Turn*, pp. 88–9.
23 *Blyth News*, 19 July 1926 mentions a man of this name taking the oath as a JP.
24 TNA, *CAB 27/331*.
25 TNA, *HO 144/6904*.
26 *Sheffield Daily Telegraph*, 5 August 1926.
27 TNA, *HO 144/6904*.
28 TNA, *HO 144/6904*.
29 *Sheffield Daily Telegraph*, 31 July 1926.
30 P. Wyncoll, *The Nottingham Labour Movement 1880–1939*, p. 200.
31 MRC, *MSS.292/252.62/95*.
32 MRC, *MSS.292/252.62/97*.
33 TNA, *CAB 23/52/25*.
34 Much of this information comes from TNA, *T 162/302*.
35 TNA, *ADM 116/2312*.
36 See TNA, *CAB 24/178*.
37 TNA, *T 162/302*.
38 S. Benton, 'Sheffield', pp. 431–3; G. Barnsby, 'The Black Country', p. 196.
39 G.A. Phillips, *The General Strike*, p. 141.
40 MRC, *MSS.292/252.62/113*.
41 MRC, *MSS.292/252.62/135* and *MSS.292/252.62/99*.
42 See E.A. Radice & G.H. Radice, *Will Thorne*, pp. 104–5 for the NUGMW leaders' attitude to the general strike.
43 G.A. Phillips, *The General Strike*, p. 142.
44 MRC, MSS 292/252.62/29.
45 The chairman was Jimmy Rowan, general secretary of the ETU.
46 MRC, *MSS 292/252.62/29*.
47 MRC, *MSS 292/252.62/102*.

48 MRC, *MSS 292/252.62/76*.
49 MRC, *MSS 292/252.62/29*.
50 MRC, *MSS 292/252.62/29*.
51 MRC, *MSS 292/252.62/99*.
52 MRC, *MSS 292/252.62/105*.
53 MRC, *MSS 292/252.62/76*.
54 MRC, *MSS 292/252.62/146*.
55 MRC, *MSS 292/252.62/100*.
56 MRC, *MSS 292/252.62/123*.
57 MRC, *MSS 292/252.62/113*.
58 TNA, *HO 144/6894*.
59 J.T. Murphy, *The Political Meaning of the Great Strike*.
60 J. Klugmann, *History of the Communist Party of Great Britain*, vol. 2, pp. 133–5.
61 MRC, *MSS/292.252/62/146*.
62 H. Francis, 'South Wales' in J. Skelley (ed.), *The General Strike, 1926*, pp. 238–9.

10 THE STATE'S OFFENSIVE

1 C. Farman, *The General Strike, May 1926*, pp. 187–8.
2 TNA, *CAB 23/52/26*.
3 A. Perkins, *A Very British Strike: 3 May–12 May 1926*, p. 179.
4 TNA, *CAB 27/331*.
5 MRC, *MSS.126/TG/11/1/10*.
6 TNA, *CAB 27/331*.
7 J. Attfield & J. Lee, 'Deptford and Lewisham', pp. 263–4; J. Jacobs, 'From Hackney', pp. 362–3.
8 TNA, *HO 144/6751*.
9 TNA, *WO 32/3455*.
10 J. Symons, *The General Strike*, pp. 184–5.
11 TNA, *WO 32/3455*.
12 TNA, *HO 144/6751*.
13 See H. Watson, 'An Incident on the River Thames' in J. Skelley (ed.), *The General Strike, 1926*.
14 MRC, *MSS.292/252/62/102*.
15 TNA, *ADM 1/8705/184*.
16 J. Attfield & J. Lee, 'Deptford and Lewisham', pp. 270–1.
17 TNA, *KV 4/246*.
18 TNA, *HO 144/6751*.
19 *Chelmsford Chronicle*, 21 May 1926.
20 *Chelmsford Chronicle*, 28 May 1926.
21 TNA, *ADM 1/8705/184*.
22 For details of this incident see TNA *HO 144/6751* and *WO 30/143*.

23 *Eastern Counties Times*, 21 May 1926.
24 TNA, *WO 30/143*.
25 TNA, *WO 30/143*.
26 J. Symons, *The General Strike*, p. 190.
27 E. Frow & R. Frow, 'Manchester Diary', p. 165.
28 *Thanet Advertiser*, 10 May 1926.
29 A. Perkins, *A Very British Strike,* p. 189.
30 TNA, *CAB 27/331*.
31 TNA, *HO 144/6894*.
32 TNA, *WO 30/143*.
33 *Sheffield Daily Telegraph*, 8 May 1926.
34 MRC, *MSS 292/252.62/99*.
35 *Hull Daily Mail*, 11 May 1926.
36 MRC, *MSS 292/252.62/146*.
37 MRC, *MSS 292/252.62/100*.
38 *Merthyr Express*, 15 May 1926.
39 A. Mason, *The General Strike in the North East*, p. 72.
40 *Hartlepool Northern Daily Mail*, 14 May 1926.
41 A. Mason, *The General Strike in the North East*, p. 72.
42 M. Large, *The Nine Days in Birmingham: The General Strike 4–12 May 1926*, p. 39.
43 TNA, *HO 144/6894*.
44 TNA, *CAB 23/52/26*.
45 TNA, *CAB 24/179*.
46 *Dundee Evening Telegraph*, 12 May 1926.
47 TNA, *WO 30/143*.
48 TNA, *CAB 27/332*.
49 TNA, *ADM 1/8697/70*.
50 *Buckingham Advertiser and Free Press*, 22 May 1926.
51 TNA, *WO 32/3455*.
52 C. Farman, *The General Strike, May 1926*, pp. 203–9.
53 *Hansard*, 6 May 1926.
54 *Dundee Evening Telegraph*, 8 May 1926.
55 MRC, *MSS.21/3285/12*.
56 *Hansard*, 10 May 1926.
57 MRC, *MSS.292/252.62/57*.
58 MRC, *MSS.292/252.62/107*.
59 MRC, *MSS.292/252.62/145*.
60 MRC, *MSS.292/252.62/107*.
61 MRC, *MSS.292/252.62/25*.
62 MRC, *MSS.292/252.62/25*.

63 MRC, *MSS.292/252.62/25*.
64 A.L. Goodhart, 'The Legality of the General Strike in England' in *Yale Law Journal* 36, pp. 465-6.
65 TNA, *CAB 24/179*.
66 TNA, *CAB 23/52/27*.
67 T. Jones, *Whitehall Diary*, vol. 2, pp. 45–7.
68 C. Farman, *The General Strike, May 1926*, pp. 211–13.
69 TNA, *CAB 23/52/28*.
70 J. Symons, *The General Strike*, p. 189.
71 *Liverpool Evening Express*, 27 May 1926.

11 SURRENDER

1 MRC, *MSS.292/252.62/76*.
2 TNA, *CAB 27/332*.
3 C.R. Potts, *The GWR and the General Strike*, p. 46.
4 See for example the letter from the Harrogate Typographical Society in MRC, *MSS.292/252.62/147*.
5 M. Large, *The Nine Days in Birmingham*, pp. 33–4.
6 *British Worker*, 6 May 1926.
7 G. Blaxland, *A Life for Unity*, p. 196.
8 B. Turner, *About Myself 1863–1930*, p. 313.
9 A. Bullock, *The Life and Times of Ernest Bevin*, vol. 1, p. 324.
10 M. Bondfield, *A Life's Work*, p. 269.
11 B. Pearce & M. Woodhouse, *A History of Communism in Britain*, pp. 101–4.
12 K. Morgan, *Bolshevism, Syndicalism and the General Strike*, pp. 130–1.
13 K. Morgan, *Bolshevism, Syndicalism and the General Strike*, p. 234.
14 J. Campbell, *F.E. Smith*, p. 774.
15 R. Rhodes James, *Memoirs of a Conservative*, p. 243.
16 H. Fyfe, *Behind the Scenes of the Great Strike*, pp. 51–2.
17 T. Jones, *Whitehall Diary*, vol. 2, p. 41.
18 T. Jones, *Whitehall Diary*, vol. 2, p. 43.
19 T. Jones, *Whitehall Diary*, vol. 2, p. 43.
20 G. Blaxland, *A Life for Unity*, pp. 199–201.
21 O. Sitwell, *Laughter in the Next Room*, pp. 225–8.
22 *Hansard*, 5 May 1926.
23 T. Jones, *Whitehall Diary*, vol. 2, p. 37.
24 *Western Daily Press*, 8 May 1926.
25 A. Perkins, *A Very British Strike: 3 May–12 May 1926*, pp. 168–9, 181.
26 H. Fyfe, *Behind the Scenes of the Great Strike*, p. 63.
27 *Bath Chronicle and Herald*, 8 May 1926, *Portsmouth Evening News*, 8 May 1926.
28 H. Fyfe, *Behind the Scenes of the Great Strike*, p. 59.

29 MRC, *MSS.292/252.62/21/27*.
30 R. Rhodes James, *Memoirs of a Conservative*, p. 249.
31 P. Williamson & E. Baldwin (eds.), *Baldwin Papers*, p. 181.
32 MRC, *MSS.292/252.62/21/8*.
33 G.A. Phillips, *The General Strike*, p. 225.
34 H. Samuel, *Memoirs*, p. 187. Segrave would die four years later while attempting to break the world water speed record on Windermere.
35 TNA, *CAB 23/52/27*.
36 R. Taylor, 'Citrine's Unexpurgated Diaries, 1925–26: The Mining Crisis and the National Strike' in *Historical Studies in Industrial Relations* 20, p. 91.
37 G.A. Phillips, *The General Strike*, p. 227.
38 MRC, *MSS/292.252/62/28*.
39 A. Bullock, *The Life and Times of Ernest Bevin*, vol. 1, pp. 329–30.
40 W. Citrine, *Men and Work*, pp. 194–5.
41 G.A. Phillips, *The General Strike*, p. 227.
42 A. Bullock, *The Life and Times of Ernest Bevin*, vol. 1, p. 334.
43 TNA, *CAB 24/179*.
44 TNA, *CAB 24/179*.
45 J. Campbell, *F.E. Smith*, pp. 775–6.
46 A. Bullock, *The Life and Times of Ernest Bevin*, vol. 1, p. 337.
47 *British Worker*, 12 May 1926.
48 B. Turner, *About Myself 1863–1930*, p. 312.

12 THE SECOND GENERAL STRIKE

1 K. Laybourn, *The General Strike Day by Day*, p. 127.
2 C. Farman, *The General Strike, May 1926*, p. 236.
3 *Hansard*, 12 May 1926.
4 *British Gazette, 13 May 1926*.
5 R.P. Hastings, 'Birmingham', pp. 223–4.
6 MRC, *MSS.292/252.62.75*.
7 P. Wyncoll, 'The East Midlands', pp. 188–9.
8 MRC, *MSS.292/252.62/68*.
9 B. Johnson, *Nine Days that Shook Mansfield: The General Strike in the Mansfield Area*, p. 61.
10 D. Brandon, *The General Strike 1926*, p. 179.
11 G.A. Phillips, *The General Strike*, pp. 245–6.
12 J. Attfield & J. Lee, 'Deptford and Lewisham', p. 276.
13 MRC, *MSS.292/252.62/68*.
14 M. Large, *The Nine Days in Birmingham*, p. 39.
15 *Daily Herald*, 14 July 1926.
16 MRC, *MSS.292/252.62/120*.

17 MRC, *MSS.292/252.62/76*.
18 MacDougall, 'Edinburgh', p. 153.
19 MRC, *MSS.292/252.62/120*.
20 MRC, *MSS.292/252.62/121*.
21 MRC, *MSS.292/252.62/145*.
22 C. Farman, *The General Strike, May 1926*, p. 235.
23 MRC, *MSS.292/252.62/120*.
24 MRC, *MSS.292/252.62/120*.
25 MRC, *MSS.172/GS/5*.
26 TNA, *CAB 27/332*.
27 MRC, *MSS.126/TG/11/1/10*.
28 A. Tuckett, 'Swindon', pp. 304–5.
29 *Gloucestershire Echo*, 14 May 1926.
30 R.A. Florey, *The General Strike of 1926*, pp. 155–6, *Daily News* 14 May 1926.
31 TNA, *CAB 27/332*.
32 *Hansard*, 13 May 1926.
33 *Hansard*, 13 May 1926.
34 C.R. Potts, *The GWR and the General Strike*, pp. 97–100.
35 MRC, *MSS.292/252.62/18*.
36 J. Symons, *The General Strike*, pp. 211–12.
37 C. Farman, *The General Strike, May 1926*, p. 242.
38 TNA, *CAB 27/332*.
39 TNA, *CAB 27/332*.
40 MRC, *MSS.292/252.62/18*.
41 A. Mason, *The General Strike in the North East*, p. 95.
42 G.A. Phillips, *The General Strike*, p. 246.
43 K. Laybourn, *The General Strike Day by Day*, pp. 132–3.
44 K. Laybourn, *The General Strike of 1926*, pp. 91–2.
45 MRC, *MSS.126/TG/11/1/10*.
46 *Hull Daily Mail*, 19 May 1926.
47 *Hull Daily Mail*, 17 May 1926.
48 MRC, *MSS.126/TG/11/1/10*.
49 *Eastbourne Chronicle*, 22 May 1926.
50 *Daily Mirror*, 14 May 1926.
51 R.H. Saltzman, *A Lark for the Sake of Their Country*, pp. 155–60.
52 *Yorkshire Evening Post*, 14 May 1926.
53 See for example *Western Morning News*, 13 May 1926.
54 MRC, *MSS. 126/TG/11/5/3*.

13 THE EXPERIENCE OF DEFEAT

1 C. Farman, *The General Strike, May 1926*, pp. 246–7.

2 G.A. Phillips, *The General Strike*, p. 254.
3 MRC, *MSS.292/252.62/4*.
4 G. Blaxland, *A Life for Unity*, pp. 206–7.
5 MRC, *MSS.126/TG/11/1/8*.
6 MRC, *MSS.126/TG/11/1/36*.
7 *The Record*, May-July 1926.
8 MRC, *MSS.292/252.62/28*.
9 G.A. Phillips, *The General Strike*, p. 256.
10 MRC, *MSS.292/252.62/33*.
11 *The Record*, May-July 1926.
12 C. Farman, *The General Strike, May 1926*, p. 260.
13 P. Renshaw, *The General Strike*, pp. 236–7.
14 C. Farman, *The General Strike, May 1926*, p. 250.
15 C. Farman, *The General Strike, May 1926*, p. 248.
16 A.J. Cook, *The Nine Days: The Story of the General Strike Told by the Miners' Secretary*, p. 21.
17 MRC, *MSS.292/252.51/8*.
18 P. Davies, *A.J. Cook*, pp. 128–9.
19 S. Bruley, *The Women and Men of 1926: A Gender and Social History of the General Strike and Miners' Lockout in South Wales*, pp. 47–50.
20 P. Ryan, 'The Poor Law in 1926' in M. Morris, *The General Strike*, pp. 362–3.
21 J. McIlroy, A. Campbell & K. Gildart (eds.), *Industrial Politics and the 1926 Mining Lockout: The Struggle for Dignity*, p. 89.
22 J. McIlroy, A. Campbell & K. Gildart (eds.), *Industrial Politics and the 1926 Mining Lockout*, pp. 219–20.
23 MRC, *MSS.292/252.62/8/66*.
24 *Daily News*, 8 November 1926.
25 P. Davies, *A.J. Cook*, pp. 115–16.
26 P. Williamson & E. Baldwin (eds.), *Baldwin Papers*, p. 184.
27 P. Renshaw, *The General Strike*, pp. 237–8.
28 C. Farman, *The General Strike, May 1926*, pp. 248–9.
29 P. Williamson & E. Baldwin (eds.), *Baldwin Papers*, p. 188.
30 C. Farman, *The General Strike, May 1926*, p. 255.
31 T. Jones, *Whitehall Diary*, vol. 2, p. 66.
32 C. Farman, *The General Strike, May 1926*, p. 257. This referred to the British Expeditionary Force's organised retreat at the Battle of Mons in the early weeks of the First World War.
33 P. Davies, *A.J. Cook*, pp. 127–30. Many safety men had left the Federation and returned to their own specialist unions as a result of victimisation after the 1921 lockout. See A. Campbell, 'Reflections on the 1926 Mining Lockout' in *Historical Studies in Industrial Relations* 21, pp. 148–9.

34 K. Laybourn, *The General Strike of 1926*, pp. 95–6.
35 MRS, *MSS.292/252.62/28*.
36 MRC, *MSS.292/252.62/42*.
37 MRC, *MSS.292/252.62/42*.
38 *Report of proceedings at a Special Conference of Executives of all affiliated unions to consider the Report of the General Council on the National Strike*, p. 9.
39 *Report of proceedings at a Special Conference of Executives of all affiliated unions to consider the Report of the General Council on the National Strike*, p. 12.
40 *Report of proceedings at a Special Conference of Executives of all affiliated unions to consider the Report of the General Council on the National Strike*, pp. 33–6.
41 *Report of proceedings at a Special Conference of Executives of all affiliated unions to consider the Report of the General Council on the National Strike*, p. 53.
42 *Report of proceedings at a Special Conference of Executives of all affiliated unions to consider the Report of the General Council on the National Strike*, pp. 43–4.
43 *Report of proceedings at a Special Conference of Executives of all affiliated unions to consider the Report of the General Council on the National Strike*, p. 45.
44 MRC, *MSS.292/252.62/68*.
45 MRC, *MSS.292/252.62/74*.
46 P. Wyncoll, *The Nottingham Labour Movement 1880–1939*, p. 207.
47 MRC, *MSS.292/252.62/68*.
48 MRC, *MSS.292/252.62/33*.
49 G.A. Phillips, *The General Strike*, p. 281.
50 MRC, *MSS.292/252.62/33*.
51 P. Renshaw, *The General Strike*, p. 241.
52 G.A. Phillips, *The General Strike*, pp. 277–8.
53 G.A. Phillips, *The General Strike*, pp. 278–9.
54 P. Ryan, 'The Poor Law in 1926', pp. 365–70.
55 G.W. McDonald & H.F. Gospel, 'The Mond-Turner Talks, 1927–1933: A Study in Industrial Co-operation' in *The Historical Journal* 16(4), pp. 810–13.
56 K. Laybourn, *The General Strike of 1926*, p. 113.
57 P. Foot, *The Vote: How It Was Won and How It Was Undermined*, pp. 280–2.
58 A. Clinton, *The Trade Union Rank and File*, pp. 147–9.
59 W. Citrine, *Men and Work*, pp. 253–4.
60 C. Andrew, *The Defence of the Realm*, pp. 153–5.
61 *Hansard*, 13 February 1946.
62 P. Davies, *A.J. Cook*, pp. 161–8.
63 *Sunderland Daily Echo and Shipping Gazette*, 24 October 1931.
64 *Daily Herald*, 6 November 1931.
65 *Birmingham Daily Gazette*, 3 November 1931.

66 D. Smith, 'The Tonypandy Riots, 1910 – Winston Churchill's Nemesis' in *Finest Hour* 193, p. 15.
67 P. Williamson & E. Baldwin, *Baldwin Papers*, p. 190.

14 THE LEGACY OF 1926

1 L. Trotsky, 'Notes on the Situation in Britain 1925–26' [https://www.marxists.org/archive/trotsky/works/britain/ch12.htm]
2 G. Lansbury, *The Secret History of the Great Strike and the Blackleg State*.
3 TNA, *WO 32/3455*.
4 TNA, *HO 144/6116*.
5 TNA, *HO 144/6116*.
6 *Report of proceedings at a Special Conference of Executives of all affiliated unions to consider the Report of the General Council on the National Strike*, p. 58.
7 J. Klugmann, *History of the Communist Party of Great Britain*, vol. 2, pp. 135–8.
8 *Workers' Weekly*, 30 April 1926.
9 See L. Trotsky, 'The Struggle for Peace and the Anglo-Russian Committee' in *Writings on Britain*, vol. 2.
10 See for example P. Taaffe, *1926 General Strike: Workers Taste Power*, ch. 11, T. Cliff & D. Gluckstein, *Marxism and Trade Union Struggle: The General Strike of 1926*, ch. 24.
11 M. Cole (ed.), *Beatrice Webb's Diaries 1924–32*, pp. 92–3.
12 R.H. Saltzman, *A Lark for the Sake of their Country*, pp. 177–8.
13 J. Galsworthy, *A Modern Comedy*, p. viii.
14 R.H. Saltzman, *A Lark for the Sake of their Country*, pp. 186–94.
15 I. Haywood, ' "Never Again?": Ellen Wilkinson's *Clash* and the Feminization of the General Strike' in *Literature & History* 8(2), p. 36.
16 G.D.H. Cole, 'The Striker Stricken' in *Historical Studies in Industrial Relations* 22, pp. 109–28.
17 See for example B. Turner, *About Myself 1863–1930*, p. 315.
18 J. McIlroy, 'Memory, Commemoration and History – 1926 in 2006' in *Historical Studies in Industrial Relations* 21, pp. 75–8.
19 A. Campbell, 'Reflections on the 1926 Mining Lockout' in *Historical Studies in Industrial Relations* 21, p. 181.
20 J. McIlroy, 'Memory, Commemoration and History – 1926 in 2006', pp. 78–80.
21 See R. Luxemburg, *The Mass Strike, the Political Party and the Trade Unions*, ch. 3.
22 *Plebs*, Vol. 18 No. 7, p. 254.

Index

Ablett, Noah 197
Abraham, William (Mabon) 14
AEU *see* Amalgamated Engineering Union
All-Russian Co-operative Society (ARCOS) 265
Allen, Jim 279
Amalgamated Engineering Union (AEU) 45, 100
Anderson, John 113
Anglican Church, appeal for peace 131, 215–217, 253–254
antisemitism 143–144
ARCOS *see* All-Russian Co-operative Society
aristocracy
    ending of the General Strike 214–215
    impact of the Strike on 276–277
    ownership of mining companies 7
the Army
    ending of the General Strike 213
    escalation of unrest towards end of Strike 196–207
    during the General Strike 133–135, 138–143, *186*, 187–207
    mutinies in 56
    use of to oppose strikes 59, 60
ASLEF *see* Associated Society of Locomotive Engineers and Firemen
Asquith, Herbert Henry 17, 201
Associated Society of Locomotive Engineers and Firemen (ASLEF)
    1919 strike 43–44
    during the General Strike 168, 173
    resumption of Strike 234
    after the General Strike 250–251, 257
Astbury judgement 204–205, 209, 257, 261
Asylum Workers' Union 85–86
Automobile Association (AA) 59, 118–119

Bailey, Abe 218
Baldwin, Alfred 6–7
Baldwin, Stanley
    BBC address 132–133
    becoming PM 60
    biographical details 7
    British Gazette 127–128
    Church's appeal for peace 217
    ending of the General Strike 213–214, 221–222, 228
    illegal strikes bill 205–206
    immediate precursors to the General Strike 89–91
    intervention in reinstatement of workers 237
    landslide victory 62–64
    lead up to the General Strike 75–84
    political career following the Strike 268
    "road to anarchy and ruin" 127, 271
    after the General Strike 254
    trade disputes and trade unions bill 263, 266–267
    trade union movement 65–66
Beckton Gasworks 33–34
Bevan, Nye 44, 96
Bevin, Ernest
    concern about arrest warrant 206
    elected to represent TGWU 49
    ending of the General Strike 211–212, 222–223
    forming the TGWU 21, 40
    during the General Strike 148, 154
    lead up to the General Strike 81–82, 85–86
    response to Russia 56
    resumption of Strike 233–234
    after the General Strike 247–248, 257–258, 259, 265–266
    victimisation attempts 234, 240
bicycles, increased use during the General Strike 103, 149–150
Billy Elliot 5
Birkenhead, Lord (Frederick Edwin Smith) 8, 65–66, 87, 132, 141, 213, 222
Birmingham Worker 142–143
Black Friday 22, 45, 60–61
'black juice' 180, 272
blacklisting of trade unionists 260–261
Blaxland, Gregory 77
Bolshevik revolution 46–47
Bolshevism 51–55
Bondfield, Margaret 150, 160, 212, 248
Bower, Phil 141
Bramley, Fred 49
Brassed Off 5
British Broadcasting Company (BBC)
    early BBC 130–133
    ending of the General Strike 227–228
British Fascists (BF) 72, 135–136
British Gazette
    Churchill in charge of 127–128, 130
    dock siege 190–191
    ending of the General Strike 216–217
    endorsement of military intervention 187–207

Index

lead up to the General Strike 91
production by *Morning Post* office 126
reinstatement of workers 236–237
union leaders' communication 151
voluntary workers 114
British Legion 110
British Worker
   demand for 130
   ending of the General Strike 210, 223
   during the General Strike 151–152, 153–154, 184
   origin and production 128–129
   after the General Strike 259
   voluntary workers 231
broadcast media
   early BBC 130–133
   ending of the General Strike 227–228
   literary and television portrayals of the General Strike 276–279
Bromley, John 212, 267
Bryant & May match factory 33–34
Building Trade Workers 260
Burns, John 35–36
Burr, J. Stuart 282
Burton, Nancy 109
buses, in the General Strike 99, 103
   police force assistance 138
   reinstatement of workers 241–243
   sabotage 170–171
   voluntary workers 110–111, 115–116
'butty' system 10–11

Campbell, John Ross 62–63
car ownership 70, 118–119, 149–150
cars, in the General Strike 103
   see also road haulage
cartel practices 7–8
Cartwright, Edith 253
Casson, Lewis 149
Chamberlain, Neville 198, 213, 229, 254, 262
Chambers of Commerce 109
Charlesworth, Jack 175
check-weighmen 13
chemical industry 100
Christian opinion of the General Strike 215–217
Church of England, appeal for peace 131, 215–217, 253–254
Churchill, Winston
   addressing radicalism 47
   appointment as chancellor 65
   and Bolshevism 55
   in charge of *British Gazette* 127–128, 130
   Civil Constabulary Reserve established 199–200
   civil servants' rights 176–177
   ending of the General Strike 213, 214
   gold standard 24
   as interventionist 55
   lead up to the General Strike 90
   NSFU strike 37–38
   opposition to 1925 subsidy 26
   political career following the Strike 268

   after the General Strike 254
   use of military 15, 59, 60, 189
Citrine, Walter
   appointment as TUC acting general secretary 25, 49
   cartoon portrayal 277
   during the General Strike 154, 176, 203
   lead up to the General Strike 84, 86, 87, 88–89
   after the General Strike 249, 256–257, 259, 264–265
Civil Constabulary Reserve (CCR) 199–200
civil servants, trade union rights for 176–177
Clark, Dorothy 231
co-operative movement 11
Co-operative Wholesale Society 158, 182
coal
   embargo on 25–26
   historic importance 3–4
   human labour as dominant in Britain 4–5
   international economics' impact on prices 13, 16–20, 23–25
   lead up to the General Strike 78–79
   price-fixing 7–8
Coal Commission *see* Samuel Commission
coal embargo 249
coal mines bill 254–255
coal subsidy
   ending of the General Strike 215, 216, 218, 219–221
   lead up to the General Strike 48, 68, 75
   Lloyd George's views 201
Cole, G. D. H. 277
communism
   ending of the General Strike 212–213
   government of Lloyd George 51–55, 56
   government of Stanley Baldwin 62–72
   legal disputes 67–72
   perception as dangerous worldview 52–54
   the security services response to 143–145
   after the General Strike 264–265
Communist Party of Great Britain (CPGB) *186*
   attempt at revolution 273–275
   criticism of TUC's handling of the General Strike 183–185
   interaction with trade union movement 46–48
   lead up to the General Strike 77–78
   military activism 141–143
   in the North-East 157
   resumption of Strike 235–236
   Russia-British relations 51–54
   the security services response to 144
   after the General Strike 256–257, 264–265
Connolly, Martin 120–122
construction industry 85, 97
Cook, Arthur James *74*
   Co-operative Wholesale Society 158
   early life 6
   illness and death 267
   imprisonment and raid on house 22
   lead up to the General Strike 75, 76–78, 87–88
   mining injuries and deaths 9
   opposition to WW1 exploitation 17–18

318   *Index*

rejection of 1921 agreement 24–25
the security services response to 144
after the General Strike 250–252, 253–254, 256
syndicalism 39
Unofficial Reform Committee 15
wage stagnation 14–15, 16
Councils of Action
   escalation of unrest towards end of Strike 198
   foundation of 56
   during the General Strike 148, 158
   lead up to the General Strike 78
   see also National Council of Action
counter-espionage 58–59
Court of Inquiry 25, 205
CPGB *see* Communist Party of Great Britain
Cramp, Charlie 211, 238, 267
criminalisation of protest 281
Croft, Harold 104

Daily Herald
   announcing the Strike 94
   British Fascists news story 135–136
   editorial direction 129–130
   lead up to the General Strike 91
   union leaders 151
Daily Mail 88–90
datum line strike 20–21
Davidson, J. C. C.
   as chief civil commissioner 60–62
   ending of the General Strike 216
   government newspaper 126, 128
   support for Baldwin's appointment 64
   voluntary workers 113
Davidson, Randall, Archbishop of Canterbury 131, 215–216
Davies, Idris 277
Dawes plan 23
Days of Hope 279
dockers union 34, 170–171, 239–240
docks, military intervention to break strike 188–191
'domestic associations' (for civil servants) 177
Downton Abbey 276–277
Dublin, 1913 union dispute 38–39
Dukes, Charles 273
Dunstan, Robert 141

Edwards, Ebby 157, 267
Electrical Power Engineers' Association (EPEA) 117
Electrical Trades Union (ETU) 100, 179, 180
Electricity Advisory Committee (EAC) 178–179, 180
emergency machinery 120–121
Emergency Powers Act (EPA)
   Birmingham Strike Committee miscommunication 198–199
   controversies over reinstatement of workers 236, 268, 281
   debate during the General Strike 201–202
   introduction of 54
   offences by communist supporters 142, 235
   parliamentary debate about scope 54, 201, 206

picketing 166, 173, 192, 196
   reactivation after end of Strike 246–247
   use of military 139
Empire Day Movement 135
engineering
   Amalgamated Engineering Union 45, 100
   confusion over TUC instructions 178
   during the General Strike 100–101, 159–160
   reinstatement of workers 229
   voluntary workers 117
Evans, Arthur 174
exchange rates 23–24
export crisis 23–24

Fabian Society 36
First World War *see* World War I
Food and Essential Services Committee (FESC) 150
food permit system 121, 158–162, 181–182
food shortages
   avoiding major shortages 158, 181–182, 272
   military intervention 188–191
foreign exchange *see* exchange rates
Forsyte Chronicles 276
Forsyth, Douglas 193
Franks, Ben 143–144
freight
   road haulage instead of rail 70, 119–120
   trains not operating during Strike 98
Fyfe, Hamilton 129, 213

Gaitskell, Hugh 115
Galsworthy, John 276
Garnett, Tom 232–233
Gazette see British Gazette
Geddes Axe 33
the General Council
   founding of 45–46
   lead up to the General Strike 78–88
   messaging during the General Strike 148–162
   order to Strike 95
   persuading workers to join the Strike 147–148
   subcommittees 148–149
   see also Trades Union Congress (TUC)
the General Strike
   attempts to prevent 75–84
   end of announced 222, 226, 227–228
   first day of 95–105
   immediate precursors 88–91
   legacy of 271–282
   length of 272
   order to Strike 95
   preparation for 84–88
   reinstatement of workers 227–243, 260–264
   resumption of Strike 234
   terminology 85, 165
   unprecedented breadth of 107–108
George V, King
   concern about picketing 187–188
   daily news updates 126
   during the General Strike 236–237

lead up to the General Strike 25, 38, 89
opinion of emergency regulations 206
after the General Strike 249, 269
gold standard 24
Gossip, Alex 259
government newspaper *see British Gazette*
graduate volunteers during strike 112, 114–115
Graves, Robert 33
Great Depression 268
Gwynne, Howell Arthur 126

Hallsworth, Joseph 181–182
Hann, George Maurice 181
Hardinge, Charles 71–72
Hartley Pit disaster 23
health and safety
    health risks of mining 10
    mining injuries and deaths 2, 9–10, 23
    road accidents during the General Strike 149–150
    voluntary workers 116
Henderson, Arthur 82–83, 90
Hepburn, Thomas 11–12
Herald see Daily Herald
hewers (mining) 8–9, 10
Hicks, George 257
Hodges, Frank 21–22
home-ownership as goal 64
Horwood, William 68
housing
    construction work 85
    mining communities 6
    rental market for the working class 32–33
human labour
    as dominant in British coal industry 4–5
    mining injuries and deaths 2, 9–10, 23
    women and children working in the mines 8
Hyde Park, as distribution centre 118, 120
Hyde Park, volunteers group *106*, 111
Hyndman, Henry 35–36

illegal strikes bill 205–207
Incitement to Mutiny Act (1797) 62
Independent Labour Party 175
Industrial Action Committee 59
industrial revolution, coal's role in 3–4, 5
industrial unionism 40
International Workers' Day 85
Irish Home Rule 34
Irish Transport and General Workers' Union (ITGWU) 38–39
Isherwood, Christopher 276

"Jix" *see* Joynson-Hicks, William
job losses, following strike 227–234
Jones, Joseph 24–25
Jones, Tom 214, 254–255
journalists *see National Union of Journalists*
Joynson-Hicks, William
    Civil Constabulary Reserve established 199–200
    ending of the General Strike 213

law enforcement 69
lead up to the General Strike 88
OMS 114
opposition to trade unionism 64–65
political career following the Strike 268
road haulage 118–119
after the General Strike 249
voluntary workers 70

Kerensky, Alexander 51–52
Keynes, John Maynard 24
King *see* George V
Klugmann, James 273–274

Labour Party
    foundation of 36–37
    overlap with trade unions 154–155
    student volunteers 115
Labour Representation Committee (LRC) 36
Laird, Cammell 260–261
land ownership in Britain 5–6
Lane-Fox, George 76
Lansbury, George 151, 169
Lansbury's Labour Weekly 271
Laski, Harold 214
Law, Bonar 60, 64
law enforcement
    actions during the General Strike 103–104
    arrests of strike leaders 197–198
    Civil Constabulary Reserve established 199–200
    escalation of unrest towards end of the Strike 195–207
    during the General Strike 133–137
    reinstatement of workers 236
    response to riots 69
    special constables' role 134–137
    after the General Strike 252–253
    Yorkshire Miners' Association mass picketing 173–174
Lawrence, D. H. 253, 268
Lawther, Will 197
leadership, crisis of 274
leadership, faith in workers 282
Lee, Jennie 115, 232
Lee, William 267
Leedham, John 137
Leeds Convention 41
legacy of the General Strike 271–282
legal context
    Campbell case 62–63
    coal mines bill 254–255
    Court of Inquiry 25, 205
    criminalisation of protest 281
    illegal strikes bill 205–207
    labour of women and children 8
    legality of the Strike 202–204
    picketing 166–168
    protection/immunity for those striking 37, 261
    after the General Strike 246–247
    tolerance of political views 67

trade disputes and trade unions bill 261–264, 266–267, 281
see also Emergency Powers Act (EPA)
Lenin, Vladimir 51–52
LGOC see London General Omnibus Company
Lindsay, Lionel 273
literary portrayals of the Strike 276–279
Liverpool transport strike (1911) 30
Lloyd George, David
   adoption of union-friendly policies 40–41
   Court of Inquiry 25
   Emergency Powers Act introduced 54
   national coal strike 19–20
   perception of the General Strike 201
   public broadcast request 131
   response to Russia 51–55, 56
   Triple Alliance 44
   during WW1 17
lockout notices
   ending of the General Strike 210, 220, 228
   lead up to the General Strike 78, 83, 87
   legacy of 277–278
   victimisation 227, 228
London District Committee 152, 179, 180
London General Omnibus Company (LGOC) 103, 138, 243
Luxemburg, Rosa 280

Mabon see Abraham, William (Mabon)
MacDonald, Alexander 13
MacDonald, Ramsey
   the Constitution 56
   ending of the General Strike 216, 236–237, 267
   lead up to the General Strike 82–83
   Leeds Convention 41
   loss of pubic confidence 62
   political career following the Strike 268
   request for BBC broadcast 131
Macquisten, Frederick Alexander 65
Macready, Nevil 43
mail see post, during the General Strike
Makower, Sylvia 114–115
Mann, Tom 30, 35–36, 37–38, 77
manufacturing industry
   contemporary context 281–282
   during the General Strike 100–101
   post WW1 conditions 32–33
   reinstatement of workers 229, 260–261
Markham, Arthur 7–8
Marx, Eleanor 36
Marx, Karl 36
Matteotti, Giacomo 72
Matthews, Jimmy 230
May Day (1926) 86–87, 195
media
   during the General Strike 125
   immediate precursors to the General Strike 88–91
   introduction of government newspaper 126
   lead up to the General Strike 82–88
   literary and television portrayals of the Strike 276–279
   press freedom 125–126
   propaganda war between *British Gazette* and *British Worker* 126–133
   Russian news reports 51–53
   see also broadcast media
MI5 (security services) 57–59, 143–145
Middle Class Union 109
the military see the Army
Milne-Bailey, Walter 89
miners
   emergence of trade unionism 11–15
   first national miners' strike 16
   health risks of mining 10
   historic importance of coal 3–5
   housing 6
   incidents, injuries and deaths 2, 9–10, 23
   job roles 8–9
   legacy of the General Strike 277–278
   popular conceptions of 8
   ramifications of WW1 16–21
   structure and development of unions 12–14, 20–28
   as varied population 5–6
Miners' Association of Great Britain and Ireland (MAGBI)
   foundation 11
   North-East strike (1844) 11–12
   structure of 12–13
Miners' Federation of Great Britain (MFGB)
   Arthur James Cook 6, 14–15
   ending of the General Strike 210–211, 219–221
   foundation and early growth 13–14
   and the General Council 46
   lead up to the General Strike 82
   Lib-Lab politics 14
   national minimum wage 16
   nationalisation 19–21
   radical leadership 22–23
   after the General Strike 248–252, 253–256, 258–259
   Treasury Agreement (1915) 16–17
   Triple Alliance 20–22
Mines and Collieries Act 1842 8
minimum wage
   efforts to introduce 16
   lead up to the General Strike 78–79
   reinstatement of workers 229
   after the General Strike 246, 256, 258–259
Mining Association 20, 25, 27, 76
mining communities
   historic patterns in Britain 5–6
   legacy of the General Strike 277–278
   living conditions 6
   see also miners
Minority Movement 147–148
Mitchell-Thomson, William 113, 131, 272
Mond, Alfred 263–264, 275
Mond-Turner talks 263, 275
Morgan, Kevin 212–213
Morning Post 126–127

Mosley, Oswald 267
Moss, Sam 136–137
Murphy, Jack 183–185, 273–274
Murphy, William Martin 38–39
Mussolini, Benito 71–72

National Citizens' Union (NCU) 109
National Council of Action 56
National Fascisti (NF) 72, 104
National Federation of Building Trade Operatives 177, 179
National Federation of Women Workers 32
National Free Labour Association 35
National Minimum Wage *see* minimum wage
National Minority Movement (NMM) 47–48
National Sailors' and Firemen's Union (NSFU) 34, 37–38, 85–86, 99, 202–204
National Society of Operative Printers and Assistants (NATSOPA) 83
'national strike' as term 85, 165
   see also the General Strike
National Trade Union Defence Committee 262
National Transport Workers' Federation (NTWF) 20–21, 39–40
National Union of Distributive and Allied Workers (NUDAW) 156
National Union of General and Municipal Workers (NUGMW) 35, 42, 175, 178, 181
National Union of Gold, Silver and Allied Trades 46
National Union of Journalists 97, 125
National Union of Mineworkers (NUM) 278, 280
National Union of Police and Prison Officers (NUPPO) 43
National Union of Railwaymen (NUR)
   foundation 39–40
   the General Strike 95, 98
   Triple Alliance 20–21
National Union of Vehicle Builders 230
nationalisation
   effects of 19–20
   during WW1 18–19
   ending of the General Strike 246
   Russian news stories 52
   Samuel Commission 27, 75
NATSOPA *see* National Society of Operative Printers and Assistants
the Navy
   dock siege 190–191
   during the General Strike 140–143
   mutinies in 57
   Sea Division of Civil Constabulary Reserve 200
Negotiating Committee (of the TUC) 81, 82–83, 87–88, 218–221, 250
new unionism 178
Newspaper Proprietors' Association 126
newspapers
   first day of General Strike 96–97
   during the General Strike 125, 153
   immediate precursors to the General Strike 88–91
   introduction of government newspaper 126
   lead up to the General Strike 82–88
   press freedom 125–126
   propaganda war between *British Gazette* and *British Worker* 126–133
   reinstatement of workers in print industry 231, 240–241
   Russian news reports 51–53
   see also British Gazette; *British Worker*; printing unions
NSFU *see* National Sailors' and Firemen's Union
NUGMW *see* National Union of General and Municipal Workers
NUR *see* National Union of Railwaymen

October Revolution 52
Official Secrets Act 62
Organisation for the Maintenance of Supplies (OMS) 70–71, 112–113, 120, 169

Page Arnot, Robin 157
Pankhurst, Sylvia 55–56
paperworkers' union 230–231
pay *see* wages
Peaky Blinders 277
Percy, Eustace, Lord 70
permit system for food 121, 158–162, 181–182
petrol industry 193
picketing 165–175
   escalation of unrest towards end of Strike 195–207
   food shortages 188–190
   personal safety concerns 191–192
   reinstatement of workers 236, 239
   after the General Strike 252–253
police
   actions during the General Strike 103–104
   arrests of strike leaders 197–198
   Civil Constabulary Reserve established 199–200
   escalation of unrest towards end of Strike 195–207
   expectation to deal with riots 69
   during the General Strike 133–137
   reinstatement of workers 236
   special constables' role 69, 114, 134–137, 192–194, 199
   after the General Strike 252–253
   Yorkshire Miners' Association mass picketing 173–174
Pollitt, Harry 46–47, 253, 267
Port of London Authority (PLA) 140–141, 188–191
Post see Morning Post
post, during the General Strike 103
pound sterling *see* exchange rates
power industry
   confusion over TUC instructions 178–179
   during the General Strike 150, 178
   voluntary workers at power stations 117
Powers and Orders Committee, rebranding of 150
   see also Strike Organisation Committee
press freedom 125–126
price-fixing 7–8
printing unions

exemption for *British Worker* 128
first day of General Strike 96–97
during the General Strike 153
National Society of Operative Printers and Assistants 83
press freedom 125–126
reinstatement of workers 231, 240–241
propaganda, war between *British Gazette* and *British Worker* 126–133, 153–154
property-owning democracy 64
Pugh, Arthur 49, 81, 221, 222, 258
Purcell, Alf 206, 212
Purvis, Thomas 174

Quaile, Mary 150

radicalism
    addressed by Churchill 47
    and communism 53
    miners' unions 15–16
rail strike (1919) 59
rail strikes, as part of General Strike 91, 98–99
    ending of the strike 209
    sabotage 171–172
    voluntary workers 110, 112, 115–117
Railway Clerks' Association (RCA) 97
railwaymen
    1919 strike 43–44
    lead up to the General Strike 77
    post WW1 conditions 32, 39–40
    reinstatement of workers 229–230, 236, 237–239
    see also National Union of Railwaymen
'The Red Flag' 67, 96, 251–252
Red Friday 48, 66, 68, 102, 201, 248
reinstatement of workers, following the General Strike 227–243, 260–263
    blacklisting of trade unionists 260
Reith, John 130–131, 216
revolution
    failure of 244, 245–269, 273–275
    fear of 55, 59, 272–273, 275
    see also communism
the Rhondda, South Wales 5–6
Rhys, Samuel 15
rioting
    during the General Strike 133–134
    miners' disputes 14–15
    role of police 69
    Thameshaven riots 191–193, 194–195, 200
    use of military 15, 139–140
road haulage
    instead of rail during the Strike 70, 118–120
    job losses 230
    not involved in Strike 85, 98
    sabotage 170–171
roadblocks 103–104
Rotary Clubs 109
Rowlinson, Ernest 182
Royal Automobile Club (RAC) 118–119

Royal Commission on the Coal Industry *see* Samuel Commission
Rufford Pit Communist Group 50
Russian revolution 41–42, 51–52
Ryall, William Bolitho 104–105

safety conditions *see* health and safety
salary *see* wages
Samuel Commission 74
    ending of the General Strike 215
    lead up to the General Strike 49, 75–84
    print run 27
    recommendations 27–28, 75–76
    during the Strike 218
    after the General Strike 250
Samuel, Herbert 217–221, 222, 250, 258
    see also Samuel Commission
Samuel memorandum 219–221, 246, 258
Sankey, John 19
Scargill, Arthur 279–280
Scoulding, Tom 239–240
seafarers' union *see* NSFU
Secret Service Bureau 58–59
security services 57–59, 143–145
security state 55
sedition charges 104
Segrave, Henry 218
Sexton, James 257
shipbuilding
    confusion over TUC instructions 178
    during the General Strike 100, 176
shipping, in the General Strike 99
Shop Assistants' Union 181, 212, 261
Simon, John 201–202, 204, 205–206, 211
Sitwell, Osbert 214
Slesser, Henry 67, 202
Smillie, Bob 44
Smith, Dai 268
Smith, Ernest 23
Smith, Frederick Edwin *see* Birkenhead, Lord
Smith, Herbert 74
    biographical details 23
    ending of the General Strike 212, 214
    lead up to the General Strike 79
Social Democratic Federation (SDF) 35–36
socialism
    in 1880s 35–36
    fears about 65, 201
    and the mining industry 7
    place of the Labour Party after the General Strike 275
    trade union movement 36
    see also communism
Socialist League 35
South Wales, site of the largest coalfield in the world 5–6
Soviet trade unions 249
special constables' role 69, 114, 134–137, 192–194, 199
Spencer, George 255
sports, during the General Strike 133–135

Index

Squance, William 173
Stanford-le-Hope 192
Stanton, Charles 14–15
STC *see* Supply and Transport Committee
Steel-Maitland, Arthur 80, 218–219, 262–263
steelmaking 100
STO *see* Supply and Transport Organisation
Stoker, William 104
Strachey, John 267
Strike Organisation Committee (SOC) 150, 160, 175–181
strike wave (2022–23) *270*, 282
strikebreaking
    in the 1890s 35
    escalation of unrest towards end of Strike 195–207
    first day of General Strike 97–105
    picketing and sabotage 165–175, 188–192
    role of the police, army and navy 134–143
    special constables' role 134–137
    use of road transport 118–122
    voluntary workers 107–118
strikes, history of prior to General Strike
    1919 strike 43–44
    government means of prevention 37, 59
    history of in Britain 33–40
    Industrial Action Committee 59
    legal protection 37
    in the military 57
strikes since the General Strike *270*, 278–282
students as volunteers 112, 114–115
    see also voluntary workers
suffragettes 55–56
Summerbell, Thomas 231
Sunday Worker 186, 256
Supply and Transport Committee (STC) 59–61, 69–70, 213, 239
Supply and Transport Organisation (STO) 61, 108, 118, 162
Swales, Alonzo 48–49
Symons, Julian 110, 206
syndicalism 39

Taff Vale judgement 36
The Tatler 112, 119
Tawney, R. H. 254–255
Taylor, Sidney 177
television portrayals of the Strike 276–279
Territorial Army (TA) 142, 197, 199
textile industry 43, 180, 183
TGWU *see* Transport & General Workers' Union
the Thames, complete strike along 188–191
Thameshaven riots 191–193, 194–195, 200
Thomas, Jimmy
    ending of the General Strike 206–207, 210, 211, 214–215, 222
    in the General Council 49
    lead up to the General Strike 77, 80, 82, 83–84, 87, 90
    as moderate leader 56, 210, 211
    reinstatement of workers 238–239
    after the General Strike 250–251, 259, 266
    strike call on miners' behalf 76–77

Thorne, Will 33–34, 150, 178
Tillett, Ben 34, 36
Tobacco Workers' Union 180
Tonypandy riots 15
Tracey, Herbert 129
trade disputes and trade unions bill 261–264, 266–267, 281
trade union movement
    adversarial relations with government 65–66, 69
    and communism 46–48, 54
    ending of the General Strike 232–233
    ending of the Strike 211–214, 221
    and the General Council 147–148
    lead up to the General Strike 84
    picketing 169–170
    Trades Councils 154–155
trade unionism
    in the 1890s 36
    in contemporary times 280–282
    formation of General Council 45–46
    history of in Britain 33–40
    industrial unionism 40
    mining unions - origins of trade unionism 11–15
    mining unions - structure and development 12–14, 20–28
    perception after the General Strike 261
    post-war decline 44–45
    ramifications of WW1 16–21
    and syndicalism 39
Trades Councils 154–155
Trade Disputes Act (1906) 37, 65–66, 166, 204
Trades Union Congress (TUC)
    British Worker founded to provide pro-TUC news 128–133
    confusion over instructions during the General Strike 178–179
    criticism by Communist Party 183–185
    ending of the General Strike 209–213, 221, 223, 232–233
    failed revolution *244*, 245–269
    first day of General Strike 96–105
    foundation 45
    function and evolution 45–46
    illegal strikes bill 205–207
    immediate precursors to the General Strike 88–91
    Irish workers assisted by 38–39
    lead up to the General Strike 76–88
    legacy of the General Strike 271–282
    Negotiating Committee 81, 82–83, 87–88, 218–221, 250
    printworkers 125–126
    pyrrhic victory 260
    reinstatement of workers not guaranteed 227–243
    resumption of Strike 234
    support of miners 25–26
    widespread obedience to orders 102
    see also the General Council
trains not running *see* rail strikes, as part of General Strike

trams, in the General Strike 99, 110–111
  attempt to reinstate services 179–180
  reinstatement of workers 241
  sabotage 169, 170–171
Transport & General Workers' Union (TGWU)
  amalgamation 45
  food permit system 160
  forerunners of 35
  formation 21, 40
  during the General Strike 101, 176
  reinstatement of workers 229, 230, 240, 241
  rioting 196
  after the General Strike 247–249, 260, 261
transport services
  picketing 167–173
  responsibility for delivery of food 181–182
    see also bicycles, buses, rail strikes, Supply and Transport Committee; Supply and Transport Organisation, trams
transport unions
  first day of the General Strike 98–99
  food permit system 121, 158–162, 181–182
  Irish Transport and General Workers' Union 38–39
  moving essential supplies 150
  reinstatement of workers 241–243
  road haulage replacing rail during the Strike 70, 118–120
  Triple Alliance 20–21
    see also National Union of Railwaymen; Transport & General Workers' Union
Treasury Agreement (1915) 16–17, 40
Tress, C. W. B. 194
Triple Alliance 20–22, 26, 40, 44, 46, 251
Trotsky, Leon 271, 274
TUC see Trades Union Congress
Turner, Ben 263–264

Underwood, W. T. 230
unemployment
  in the 1930s 275
  after the General Strike 242, 260–261, 262, 268
  post-WW1 33, 100
Union of Women Matchworkers 33
Universal Colliery, Senghenydd 2, 9
Unofficial Reform Committee 15
Upstairs Downstairs 278–279

victimisation, ending the General Strike 230–234, 240, 260
Voluntary Service Committees (VSCs) 107–108, 122
voluntary workers
  British Gazette 126, 128, 130
  emergency planning 69–71
  during the General Strike *106*, 108–118, 122
  ineffectiveness 152–153
  legacy of 275–277

military intervention 189–190
turning away at the end of the General Strike 232, 241

wages
  lead up to the General Strike 76–77, 78–79
  mining compared to other occupations 10–11
  national minimum wage 16
  Samuel Commission 28
  stagnation in 1900s 14–15, 16
  after the General Strike 246, 250, 256, 258–259
  Triple Alliance 22
  war bonus 41
  wartime inflation 16–17
Watson, Harry 102
Waugh, Evelyn 276
Webb, R. H. 143
Wedgwood, Josiah 61–62
Westminster Worker 153
Whitley Councils 42
Wilden workers 63–64
Wilkinson, Ellen 277
Williams, Robert 256–257
Wilson, Havelock 85–86, 202–204, 257
Wilson, Henry 55
Wimborne, Lady Cornelia Henrietta Maria 214–215
women
  confrontations with police 253
  National Federation of Women Workers 32
  reinstatement of female workers 230–231
  role in colliery workforces 8
  taking industrial roles during WW1 33
  taking on voluntary roles 108, 112, 114, 153
Wood, Kingsley 121, 122, 157
Workers' Bulletin 184
Workers Chronicle 196
working class
  emergence of trade unionism 33–36
  legacy of the General Strike 277, 282
  post-WW1 conditions 32–33
  Red Friday 48–49
  unemployment 33
working conditions
  across industrial Britain 31–33
  mining injuries and deaths 2, 9–10
  mining job roles 8–9
  shift patterns introduced in Wilden ironworks 63–64
  after the General Strike 254–256
World War I 16–19
  Russian revolution 41–42
  shared experience of loss 33

Yorkshire Evening Post 206
Yorkshire Miners' Association 172–173

Zinoviev, Grigory 63